WOMEN LEADERSHIP IN ORGANIZATION
Socio-Cultural Determinants

WOMEN LEADERSHIP IN ORGANIZATIONS
Socio-Cultural Determinants

Sunita Singh-Sengupta

GYAN PUBLISHING HOUSE
NEW DELHI-110002

Women Leadership in Organization : Socio-Cultural Determinants

(*Women Studies, Sociology*)

Rs.640

ISBN: 81-212-0816-5

Published in 2003 in India by
Gyan Publishing House
5, Ansari Road, Darya Ganj, New Delhi-110002
Phones : 3282060, 3261060, Fax (011) 3285914
E-mail : gyanbook@vsnl.com
Website : http://www.gyanbooks.com

Laser Typesetting at: Sharma Graphic, New Delhi
Printed at: Mehra Offset Press, Delhi

Dedicated

To

My Father

Late Parmanand Singh

Contents

List of Figures

List of Tables

Preface

One of the most prominent themes to emerge is that women managers regardless of the country, in which they live and work, have similar experiences derived from their assigned status as women and such a situation is prevalent till today irrespective all other changes taking place this area has not seen much change in positive terms. Patriarchy and its masculinist value persist world wide, varying by country only in degree to which they dominate policy and legislation. These circumstances provide the background of values in which women managers have to function and create viable life style.

Women face discrimination on the basis of marital status and have to conform to masculine standards of behavior to progress through managerial rank and also has to balance societal responsibilities of parenthood and work. The organizational atmosphere has not yet changed to the level where they can accommodate, women as members fully equal to men. The widely relevant obstacle to women in the management field is the stubborn assistance of most societies to recognizing housework and childcare as roles to be shared equally by women. The result is low representation of women at the top.

The present volume addresses some of these issues. The author took the viewpoint that socio-cultural factors does affect women's share in top managerial positions.

The study is manifested through five chapters.

Chapter 1. Presents a review of what has been learned, where the investigations might lead and the conceptual framework of the present research.

Chapter 2. Highlights objectives and hypotheses framed for the study.

Chapter 3. Highlights the strategy of the main survey. In this section the variables are operationalized with the help of relevant scales followed by a note on research setting, sample and procedure of the data collection.

Chapter 4. Presents the statistical analyses of the obtained data.

Chapter 5. Interprets the findings and discusses the limitations of the present research. Suggestions for future research are given in this section.

Chapter 6. Deals with the summary of the main findings. The section covers suggestions for the policy-makers and some thought inputs for the readers.

I take this opportunity to express my heartfelt thanks to all those people and institutions who helped me at one stage or other in making this research a success.

Special thanks are acknowledged to National Productivity and Economic Centre, Nepal and P.G. Institute of Management Columbo, Sri Lanka for their assistance and co-operation in data collection.

The warmest appreciation is expressed to the Indian Council of Social Science Research, New Delhi, who provided me an opportunity to carry out such a relevant research by funding the project.

I owe a very special debt of thanks to my respondents who extended their co-operation and participated in the study.

My husband, Mr. Arijit Sengupta and my two daughters, Ms. Isha and Ms. Shreya deserve special thanks for their cooperation that they provided to me. My mother, brother and sisters owe a very hearty thanks for the support they keep providing me continuously.

Finally, I am deeply indebted to my father Late Shri Parmanand Singh Retired M.V.I who nurtured in me the basic training of hard work and success.

Sunita Singh-Sengupta

1
Introduction

The Indian Culture and Women

Research studies carried out in the area of the status of women in India during the ancient period shows that there was a widespread misconception regarding the true status of women in Indian society during the ancient times. The main cause sighted for this was due to deplorable ignorance of the original Sanskrit texts, both 'Srut' and 'Smriti' in which one finds laws, customs and traditions which define the true status of women in early times. The most authoritative text on the subject is the Rig-Veda, the primary root from which sprang all the later development of Hinduism, its many sects, school and religious systems. As a matter of fact the Rig-Veda, contains the seeds and source from which the entire course of Hindu thought has been through ages derived and followed in so many streams. It is the tree of knowledge out of which has grown so many offshoots and branches representing the various aspects of Hindu civilization (Mookherji, 1957).

The Rig-Veda shows abundant evidence pointing to the fact that women were fully equals of men as regards access to and capacity for the higher knowledge, including the knowledge of the 'Absolute' or 'Brahma'. Rig- Veda is a product of highest religious thought, which dawned on the saints and seers as a result of their contemplation in a life of complete asceticism and penance. It was to such meditative master minds that truth ', revealed itself. They gave expression to the truth, thus revealed in impassionate prayers called "Suktas". The entire Rig-Veda contained such Suktas and hymns. They were uttered in ecstasy to these seers, aptly called rishis, who were capable of direct vision of truth and represented the highest degree of spiritual enlightenment. The hymns of the rishis were inspired and were not ordinary secular compositions. Every hymn of the Rig- Veda was attributed to a rishi. Though the majority of these hymns were work of the male rishis, the Rig -Veda contained hymns, which were revealed by women seers also. The latter were called rishikas and brahmavadins (Mookherji, 1957).

The Rig-Veda speaks of the following rishikas and brahmavadins. The Rig-Veda speaks of the following rishikas, e.g., Romasa, Lopamudra, Apata, Kadru, Visvavara and several others mentioned in the mandala like Ghosha, Juhu, Vagambhrini, Paulomi, Jarita, Sraddha- Kamayani, Sarnga, Yami, Indrani, Savitri, Nodha [Purvarchchika], Akrishtabhasha, Sikatanivavari [Uttaravchchika], Ganpayana (Mookherji, 1957).

The Brahmavadinis were products of the educational discipline of brahmacharya, for which women were also eligible. The Rig- Veda referred to young maidens completing their education as brahmacharinis and then gaining husbands in whom they were merged like rivers in oceans. The Yajur -Veda sights that a daughter who has completed her brahmacharya should be married to one who is learned like her. The Atharvaveda also refers to maidens qualifying by brahmacharya the discipline life of studentship for married life in the second asrama. It is therefore, no wonder that wife along with her husband enjoyed full social status, religious rights and practiced and participated in religious ceremonies which would be invalid without wife, hence joining her husband as his full partner was a must in those days. Thus Rig -Veda accorded the highest social status to the qualified women of those days (Mookherji, 1957).

The Rig-Veda laid down the norm, the ideal and the tradition, which were followed as a law in later times. The Upanishads exhibit fully the continuance of this tradition. They tell of a learned conference of philosophers—the earliest conference of its kind in the world, which was convened at his court by Rajarshi (philosopher - king), Janaka of Videha. The royal invitation was sent to all the philosophers of those days. In the view of the many different schools of philosophy that had grown up in the country, with their different religious doctrines and practices, king Janaka thought that it was time to codify the floating mass of philosophical speculation into a regular and scientific system. The conference adopted a proper procedure by which its discussion could be regulated and made fruitful in results. The procedure was that the exponents and the representatives of the different schools of philosophy should take a prominent part in the discussion so that each might expound the special doctrines of his school. Among these participants mentioned eight principal philosophers their names being Uddalaka, Aruni, Astabhaga, Bhuju, Ushasta, Kahoda, Vidagdha, Sakalya and the women philosopher, Brahmavadini Gargi Vachaknavi. Gargi Vachaknavi was a conspicuous figure at the conference. She came forward boldly to cross lances in argument with the male philosophers. A position of authority was assumed by rishi Yajnavalka who was therefore a target to attack by Gargi (Mookherji, 1957).

The Upanishads throw further light on the intellectual life of the times in which male and females were equal participants. According to the story king Janaka, after receiving instruction from Yajnavalkya as his guru [teacher] offered him his gurudakshina. The rishi at the height of his power, prosperity, name and fame chose the gift of a kingdom. The Rig-Vedic society was based on monogamy and was patriarchal. The marriage hymn points to the practice of the bridegroom going to the brides house where he marries her and takes her to his house where she has a honoured place as the mistress of the household, looking after the functioning of the whole house. The hymn also indicated that the marriage was a sacrament and indissoluble, hence widows were not remarried. The wife took part with her husband in his religious ceremonies. If the girl's parents died her brothers looked after her. The institution of monogamy was itself eloquent recognition of high social status of women. The Vedic tradition continued to later the Vedic times The Rig- Vedic female rishis were called as Ghosha, Romasa, Lopamudra and Visvavara brahmavadinis.

The great grammarian Panini who lived before 500 B.C., in his work named Ashtadhyavi City illustrated of his grammatical rules to show how women were going in for regular Vedic studies like men. Thus the information Kathi means a female student of the Katha Sakha of the Veda in that particular rescission. Similarly the term Bahrichi means a female student who was well-versed in many hymns, i.e., the Rig-Veda. Learned ladies of those times naturally figured and functioned as teachers. Some grammatical passage show that women had other careers to them apart from a mere literary career. The great grammarian, Patanjali, author of that monumental masterpiece known as Mahabhashya, uses the formation Saktiki to indicate a female bearer of spear. In this connection we are reminded of the Amazonian bodyguard of armed women employed in his palace by the emperor Chandragupta Maurya as described by Megasthenes, the Greek ambassador to his court (Mookherji, 1957).

If we look into the Buddhist philosophy we find that it kept up with the tradition of brahmanical religion. According to this tradition womanhood was given an honoured place in social life. Women were made eligible for admission to what was known as the "Bhikshunis-Sangha", the order of nuns, which opened them avenues of culture and social service and ample opportunities for public life. The young Buddhist church of those early days was also able to attract sympathy and generosity of many a lady. Only that of the merchant Prince Anathapindika equals the munificence of the matron Vishaka was the head of an illustratous band, which included names like Amrapali of Vaishali and Suppiya of Benaras. The Buddhist fully appreciated the hospitality and the offering of financial support from individual women of sincere religious devotion. Apart from these remarkable characters among Buddhist women, the order of the nuns are accounted in the sacred texts. Some Buddhist nuns achieved great distinction by prominent part they took in the work of the early Buddhist reformation as are mentioned in the commentary of Dharmapala. It will be apparent from these examples that the Buddhist convents opened out to women opportunities for education, self-culture and varied spheres of social service, in which they made themselves the equals of men, supplementing their work in the spread of their faith (Mookherji, 1957).

The period from the invasion of India by Mohammed of Ghor to the establishment of British authority in Bengal in the second half of the eighteenth century witnessed in general a deterioration of the position of women in India. With the 15th century the situations underwent a change. The general revival of Hindu life, which the period witnessed also, led to a considerable improvement in the status of women. Conditions in South India were of course different. As society was much more settled and was not subjected to the pressure of continuous invasion, the position of women underwent no serious deterioration.

In the field of administration Indian women produced some notable figures during this period. There was Rudrama Devi, the Kakatiya queen of whom Marco Polo speaks; Razia Begum (13th century) of whom it was said that her one weakness was that she was a woman; Chandbibi, who appeared on the ramparts of the fort of Ahmednagar dressed in male attire and put heart in the defenders of that town against the prowess of Akbar himself; Tarabai, the Maharashtra heroine who was the life and soul of Maharashtra resistance during the last determine onslaught of Aurangzeb; Managammal, whose benign rule is still a green memory in the south, and Ahalyabai Holkar, to whose administrative genius Sir John Malcolm has paid a magnificient tribute. These are but a few outstanding names among the great women that India can boast of during this period (Panikkar, 1957).

But the general state of Indian womanhood cannot well be judged by the lives of the princesses and the queens. However, the reality is that in contrast to the joyous celebration at the birth of sons, girls generally receive a muted if not a totally cold reception. The religious merit reaped at the birth of a daughter is minimal; her entry into the world is accompanied by foreboding on the part of the parents. Thus, Indra's charioteer Matali, father of the beauteous Gunakeshi laments: Alas, the birth of a daughter in the families of those that are well behaved and high-born and possess reputation and humility of character, is always attended with evil results. Daughters when born in respectable families always endanger the honour of these families, their maternal and paternal families and the families into which they are adopted by marriage. And though King Drupada, for very good reasons of his own, wishes for the birth of a son, he seems to go to ludicrous lengths to deny the sex of the daughter who is finally born, futilely begs Shiva to change her sex and (after her birth) conceals her real identity and performs the rites prescribed for a male child (Kakar, 1979, p.16).

The greatest drawback of Indian tradition seems to be its relative rejection of girls. Even in the myths of abandonment of children in the Mahabharata, Menaka's abandonment of her new born daughters Pramdavara and Shakuntala is counterbalanced by Kunti abandoning the infant Karna. It is more in its exaggerated emphasis on sons, in the joyous din at the birth of male children, that the silent rejection of female infants stands out so clearly and has had such grave consequences for Indian women and society (Kakar, 1979, p. 32).

The Social Reality: Asian Perspectives

Asian countries are characterized by patriarchal family system where children are expected to be obedient to their parents and to pay them respect. In return, the father, as the chief head of the family, is expected to be benevolent to family members by caring for their welfare. Thus, large patriarchal families are authoritarian, with strict hierarchical orientation. Because large families were traditionally cohesive and self-sufficient 'in-groups' with a common destiny, their social values and interpersonal relationships tended to be oriented to and characterised by nepotism, particularism and informalism in terms of blood ties, residence, school background, etc. (Son-Ung Kim, 1999).

The society gives higher status and privileges to men as compared to women. Men are perceived to be assertive and commanding whereas women are expected to comply, obey and be submissive and docile. The differentiation labeled by the virtue of being men or women can be easily observed in day to day interactions. The inequality is even expressed in the behaviour of Indian mother towards her children (son or daughter) while rearing them. Men are supposed to maintain external contacts whereas women are primarily supposed to fulfill family responsibilities. The society expects that a female should have genuine concern for family members, should make sacrifices for them and adhere to the normative behavioural a pattern (Singh-Sengupta, in press).

From very early childhood the cultural expectations of boys and girls begin to diverge radically. The Indian daughter is not severed from the company of her mother and the other woman in the household, although like her brothers she continues to be cared for by her mother, albeit more casually than before, as she gradually learns to be like her mother by taking care of herself as well as the other younger children in the family. Late childhood also marks the beginning of an Indian girl's deliberate training in how to be a good woman, and hence the conscious inculcation of culturally designated feminine roles. She learns that the 'virtues' of womanhood, which will take her through life, are submission and docility as well as skill and grace in various household tasks (Kakar, 1979, p. 38).

Research studies states that such a problem related to the status of women does not persist only within our society but among most societies, of the world and this has in the present times emerged as a fundamental crisis in human development. This has led to sex inequality inherent in our traditional social structure based on caste, community and class and have a very significant influence on the status of women and their problems in different spheres. Socially accepted rights and expected roles of women, norms governing their behaviour and the others towards them vary among groups and region. The stage and methods of development and the position held by the group in the social hierarchy also closely affect them. All this makes broad generalization regarding women's status unrealistic.

If we look to other Asian countries (i.e., Korea, Bangladesh, Sri Lanka and Nepal) we find more or less the same social arrangements. The society seems to be collectivist in its orientation. The family system seems to be patriarchal in nature. Obedience to elders and conformity to rules seem to be preferred values. The youngers show deference and respect to elders and elders in return express affection and provide shelter and guidance to the younger (Singh-Sengupta, 1990). Son-Ung Kim (1999) reports the same in Korean culture. Perera (2000) founds the similar trend in Sri Lanka, "...a woman has to run the home, handle the basic needs of the family, in addition provide emotional support to the family" (p. 78).

Influence of Socio-Cultural Factors on Organizations

Organizations operate in the social milieu and therefore the socio-cultural factors greatly influences it. The people bring these values into the organizations. Despite their imported technologies Indian work organizations are strongly influenced by its socio-cultural factors. There is some evidence that work relationship is not quite contractual. There is strong preference for personalized relationship (Dayal, 1976; Singh-Sengupta, 1990; Sinha, 1980). Excessive dependency seems to be a dominant orientation of the Indian executives (Chattopadhyay, 1975; De, 1974; Sinha, 1970). Weak work values and strong status orientation are found to be pervasive. Agarwal (1976) has attempted to identify the linkages between social and work values. Chattopadhyay and Rao (1970) found that aspirations and worries of industrial workers as well as managers are mostly centered around their self and family. They want to be informed and consulted by their family, because they carry on the familial modes of Indian nurturant superior (Sinha, 1980a). Dayal (1976) has noted that social relationship and organizational performance is not separated in India. Loyalty often gets priority over efficiency. Intrinsic work values are sure to suffer in such a personalized work culture.

Culture and values. People's self-concepts reflect internalization of the values, beliefs and meanings from the larger culture in which they (and organizations) are embedded (Frez and Early, 1993). Scott and Lane (2000) suggest that people's perceived overlap with an organization will enhance their self-esteem, (i.e., the attractiveness of the overlap) only to the extent they view prototypical characteristics of the organization as consistent with norms, values, and definitions of the embedding culture.

Sinha (1980b) has identified some salient features of the Indian social system, which can further exemplify the linkages between social norms and values and organizational behaviour. Indian social institutions and relationships are hierarchically structured where there are meticulously elaborated rules and rituals which are expected to be rigidly conformed to (Kothari, 1970). Hence, Indian tend to arrange themselves in superior-subordinate relationship (Kakar, 1978) which is bound ideally by affective intimacy (Roland, 1980), i.e., *sneh* (affection and care) for the dependents and subordinates and *shradha* (deference) for the superiors. This vertical solidarity (Srinivas quoted by Marriot, 1977) of superior and subordinate is often a part of a social collectivity to which Indians willingly submit. They do not, however, dissolve their individuality or forget their self-interest. The finely differentiated roles and positions within a collectivity allow them to protect and in fact enhance their self- interest by developing mutually helpful dyadic cliques within the collectivity. Indians use collectivities for their individual interests. They cultivate linkages with a number of collectivities which are themselves graded into relatively central or peripheral in importance for the individuals compromising them. Indians disposition to grade people into "own" (*apna*) and "others" (*paraya*) reflects a universal phenomenon of categorizing persons into in-groups and out-groups. Yet the meticulous extent to which Indian carry this frame (Singh-Sengupta, 1990; Sinha, 1980b) to demarcate social groups and persons within the groups are phenomenal. For "own" and in-group members, Indians are all-sacrificing, loving, affectionate, and loyal. For outsiders, they are callous, manipulative and exploitative. Quite often the only in-group which remains crucial in the minds of Indians is the nuclear family; and the entity which stands distinct, though a lonely, within the family is the "I" of the person. Thus, the gyroscopic "I" and the multiplicity of the social collectivities around the "I" create in Indians a contextual orientation (Roland, 1980) which is quite congruent with their concept of a world which is believed to be fluid (*sansar*). Indians as a result, tend to tolerate ambiguity and differences in views and try to live with the things which are not under their control, and yet manifest manipulativeness and gamesmanship (Ganesh and Malhotra, 1975) which are critical for their survival and prosperity.

Spill-Over to Organizations. Cultural values underlie people's attitudes and behaviour. Thus, they shape individuals' perceptions and expectations about work, as well as the way they interact with their colleagues in the workplace. Furthermore, cultural values also provide guidelines for making decisions. Accordingly, cultural values have many implications for the ways in which organizations are managed in different cultural settings.

Socio-cultural factors are fundamental in determining women's status and position in the labour market. Our experiences show that cultural barriers like traditional stereotypes of women hinder women's career progress. There are two very strong pulls. On the one hand there is ambition, career, and the desire to achieve. On the other, the pull of the family and children is stronger because that is a role the woman sees as her's (Seth, 1998). But how many men turn down promotions because of domestic chores and kids' homework? Not only does culture influence individual's behaviour and the ways they interact with others, it also affects the values, norms, and expectations prevailing in the workplace. Meenakshi Madhvani, a CEO of Carat India writes, " the work culture will not change unless people are willing to set aside the gender issue" (Business World, 1998:79). The 'masculine' organizational culture is also found to be a major impediment to women's progress into managerial positions (Alvesson and Billing, 1997; Marshall, 1993).

Thus, cultural values underlie people's attitudes and behaviour. They shape individuals' perceptions and expectations about work, as well as the ways they interact with their colleagues in the work place. Furthermore, cultural values also provide guidelines for making decisions. Accordingly, cultural values have many implications for the ways in which organizations are managed in different cultural settings. Previous cross-cultural research showed that national culture profoundly influence management thought, strategic decision making, organizational culture, organizational structure, and leadership behaviour (Boyacigiller and Alder, 1991; Lachman, Nedd, and Hinings, 1994; Lau and Ngo, 1996; Offermann and Hellmann, 1997; Schneider and DeMeyer, 1991). More importantly, cultural values are found to have significant impacts upon HR policies and practices in organizations (Gomez-Mejia and Welbourne, 1991; Laurent, 1986). To a certain extent, these policies and practices determine the career paths and status of men and women in organization.

Culture encompasses patterned ways of thinking (Kluckholm, 1954), mental programs (Hofstede, 1980), and shared meaning systems (Shweder and Levine, 1984). To a large degree, culture provides an interpretive framework through which individuals make sense of their own behaviour, as well as the behaviour of collectivities in their society.

The impact of national culture on the employees work behaviour, specially, in terms of work related values were intensely examined by Geert Hofstede (1980, 1991) who suggested four dimensions to interpret behaviour at workplace in one's socio-cultural context. These dimensions were:

(1) **Power distance** measures human inequality in organizations looking at the boss's decision-making style, employees' fear of disagreeing with the superior, and how subordinates prefer a boss to make decisions. Essentially, it looks at how less powerful people validate the power structure. Cultures with a low score tend to respect individuals, strive for equality and value happiness.

(2) **Uncertainty avoidance** explains each society's search for the truth and the anxiety people feel in a situation with conflicting values or unstructured outcomes. Cultures with high uncertainty avoidance try to minimise the anxiety with a thorough set of strict laws and behaviour norms. Low uncertainty avoidance cultures tend to have fewer rules and more acceptance of diversity of thought and behaviour.

(3) **Individualism** looks at the degree to which people are parts of groups or on their own. In collective societies, everyone is born into a strong clan of uncles, aunts and cousins (even third and fourth) who are part of one unit. Each person contributes to the group and at some time receives care from the group. Loyalties are to the group above everything else. In more individualistic societies, people are more or less on their own and are expected to take care of themselves and their immediate family.

(4) **Masculinity** versus its opposite, femininity examines how roles are distributed between sexes. The predominant pattern of socialization worldwide is for men to be more assertive and women to be more nurturing.

Women in Organizations

Understanding of women's issues necessitates the processual dimensions of her economic, social and cultural construction from a historical viewpoint. It further necessitates analysis of contextual variations. Any action for the emancipation necessitates understanding of her status. The need for radical restructuring is not denied but also one cannot wait for total transformation, nor use it as an argument against localized efforts for the action related to specific areas for providing healthcare, education and employment. Social transformation is the end aim. However, there are specific issues, micro-level oppression, prejudices in every life, set notions and fixed mind-sets, which need to be taken up for struggle for improvement, emancipation, conscientisation and empowerment of women. This necessitates partnership of men, their involvement and their conscience building (Powell, 1990).

Women in Organizations: A Review of Research Results

Women in organizations is a subject of popular interest. Sometimes one even gets the impression that the representation and functioning of women in senior managerial jobs is believed to be the crucial issue in gender equality, at least in the context of management/organization studies. Women in organization is a large and expanding topic. Given that only a very small percentage of the top jobs in business and public administration are held by women in most countries, the lack of equality is especially striking in this part of the labour market. The following are some of the questions that are being asked. Why are there so few female managers, especially at senior levels? Do men and women differ in terms of leadership abilities and style of managing? Is there perhaps a specific female form of leadership which, if not actually practised, is preferred by a majority of women? Are prejudices and other obstacles preventing women from attaining and/or occupying managerial positions? Or do females often express other values and orientations than to exercise authority over others?

The interest in raising and answering these questions seems to be part of an international trend which started in the USA, where the theme has been a popular one for at least the last 25 years. The past and present situation in the USA can perhaps be illustrated by quoting the titles of some of the books and articles in this field. Early titles included for example *Breakthrough. Women into Management* (Loring and Wells, 1972); *Bringing Women into Management* (Gordon and Strober, 1975); and *Men and Women of the Corporation* (Kanter, 1977). Later books included titles such as *Management Strategies for Women*, or *Now That I'm the Boss, How Do I Run This Place*? (Thompson and Wood, 1981); *Women Managers: Travellers in a Male World* (Marshall, 1984); *Feminine Leadership, or How to Succeed in Business Without Being One of the Boys* (Loden, 1986); and *The Female Advantage* (Helgesen, 1990).

There is a wide variety of social science and more popular, practitioner-oriented writings on the topic. They range from careful, measurement-oriented studies in which sex is added as a variable—often without much inspiration or originality in comparison with older, non-gender leadership research—to normative writings, based on the convictions, impression and/or empirical studies of the author, on ways in which women lead or organize. Within these writings, the gender-as-a-variable perspective is the most common, even though there are also a number of feminist standpoint position texts on gender and management. Many of these, however, maintain a rather weak version of the standpoint position, putting forward the idea of women's unitary and—in relation to men different ways of being/relating to others, but embracing a positive rather than critical view on male/female compatibility.

This section will provide an overview and discussion of empirical research in the field (Source: Alvesson and Billing, 1997, pp.134-151). At first contemporary changes in leadership and management will be briefly addressed. We will then review the state of the art of empirical and other work on the most common themes concerning women and leadership: explanations for the limited number of women in managerial jobs, including family matters; discrimination and processes of selection; style of leadership of women compared to men; difficulties facing women managers, including stress level and the facing of negative stereo—types.

Gender and Organizational Culture

In this section we will talk about the workplace relations from a cultural point of view. It is organizational level cultures and related issues, such as occupational cultures, that are of interest.

Organizational Culture

Interest in organizational culture existed long before the 'corporate culture boom' of the early 1980s, but since this time a broader and more consistent interest in this area has emerged. There is enormous variation in the definitions and even more so in the use of the term 'culture' in organization theory, particularly among practitioners. Culture certainly has no fixed or broadly agreed-upon meaning in anthropology (Ortner, 1984)—a discipline that many organizational culture authors draw upon—but the variation within the latter group is probably greater than within anthropology and most other cultural disciplines. This has partly to do with the fact that organizational culture literature varies substantially in terms of both purpose and depth. Many studies are narrowly management-oriented and pragmatic while others are interested in broader, more reflective forms of understanding which include more complex aspects of culture which cannot be 'managed' or controlled. A lot of these views of culture are pretty vague. Many who talk about culture refer to everything, and thus nothing.

We use the concept of culture to characterize a set of meanings, ideas and symbols that are shared by the members of a collective and that have evolved over time. Talking about culture then means 'talking about the importance for people of symbolism—of rituals, myths, stories, and legends—and about the interpretation of events, ideas, and experiences that are influenced and shaped by the groups within which they live' (Frost et al., 1985, p. 17). Culture then directs attention to (1) what is shared by a group and departs from highly individualized ideas and circumstances; (2) the ideational level, that is what is on people's minds, their ideas and beliefs rather than how they behave or something else tangible (although the meaning of behaviour or material is a cultural phenomenon); and (3) the non-rational aspects, the value-laden, partly non-conscious dimensions of social life, including emotional aspects. Culture is thus not measurable, at least not in any simple sense. To understand cultural meanings calls for interpretation - unpacking the deeper aspect of a phenomenon. What surfaces in vocabulary, behaviour, practices and material artefacts must be deciphered. The more interesting cultural meanings are non-conscious and call for considerable depth, including imagination, creativity and tolerance of uncertainty, in interpretative work (Ehn and Löfgren, 1982; Geertz, 1973).

Culture may refer to an entire society or any collective within it, such as a class, a region or a social movement. It may also refer to other entities, for example an organization, a part of it or an occupation. In the present case, organization-related cultural phenomena are not restricted to issues considered to be unitary and unique for a specific organization, but may refer to much broader cultural phenomena, such as industrial-level or Western management culture ideas and meanings, or narrower cultural objects of study, such as group or workplace-level cultural issues. In gender studies it is apparent that the shared orientations of men and women in an organization may differ, despite a possible existence of a set of common values, beliefs and understandings among those working there, i.e. an organizational culture. But men and women-specific orientations may reinforced, weakened or even almost disappear as gendered meanings values overlap or are crossed by cultural formations associated with occupations, classes, work groups and so on. In one organization there be male engineers and female secretaries with highly different orientation In a Finnish study it was found that dominant cultural values of initiative and boldness hardly included the female, low-level employees (Aaltio Marjasola, 1994). In another organization, young female professionals expressed other orientations than somewhat older low-level female staff in many respects showed more cultural similarities with the male professionals (Sundin, 1993).

A qualified cultural study thus calls for attention to a variety of configurations in an organization. Sometimes a unique and unitary organizational culture may be of interest to focus on, sometimes a variety subcultures will be central in the study. Before making crucial choices terms of level and adequate conceptualization of interesting cultural a number of different possibilities must be considered (Alvesson, 1993). Sometimes conventional organizational divisions may mislead rather sensitize cultural analysis.

The cultural approach in organization studies proceeds from the assumption that the ideas, the definitions of reality and the meanings which are shared in common by a collective (a company, a work group, for example) are a central—perhaps even the central—feature of organizations. This approach draws attention to the question 'How is organization accomplished and what does it mean to be organized?' (Smircich, 1983, p. 353). More or less integrated patterns of common ideas and meanings constitute the core of structures, which denote relative stability in an organization. They have their roots in, and are influenced by, various social and material practices. They do not persist unchanged, but are recreated and reinforced (and sometimes weakened or changed) in a multitude of different situations, in everyday language, in actions and in material structures and in a multifaceted network of symbols, meanings and significations (Alvesson and Berg, 1992; Frost et al., 1985, 1991; Martin, 1992; Smircich, 1983, etc.).

Culture is the framework that guides action and social relations, 'the medium of life' (Czarniawska-Joerges, 1991). It facilitates social life, but also includes elements of constraints and conservatism as it tends to freeze social reality: to subordinate people to dominating ideas, beliefs and taken-for-granted assumptions. Even though there are also cultural meanings and values in organizations that are pro-equality, in gender studies critical aspects of the gendered subtext of organizational life are often of the greatest interest (Alvesson and Billing, 1997, p. 105).

As we have said, culture involves assumptions and ideas that are taken for granted. This quality means that questioning, or at any rate serious questioning, of existing social conditions is not pronounced. Basic social conditions tend to be taken for granted and the social world will be regarded as natural, neutral and legitimate (Deetz and Kersten, 1983; Frost, 1987). There is often limited awareness that social reality can be experienced and understood in radically different ways, and that an infinite number of approaches are possible. An acceptance of this calls for selectivity in the view of experienced social conditions, and 'complementary' selectivity in interpreting and assessing what is heard and seen. Culture closes minds. Behaviour assumed to be feminine is for example seen as natural and self-evident when performed by females, but surprising, odd and unnatural when characterizing a man and vice versa.

The creation and recreation of meaning is not primarily located in the heads of people, although something must happen there too for culture to 'work'. Rather it comes in the form of a traffic in significant symbols, which guides thinking, feeling and social interaction. Meaning, from a cultural point of view, is social and public. Its natural habitat is the market place and the town square, according to Geertz (1973, p. 45), and, one could add, meetings and other social actions and events in a company. But also stories, vocabularies and artefacts physical objects such as buildings, equipment and office arrangements embodying meaning - may be seen as cultural expressions. The gender relations, as an important social phenomena thus, influence the fundamental functioning of organizations and our general way of thinking about aims, rationality, values, leadership and so on (Calás and Smircich, 1992a, 1992b). This kind of thinking works well with a cultural approach. One may talk of a gendered-organizations perspective rather than a gender-in-organizations approach (Hall, 1993) as a way of illuminating the gendered nature of organizational and occupational cultures. This means that 'gender is not simply imported into the workplace: gender itself is constructed in part through work' (Leidner, 1991, p. 170). Gender is thus partly seen as an organizational accomplishment-and not something that is fixed and ready and then the object for certain arrangements and mechanisms in organizations. Workplace culture thus is seen as constructing beliefs about and self-understandings of men and women, what is masculine and feminine, thus shaping gender identities.

Gender can function as a perspective or as an inspiration for a set of metaphors for the understanding of organizations (Billing and Alvesson, 1994; Gherardi, 1995). Gender dimensions can thus be observed also on a more abstract level than simply in relation to the concrete circumstances and relations of men and women.

Gendering organizational culture theory thus provides an approach for an exploration of cultural meanings of physical objects, actions and verbal expressions loosely coupled to the specific mix of sexes - or even lack of a mix (in one-sex only contexts) - directly involved. All kinds of organizational structures and processes are seen as carriers of cultural meaning, drawing upon and producing gendered ideas, values and assumptions. This does not mean that everything is treated in terms of gender, but that everything is carefully considered in these terms before one finally decides if and how to treat subject matter. Business language and practices, such as corporate strategy, campaign, conquests of markets, raiders or take-overs, may, for example, be conceptualized in terms of dominating masculinities (Knights and Morgan, 1991), but the origin of, for example, strategy in the military is not in itself sufficient to say that all corporate strategy talk and practice express masculinity.

The cultural patterns of organizations may be of particular interest to investigate in the following ways: (1) how cultural meanings interact with gender division of labour - both in terms of how organizational structure brings about certain meanings (Kanter, 1977) and how these cultural meanings contribute to a certain sex distribution in the organizational structure; (2) how dominating values and beliefs are culturally defined as, or associated with, maleness or - but probably more rarely - femaleness, and thus in different ways guide everyday organizational life and social interaction; (3) how organizations play a part in the socializing processes in which people acquire, mould, change, broaden or constrain gender identities; and (4) how organizational goals, structures and social relations lead to 'external' consequences, for example, for social life outside the core organization, or for the environment, due to their gendered nature. Investigating masculine domination in certain types of organizations may, for example, throw light on control and exploitation of customers and nature. As mentioned in earlier, the cultural meaning of jobs is highly significant for the division of labour. Many ideas on gender are culturally shared well beyond the individual organization or occupation. Images and self-understandings of women associating them with subordination, domesticity and sexuality which constitute an integrated part of any culture that account for the distribution of women in certain types of service jobs. The cultural meaning of a 'woman' may thus include the more or less explicit and conscious element of a service-provider. (The meaning may well be partly non-conscious.) But there is an enormous variation in this respect between different contexts, associated with wide although uneven and often contradictory changes taking place. The images and self-understandings may be more or less embraced by different groups—of men as well as women —and thus be noticeable to different extents and in various ways in different organizational contexts. Also within a specific industry there may be clear variation between different organizations in the same field in terms of gender meanings, as Blomqvist (1994) shows in a study of 17 Swedish knowledge-intensive companies. Organization culture studies are thus interested in local variation and uniqueness as well as broader cultural phenomena in the context of organizations. Specific organizational cultures form fine-tuned nets of meaning that subtly inform and encourage people to play out gender in certain ways and discourage them from doing so in ways that are not socially sanctioned.

Organizational Culture and Women Managers

As a result of the subordinate status of women in management, and the devaluation of feminine values in the business environment, the first female executives to succeed in breaking through the glass ceiling into corporate management adhered to many of the rules of conduct, norms and standards that spelled success for their male counterparts.

Because they were breaking new ground, these women did not have role models, and because there was a general lack of recognition of women's ways of leading, they also tended to lead like men in a command-and-control style of management. Indian experiences confirm that the first wave of women executives were under pressure to conform to and assimilate a dominant masculine corporate culture and to counteract the traditional stereotypes that men held of women. In so doing, they rejected some of their own feminine values and culture. Yet they dared not go too far in adopting male patterns of behaviour lest they pose a threat to the position of men. They were expected to be tough, though not macho; they had to be ambitious, but could not expect equal treatment in terms of pay, perks and promotion. Women dared not lose their femininity altogether, but their femininity was also not valued.

Very few companies have moved women into the executive ranks. What has prevented women's movement into management and, especially, into the executive suite? What have countries, companies, and women themselves done to increase women's representation in management? Until the late 1970s, women were virtually invisible as managers, and their absence was generally considered a non-issue. Since then, women managers have become increasingly visible in our country.

From one perspective the picture is positive. In each state, changing societal patterns have resulted in significant increases in the number of women managers. These patterns include favourable economic and demographic conditions, supportive government policies, changing family roles and emerging support systems. In addition, women show positive responses to their new opportunities.

From another perspective the picture is not so rosy. Each region tells a similar stow of a society in which men control the centres of political and economic power, and of a profession controlled primarily by men -- a profession in which women remain relative newcomers, especially at the top. In all states, major barriers still hold back women's progress in management. Beyond the international commonalties underlying women's exclusion from the centres of managerial power and authority lies the uniqueness of local conditions in each country that has produced the variety of women's experiences worldwide.

Male and Female Workforce. Things are changing and women are slowly being recognized as an important part of the workforce, yet they remain concentrated in a narrow range of activities. Apart from the traditional professions, the presence of women in the new professions is as little as to be unimportant. Examination of the preferences of women for careers reveals that very few of them want to go in for new professions. Most women still prefer the traditional occupation in which they already have a monopoly. On one hand, the women are placed on a pedestal and given a very high place, and, on the other hand they are still being treated as second to men in all regards. We have always heard of a woman being behind the man never alongside. There is thus a contradictory attitude towards women as goddesses and as second grade citizen. This contradiction is found in the field of employment also.

What decides, which work is for women, is not its nature or physical and psychological or mental burden it carries, but the symbolic significance of the work society. Greater the social desirability of the work, lesser the chances of women dominating in that field. Lesser the importance of the work, greater is the chances of women being identified with it. All societies seem to prefer men in the most valued jobs. Interestingly even in the fields in which women are dominant in proportion for instance teaching, IT professions, the top positions are held by men. Women are at best tolerated in most crucial fields. Those who do not manage to enter and succeed in these spheres are regarded as having certain unusual, in fact abnormal traits, which explain and justify this deviation and inconsistency. Thus even in the limited fields in which women work, they do not occupy the key positions. They are mostly found in the supervisory positions, whereas men are seen occupying positions, which involve organization, planning and policy-making (Powell, 1990).

Image of Women Managers in Organization. The leading argument over the years has been that the abilities and attitudes of the male and female managers are thought to be different. The argument has been most successfully kept to keep women out of management. The image of a women manager has certain beliefs associated with it. These tend to make a women see unsuitable for managerial posts. In the Indian society there are certain research evidence that shows the presence of sex differences in respect of such variables such as job complexity, internal motivation to work, satisfaction with pay, security and supervision, global satisfaction, etc. among women bank employees. Such research evidence for managerial job is however scanty (Devanna, 1987).

Many other factors mitigate against full and equal participation of women in a male- dominated profession like management. Spencer and Podmore (1983) have identified certain factors that contribute to professional marginalisation of women in male-dominated professions, the most important of which from the point of view of the study carried out could be broadly viewed under two groups:

1. Stereotypes about the nature of professions and about women who work in them, and
2. The assumed lack of professional commitment among women because of their domestic commitments and consequent effects on their prospects for promotion.

The studies carried on the first aspect within an Indian society indicate that sex role stereotypes are to be still found widely prevalent within the society in spite of all the economic and social development taking place in the country. Finding of research in this area also indicate some of these popular beliefs are that a strong consensus about the differing characteristics of men and women existed across groups which differ in sex, age, religion, marital status and educational level and secondly the characteristics ascribed to men are valued more positively than the characteristics ascribed to women (Brevarman et al.1972). Numerous other investigators have also noted the existence of sex role stereotypes. These stereotypes are widely held (Lunnenborg, 1970), persistent (Fernberger, 1948) and highly traditional (Komarovsky, 1950; McKee and Sherrifs, 1959). These have also been found to affect personnel decisions regarding women (Joshi, 1988).

Attitudes and Perceptions. There are certain attitudes and perceptions, which differentiate men and women as managers, and they are broadly classified under the following heads. Attitudes form central role in the formation of people's beliefs and behaviours. Yet it is seen that attitudes are intangible and unobservable. People are often unaware of their specific attitudes and the manner in which they affect their behaviour. Many attitudes are developed and maintained in a non-logical fashion, experientially and unsystematically, rather than as the result of rational analysis. Attitudes are however powerful influences on the behaviour of the people at work. Hence we find that if a specific attitude is formed regarding any person or group, e.g., women managers it is likely that it would affect their future development in the society. This sort of behaviour can range from preferential treatment to discriminatory action as is the case for the women managers about whom the society and that form certain attitudes is being followed.

This necessitates the fact to know the image of women managers held by the society and to examine through research study as to how much of it can be justified and on what grounds and how much is just not justified (Dipboye, 1975).

The image of a women manager (Devanna, 1987) is thought to be is follows:

Women are said to take up jobs only out of economic pressure. They are in other words forced to work. There is no real drive or ambition in them. They do not aim at self-actualization or self-realization through their work.

Women tend to absent themselves from work more often than men due to family reasons. They tend to give priority to family work over their professional work.

Women change jobs often due to their husband's shifting to another city. They follow their husband's wherever they go, as they consider the man's job more important as compared to their own.

Women snatch jobs from men who are the true breadwinners of their families and require the jobs more than the women.

Women work only for extra pocket money or pin money.

Women do not make good bosses, for they are too timid and socially oriented to be tough. Interestingly, a complaint against women bosses is that they are too insensitive and considerate.

Women cannot handle crises. They are good only for routine work, which requires no decision- making or problem solving. They cannot work in the face of uncertainties.

Women cannot work in jobs involving odd hours. They are fit only for nine to five jobs.

Women do not make good managers, as they cannot.

Marriage tend to cut short the career of women with the result that their education and training go waste.

All these beliefs regarding the women managers imply that women are not ambitious, talented or committed enough to succeed as managers. Their social image clashes with the image of the professional managers. However, these are nothing but popular myths which are not true and present a distorted picture (Devanna, 1987).

Problems Faced by Women Managers

Women do not enter workforce only due to economic strain but also because of ambition to achieve something in life. They do not absent themselves from work any more than men. In fact women managers at the middle and top levels in the organization are at an age when their children have grown up and their families do not require so much attention. Similarly, women do not change jobs because of their husbands shifting to another city but due to lack of opportunity to rise in their organizations. It is also wrong to see only men as breadwinners and women as mere helpers. Women can also play the role of breadwinners like men do. It is also seen that women always do not earn for pin money but to achieve economic independence. Again it is seen that marriage and motherhood may not necessarily cut down short their careers. An increasing number of women are now combining marriage with employment and managing to keep a balance between the two.

There is again a saying that women make bad bosses because they are not strong enough. The problem is that if women are polite, they are seen as timid, ineffectual persons and if they are tough, they are criticized for being insensitive and inconsiderate. Their success is as much an object of criticism as their failure. Women are treated as unsuitable for managerial posts also because their family preoccupations do not allow - problem is that of the image of women. If they do agree to travel or work long hours, they are accused of neglecting their family life. The difficulty of women managers is that they are criticized if they succeed or do not, in both ways. All these myths play an important role in restricting women to enter into the field of management.

Even if they manage to enter the male-dominant sphere, they still have to face other problems. The difficulty that a women manager has to face is of different types. First of all there is the problem of biological and psychological misconceptions regarding women. They are considered biologically inferior and psychologically less sound to men and therefore they do not fit the rigorous and difficult task of management, which is successfully carried out by men. A male manager does not need to prove his worth to his co-members but for a women manager it is a must factor. Her competency is not taken for granted but is always under scrutiny and she is always under trail. This hostile environment reflects the attitudes of male towards them (Silverstone and Ward, 1980).

The fact that there are very few women managers in the large organizations has its own implications. The women face exclusion from the male majority and tend to become alienated. They feel like interlopers rather than a part of the organization. They are the intruders in the all male bastion. Any major problem confronting women managers is that of facing hostility from the male colleagues. For an effective performance they require cooperation from their colleagues. Research studies show that men find it very difficult to take orders from the female boss. As Cussler (1958) puts it "if there is a thing women are not supposed to be it is boss".

Yet another problem faced by women managers is that of the work and family conflict. Management job requires more than just five to nine commitment. Organization makes both formal and informal demands on managers. The compatibility between career and family goals may sometimes create difficulties for the women managers. Besides, the top executives are also expected top socialize to get in contact with important people. In case of men they get the support from their wives, but it is not so easy for women executive to make the same demand on her husband. We are going to in our research study look into all these problems to study the relevance of them and also deal them in further detail independently later trying to look into the views of various researchers who have dealt each problem independently before we provide our own collection.

Gender and Work

Today's labour market is often characterized as being highly segregated, horizontally and vertically. Women and men work in different sectors and job areas and men occupy 85 to 90 per cent of the positions at the top levels of working life. The concept of segregation implies that the division of labour is not based on 'natural' skills or on the 'free will' of individuals but that it needs explanation, especially because the segregation also results in inequalities, mainly that women are concentrated within low pay areas, whereas men's jobs are better paid and offer better promotion prospects. The division of labour into 'female' and 'male' work areas is broadly considered to be a vital element in the subordination of women.

Many explanations are available when we wish to understand the gendered division of labour historically and in the present day and the resulting inequalities between the sexes. We deal with and discuss explanations at different levels: the macro-level, the meso- and the individual (micro-) level (Alvesson and Billing, 1997).

A Brief History of Work

Most cultures seem to include systems of meanings and norms prescribing different activities and characteristics for women and men. Women's work throughout the ages is described by Novarra (1980) as six tasks which pre-date the money economy and which are necessary for the human race to survive and life to be tolerable, and these functions are still women's main work areas today. These are: to bear children; to feed them and other members of the family; to clothe people; to care for the small, the sick, the elderly and the disabled; to be responsible for the education of children; and to take care of the home (including making products of use to the home). Men have shared, in varying degrees, the tasks which are needed to sustain and continue the human race, such as hunting, farming and fishing, but our image of men's work is not currently or historically drawn from the six tasks, argues Novarra (1980).

In the pre-industrial family women and men both produced goods for the household and women also took care of the home and the people living there. Work was then not regarded as separated from private life. People produced from day to day what they needed for their existence. Wage labour was a rare phenomenon. Today most of us are dependent upon selling our labour power for wages, and if we are unemployed we are dependent upon financial support, primarily from the state.

Although women's and men's tasks overlapped in the pre-industrial era there were rather strict ideas about women's work and men's work within the specific community. What exactly is (and historically was) regarded as typically feminine or masculine to a considerable extent varied from country to country and even from one region to another. Within certain ark areas there was even a taboo against the other sex doing the job; in France and Sweden for example, milking cows was exclusively regarded as women's work until this century. Men risked ridicule, from women as well other men, if they milked cows (Shorter, 1975), and the mythical aura around milk made it unthinkable even to drink it if men had been involved its production. Besides, prestige was connected to the work men did, and lost status and power if they did women's work. It was easier for women to do men's work than the other way round. Men had more to lose. When women did men's work they were not harassed in the same way. However, it was difficult for women to achieve the status connected to men's jobs (Göransson, 1996).

On farms in Sweden it was largely men who produced the raw materials while women did the refining (Göransson, 1978) but there were also areas where women and men worked together, e.g., with the harvest. What was thought to be women's or men's work varied according to different economic and ecological preconditions (Lofgren, 1977), for instance, if men off hunting or fishing women took over responsibility for the farm in meantime. Women were considered as capable as men of taking care of farm work. In the southern part of Sweden (in the eighteenth and nineteenth centuries) in large-scale agriculture there was a stricter division tasks, with women doing work close to the farm and inside it, and men working in the field.

It is not possible to say why some work was women's and some was men's; to do so would imply a specific historical investigation of the cultural local meanings which are attached to the respective job tasks. It takes a lot of research to discover why jobs change gender. Sommestad (1992) discusses why dairying (in Sweden) changed from being a female of competency for many hundreds of years to becoming a male job in 1930s. Her study clearly shows that the gendered division of labour has nothing to do with economy/biology but is historically constructed and that work is labelled female or male on the basis of historically changeable interests and assumptions. The re-labelling process takes some time of course—it is not done in a matter of days. In the case of dairy work, the introduction of machines into the production process and the development scientific approach to milk meant that the associations between milk women eroded. Milk was now also connected with machines and technique. The inclusion of milk in a technological-scientific tradition led transcendence of the gap between milk and masculinity. Milk was nor something mysterious, taken care of by women (connected to breastfeeding), but could now be regarded as a result of a chemical process/ solution which is seen as appropriate for men to work with. When milk became scientific it lost its exclusive association with the female body and intuition and this gave men the opportunity to be involved with the hitherto taboo-laden female milk. In the UK dairying also used to be women's work but was likewise taken over by men when cheese making became more scientific (Davidoff, 1986).

It is difficult to say whether women's and men's work were regarded as equally important as some researchers tend to believe (e.g., Baude, 1992; Illich, 1982; Reskin and Padavic, 1994), while others advocate that whatever women did was regarded as less important than men's work (Hirdmann, 1988). Segregation remains today, and although the sexual division of labour is very variable there are some areas which are culturally defined as male or female respectively and dependent upon the ideas within the communities about what is suitable work for women and for men.

The industrial revolution (which started in Western Europe in the eighteenth century and continued over the following 200 years) transformed the way work was done. The work of craftsmen, for example, which was male work, was industrialized and the production was now controlled by capitalists. Many former self-employed craftsmen and farmers were forced to sell their labour power on the market. Some parts of women's production of useful items in the home were now also to be carried out on a market basis (such as textiles), first in cottage industries and later in factories, and many of these jobs were primarily reserved for (unmarried) women. In the early industrialized countries men became the large majority of the labour force while women's main responsibility was to take care of the home.

The breakthrough of industrialism and capital's need for cheap and plentiful labour power made it possible for (and/or forced) women on a greater scale (mainly working class women and children) to join in the production process, in areas unrelated to their former work in the home. This, however, carried the contradiction with it, as Engels maintained (1972), that the proletarian families were being dissolved (whether women worked or not) because, on the one hand, women could not earn anything if they fulfilled their duties in the family and, on the other hand, if they worked in industry they were unable to fulfil family obligations. Engels said that this was true of women in all sorts of occupations, from medicine to law.

In the early period of industrialization in many countries women and men faced unregulated working conditions, for example, in England there were no regulations about the length of the working day or opportunities for maternity leave. Some restrictions on the length of the working day for women were made in the 1840s in England (10 hours a day), and in the 1870s the Health of Women Act did restrict the working hours to 56.5 hours per week for women, children, and young persons employed in textile factories (Lewis and Rose, 1995). Protective labour laws were eventually carried through in other European countries, in the late nineteenth and early twentieth centuries. These provided women with some protection, maternity leave, etc., and limited the length of the working day. In many countries women were also banned from night work. Because women's labour was indispensable both for industry and the proletarian household economy, it was important that the protective labour legislation made it possible for women to reconcile paid work with family demands. 'Women's protection was not rhetorically linked to their working conditions, as in the case of men, but rather to their sex' (Schmitt, 1995, p. 128). The underlying discourse on women's work was then linked to their motherhood and family roles, thus confirming that housework and childcare were women's duties. More historians have debated the power of these discourses on protective labour laws for women and have concluded that when they were applied to women only, on the one hand they created special categories of workers (thus consolidating segregation) and on the other, in practice, they produced divisions among women, because they affected some categories of women more than others. This legislation served the purpose of 'reconciling the competing needs of women and families to meet a broader set of social purposes including sustaining the family wage male breadwinner ideology; supporting a sexually segregated labour market; and enhancing the possibilities of survival for future generations of workers' (Kessler-Harris et al., 1995, p. 23).

Industrial development also made it possible to produce on a large scale what used to be produced by the household. The development of the means of production and the needs of capital to find new markets meant that work which used to be done in the home by women (spinning, weaving, knitting, baking, butchering) was also done on a commercial basis. The industrial development made it possible to produce all consumption goods faster and cheaper than was possible in the home. Female-dominated industries increased in the late nineteenth century. One example from Sweden is bakeries, where there were (strictly) male ('soft'/white bread) bakeries and female (ordinary bread) bakeries; only in four per cent of these were men and women working together (Baude, 1992).

Because the family was no longer a production unit and could not meet its own reproductive needs any longer it became important to earn enough on the market to support the family. Women's wages were lower and perhaps more uncertain than the husbands' and the latter took on the role of the main providers or, as it was to be called later on, the breadwinners. A majority of married women became dependents and house-keepers/home-makers, and the labour force became predominantly male. This family wage model was endorsed by protective labour legislation in the late nineteenth century in many countries and is believed to have asserted woman's primary role as a mother and childrearer and also subsumed her role as provider (Kessler-Harris, 1995). In other countries, however, a family wage was never accepted by the employers and women had to accept whatever job they could get, as the families could not live on one income.

Many middle-class women only had paid work until they married, when they were primarily expected to take care of the house and children and be dependent on their husbands' wages. In working-class families women would often have to have paid work after marriage as well, in order to provide the family with what it needed. Married (middle-class) women' withdrawal from the labour market was contingent upon the idea of woman's proper place being in the home and a man's in the world of commerce (away from home). Work and family life were in many countries regarded as two separate spheres.

Reinforcing these beliefs were stereotypes of men as strong, aggressive, and competitive and of women as frail, virtuous, and nurturing, images that depicted men as naturally suited to the highly competitive nineteenth-century workplace and women as too delicate for the world of commerce. (Reskin and Padavic, 1994, p. 21)

Another reason why many married women did not work was that it was not always possible for them to get work, for example, during the depression years in the 1 930s women were discriminated against in many countries. In the USA, 84 per cent of the nation's insurance companies, 65 per cent of the banks and 63 per cent of public utilities had restrictive rule preventing married women from holding any jobs (Campbell, 1984, p. 110 cited in Alpern, 1993). State and local governments passed laws barring women from public employment; they were joined by the federal government in 1932 (Stivers, 1993). In Sweden too, unions accepted the dismissal of married women (Wikander, 1991). It should be noted, however, that not only women but also black men were discriminated against; in the 1920s in the USA 'racism in the federal government began to push black women and men out of white collar job opportunities' (Harley, 1990, quoted in Stivers, 1993).

Although many of the gender arrangements of early capitalism were continuation of the work pattern in the pre-capitalist economy, capitalism has had a crucial role in maintaining, consolidating and reconstructing patterns of segregation and sex-typing (Bradley, 1994, p. 152). In the early industries men and women competed for the same tasks, but in the new industries as well as in the public services work was 'designed' according one or the other gender (Göransson, 1996). By designating jobs as women work, it was possible to employ women more cheaply because of the low social value already put on their work, and capitalists also benefited from men trying to reserve jobs as male jobs as that resulted in the relegation women to low-paid female jobs. For example, domestic services, agricultural and light industry (textiles, tobacco and clothing) were women's jobs, women worked within the manufacturing industry, engineering and commerce. There were also jobs which men eventually took over. 'The invention of new machine or technique provides a rationale for men to redefine an old female occupation as a man's occupation, thereby increasing its social standing and driving women out to the margin' (Bradley, 1993,p. 16). As a result of the industrial revolution (and mechanizations) in Britain men eventually took over female specialities like baking, brewing and spinning (Bradley, 1993).

Some jobs which used to be men's jobs also became women's jobs eventually, e.g., clerks, tobacconists and weavers. In 1871 clerks in the UK were almost all men, while in 1930 women constituted over 40 per cent of the clerical workers. In 1911 clerks were placed in the highest of 5 social classes, class I. By 1930 clerks had fallen to class III, according to the official ranking of occupations (Kirkham and Loft, 1993). In 1870 in the USA, three per cent of the office clerks, stenographers, typists, bookkeepers, cashiers and accountants were women, whereas in 1930 women made up 95 per cent of all typists and stenographers, two-thirds of all office clerks were men, and almost half of all bookkeepers, cashiers, and accountants (Reskin and Padavic, 1994). According to Stivers (1993) it was not lack of qualifications that accounted for the small number of women in the civil service in the USA in the late nineteenth century but discrimination in hiring. In the period from 1884 to 1894 women constituted between 28 per cent and 43 per cent of those passing civil service examinations, but only seven per cent to 25 per cent of those were actually hired (Aron, 1987, p. 110, referred to in Stivers, 1993). During World War I there were significant changes in the participation of women in the public sector services, in factories, in paid and unpaid work, and women demonstrated that they could do the work as well as the men they either replaced or collaborated with (Stivers, 1993).

In both (war) periods (World Wars I and II) in the countries at war women had access to jobs which were ordinarily men's jobs. Reskin and Padavic (1994, p. 51) cite slogans designed to attract women to blue-collar jobs: 'If you can run a sewing machine you can operate a rivet gun'. They mention, for example, that women worked as conductors on the trains, and that they were building and flying cargo planes. When the war(s) ended women were laid off and transferred into low-paying jobs such as assemblers and clerk-typists and it was not until the 1970s that women were admitted into traditionally male occupations, according to Reskin and Padavic (1994). Although Bradley (1989) regards the two world wars as important challenges to sex segregation, because it was liberating experience in itself that women were able to demonstrate that they could do all sorts of tasks (from managing offices to maintaining railways), she concludes that wartime experience had little long-term impact on the structure of segregation. After World War II many women were channelled into service jobs, and many employers (in the USA) introduced marriage bars. Married women again became dependent on their husbands' wages.

In some countries, like the USA, Sweden and Denmark, the 'period of housewives' culminated around the 1950s, after which more and more women (including married women) had paid work. The increased labour demand was due to economic growth and, in the Nordic countries, to the expansion of the welfare state where childcare became a responsibility of the state; in the beginning of the 1960s around 40 per cent of Swedish, Finnish and Danish women were active in the labour market - by the 1990s this number had almost doubled. The number of women in the labour force differed very much in Western Europe, the closest number to the Scandinavian figures being West Germany with 36 per cent of women in the labour force (1970). There are (and have been) differences in family politics in the Scandinavian countries compared with the continental countries. Married women especially in Sweden and Denmark were accorded individual rights and were supported by the state in their economic independence whereas married women in continental Europe were, and are, regarded as dependent on their husbands (Borchorst, 1993). These differences in the policies of the state combined with different cultural gender ideologies have probably influenced mothers' participation in the labour market particularly.

Masculinities, Femininities and Work

A way to avoid focusing too strongly upon a particular analytical level is to use a social constructivist approach to masculinity and femininity to understand gender patterns (as well as deviations from clear patterns), e.g., segregated labour markets and division of labour in work organizations. These concepts make it possible to connect on the one hand to the overall societal culture and on the other hand to the feelings, thoughts, self-understandings and values - in short subjectivities - that characterize individuals. Expressed slightly differently, the concepts refer to how broad domains of life are culturally gendered as well as to how people conform to or transgress the social standards and guidelines for living suggested by what are culturally defined as masculine and feminine. In other words, masculinity and femininity have the advantage of making possible connections to macro as well as micro. They offer an alternative to the variable-oriented fixation on 'men' and 'women' using the bodies as a firm criterion for classification as well as being an alternative to standpoint researchers' tendency to use the female sex as a robust point of departure for ascribing experiences and interests to a unitary and unique half of humanity.

Apart from being able to throw some light on gender segregation in labour markets and work organizations, the social constructivist use of masculinity and femininity as an interpretive framework is useful for exploring a wide range of aspects of organizations, including organizational culture and leadership: This sub-section thus offers some additional illumination to some of the broader gender work patterns discussed earlier. While we still do not attempt to offer the grand explanation - and provides some ideas of value for the further study of culture and leadership in organizations.

We will to some extent say more about masculinity than femininity here - although the terms presuppose each other. One reason for this is that more work has been done on the former than the latter concept within the field of gender and organization. (There are many more books and articles including the words masculinity and masculinities than femininity and femininities.) The large majority of all gender research has emphasized women, either in variable terms or through an interest in women's perspectives, interests, values or experiences, typically in the ugh of male domination (patriarchy). The personal experiences of men have not been seen as very interesting, or perhaps as too unreliable or dubious to serve as a point of departure; instead the somewhat more distanced and problematizing concept of masculinity has served as a point of entry for studies of men, perhaps more seldom of 'men as men' but as privileged carriers of a dominating form of masculinity (or patriarchy). Only recently have a few researchers started discussing men more specifically (for example, Williams, 1993). The norms and values by which women's -and men's actions have been assessed have been defined in a 'male' way and it has not been necessary for men to reflect upon or problematize social conditions in relation to their sex in the same way that women have done.These norms and values have been and are increasingly being questioned to and the former unquestionable and 'natural' masculinity is attacked. This has encouraged (some) men to take another stance and be occupied with themselves as a relational category, as a sex which is one part of gender relations (e.g., Kimmel, 1994; Meuser, 1996). Although to some extent we concentrate on masculinity in this chapter we are still interested in gender relations and are not focusing on men perse.

Masculinity and Femininity: Some Views

Organizational and occupational structures, processes and practices may be viewed as culturally masculine and, perhaps often less salient when it comes to dominating patterns, as feminine. Masculinity and femininity are thus not essential categories but should be seen as 'products' of, or themes in, different discourses. Gendering organizations usually means paying attention to how organizational structures and processes are dominated by culturally defined masculine meanings. (Feminine meanings dominate less frequently although they may be central in some organizations.) Masculinity is a vague concept, but can be defined as values, experiences and meanings that are culturally interpreted as masculine and typically feel 'natural' to or are ascribed to men more than women in the particular cultural context. It makes sense here to recognize the variety of masculinities, avoid single masculine-feminine scales (Connell, 1987) and talk about 'multiple masculinities'. Collinson and Hearn (1994) identify five such versions in the context of organizations: authoritarianism, paternalism, entrepreneurialism, careerism and informalism (men building networks on the basis of shared masculine interests and excluding women). Variations between different classes, nations, occupations, ages, organizations and ethnic groups are sometimes pronounced when talking about masculinity and femininity. Some forms of working-class masculinity may, for example, be quite antagonistic to management and white-collar work, which is perceived as non-masculine (Collinson, 1988). Morgan, while recognizing the diversity of masculinities, suggests that they are not 'like a well-stocked supermarket', but 'are linked to each other, hierarchically, in terms of power' (1992, p. 45). He does not say very much about how. One should not neglect the possibility of various subcultures developing different forms of masculinity also in the absence of an overall hierarchy or well-connected pattern.

A typical description of masculinity stresses features such as ...hard, dry, impersonal, objective, explicit, outer-focused, action-oriented, analytic, dualistic, quantitative, linear, rationalist, reductionist and materialist' (Hines, 1992, p. 328). The concept of masculinity overlaps with what Marshall (1993, p. 124) views as male values or the male principle: self-assertion, separation, independence, control, competition, focused perception, rationality and analysis. While recognizing the multiplicity of masculinity, Kerfoot and Knights view as its core, at least in managerial and organizational work, 'a preoccupation with a particular instrumental form of "rational control" (1996, p. 79). Femininity is defined in complementing and corresponding terms. For Hines (1992, p. 314), femininity is a matter of 'the prioritizing of feelings . . . the importance of the imaginative and creative...'

Female values or the female principle are characterized by interdependence, cooperation, receptivity, merging, acceptance, awareness of patterns, wholes and contexts, emotional tone, personalistic perception, being, intuition, and synthesizing (Marshall, 1993, p. 124). Grant (1988) talks about 'nurturance, compassion, sensitivity, empathy'.

The concepts of masculinity and femininity cannot be understood in isolation. According to Kimmel (1994, p.126) masculinity is viewed as the antithesis of femininity: 'This notion of anti-femininity lies at the heart of contemporary and historical conceptions of manhood, so that masculinity is defined more by what one is not rather than what one is.' In a similar vein Hollway (1996, p. 28) argues that the idea of 'woman' has been produced 'as the negative of the masculine'.

There are considerable problems when talking about and identifying masculinity(ies) as well as femininity(ies). One issue concerns the ontological status of the mentioned ideas. Do they reflect social reality in some way or are they used for analytic purposes by the researchers? Are ideas on masculinity/femininity open to empirical impressions or are they purely in the hands of the researcher to define and use accordingly? Are the definitions cited above valid across culture and history or do they reflect contemporary Western, or only contemporary gender researchers', ideas on what is masculine and feminine? A second issue concerns how the concepts should be related to physical males/females. Are masculinity and femininity tightly connected to men and women, respectively, or can they be used also to illuminate 'non-human' phenomena such as artefacts and techniques? We start with the last question and later address the empirical vs. analytic character of the subject matter.

Some authors believe that the concept of masculinity 'may be thought of as representing the discourses and practices which indicate that someone is a man, a member of a category' (Collinson and Hearn, 1994, p. 6), and that it means 'individual signs and institutional indications that this is a male' (Hearn, 1993, p. 151). A problem with this understanding is that masculinity is associated with males, and femininity with females, defined according to biological criteria. Also men rejecting traditional masculinist orientations are defined in terms of 'other forms of masculine identity, such as that of 'the new man', the male feminist or the various forms of homosexual male identity' (Bradley, 1993, p. 22).

Another version is to relate the concepts of masculinities and femininities more loosely to physical gender (sex) and apply them to both sexes and also to 'non-sexual' phenomena - for example, nuclear power may be seen as a masculine technology irrespective of the number of females working with it or politically supporting it. When Collinson and Hearn (1994, p. 4) talk about the 'highly masculine values of individualism, aggression, competition, sport and drinking' they are clearly referring to values on which males today have no monopoly, unless one defines a male as someone who scores high on these values. Defining a male through specific values would imply that one disregards anatomy; a person may value individualism, sport and drinking, irrespective of genitals. A person may actually score high on all these dimensions, but still be seen as feminine according to some other dimensions (looks, mothering, for instance).

One way of using the concepts of masculinities and femininities without tying them essentialistically to the bodies of men and women is to treat them as traits or forms of subjectivities (orientations in thinking, feeling and valuing) that are present in all persons, men as well as women, although to different degrees. Women, biologically defined, are thus typically seen as more characterized by femininities than masculinities, even though there is great variation in terms of the composition of the two (sets of) qualities. This could be called the cocktail view on gender. In the average male version, there is typically a lot of gin and not much vermouth while the female prototype includes primarily the latter with just a few drops of the stronger stuff. (End of irony).

We believe that it is acceptable and important to use the concepts of masculinities and femininities to describe cultural beliefs without connecting these very closely to men and women. Masculine meaning may therefore be traced also in language, acts and artefacts loosely coupled to sex/human bodies. To explore how people think, feel and make sense in relation to these categories is vital for understanding gender relations and gender identities. Ideas about what is masculine/feminine and what is naturally normal for men and women in relation to these qualities guide, constrain and trap people in all respects from occupational choice to acceptance/rejection of tasks in everyday working life, although people may be more or less independent in relation to these guidelines and constraints. (Facilitating such independence may be defined as one purpose of gender studies.)

A second topic concerns the extent to which the researcher proceeds from an analytic/theoretical definition to an empirically grounded, historically and culturally oriented understanding of masculinities and femininities. The first alternative means the researcher himself or herself decides what is to be defined as masculinity/femininity or follows certain research authorities. The latter version calls for a sensitive listening to and reading of when and how people in a community ascribe a masculine or a feminine meaning to a phenomenon. Empirical grounding is necessary before labelling/interpreting something as masculine/feminine. Recognizing historical variation is important here. When masculinities and femininities are used as analytical concepts, the researcher analyses the deeper gendered meaning of social phenomena irrespective of what surfaces in terms of explicit, socially recognized cultural meanings. One may interpret something as masculine even in the absence of empirical indications that natives (the people being studied) view a phenomenon in such a way. Authorities such as Jung may for example offer ideas of what it is to be understood as masculine or feminine. (Jung views these qualities as depth-psychological qualities, a part of human nature.) Masculine and feminine then refer to 'essences', basically independent of cultural and historical variation, even though manifestations may vary cross-culturally.

The researcher must be clear about the use of the concept analytically and with little or no grounding in the cultural meanings of the natives. Often researchers choose a middle way, having some feeling for cultural ideas among people in the area studied without carefully investigating how they ascribe a gendered meaning to phenomena. Caution is, however, called for before departing too far from, or speculating too wildly about, the level of meaning. A basic problem is that the terms easily incorporate commonsensical notions held by the researcher, who may be as strong a victim of prejudices as other natives. She or he can simply read in masculinities whenever she or he feels like it. Talk about masculinities easily becomes a bit arbitrary. Let us give some illustrations of this problem.

Connell (1995) claims that the hegemonic ideal of masculinity is a man who is independent, risk-taking, aggressive, heterosexual and rational. But why are these characteristics singled out? Why not reliable, mentally balanced breadwinner, sexually attractive, physically strong, placed in a high-status position, wealthy or something else? And are not rational on the one hand, and risk-taking and aggressive on the other, rather contradictory ideals? If one of these ideals is hegemonic (culturally dominating), may the other not be? Ideals like independence and aggressiveness may look good on movies for adolescents, but are not necessarily embraced in social life. In US corporate life, for example, it is rather the socially sensitive team player that is appreciated (Jackall, 1988). Connell is aware of the discrepancy between ideals and the possibility of living up to these, but this does not prevent the claim about the hegemonic masculinity from being debatable.

Another example of problems with interpretations of masculinity we found in Tewksbury who says, in a study of male strippers, that they restructure their work roles 'to emphasize the traditionally masculine ideals of success, admiration, and respect' (1993, p.168). We feel uncertain whether these ideals are best understood as masculine. Would many people experience it as unfeminine to strive for these ideals? Ferguson also seems to talk about femininity in an arbitrary way when she writes: 'Women are not powerless because they are feminine; rather they are feminine because they are powerless, because it is a way of dealing with the requirements of subordination' (1984, p. 95). This equation between femininity and powerlessness fixes a particular view on the feminine that is of uncertain relevance for understanding contemporary cultural meanings of femininities - which do not necessarily include powerlessness. It may freeze the interpretive orientation not only by being culturally insensitive, but also analytically too narrow. Powerlessness (like power) can take many forms, some of which may be seen as feminine, for instance a participatory people-oriented soft 'leadership' style may also be seen as feminine, sexual attractiveness may be a significant source of power, as may parenthood. One obvious counter-example to understanding subordinates as feminine would be private soldiers in an authoritarian army, operating in a very strict hierarchy and forced to obey. Despite their subordination, they are normally seen as highly masculine. Arguably, there may thus be masculine as well as feminine kinds of subordination, as there may be corresponding forms of superiority and power, although in the feminine case they may be less clearly recognized. There may, of course, be forms of power/subordination that are not easily or productively interpreted in gender terms. Stivers, like Ferguson, thinks that there is a 'prototypical femininity' involved when men in organizations must cater to their superiors and become sensitive to their idiosyncracies (1993, p. 22), but that their interest in being seen as 'real men' works to prevent them from acknowledging this feminine quality. That subordinates obey their bosses may, however, be recognized without necessarily calling for labelling in gender terms. Our comments do not, of course, contradict the idea that masculinities often rank higher —in relation to monetary rewards, social status and symbolic power —thin femininities, although there may be changes underway (Alvesson and Billing, 1997). It should be noted, however, that in organizational contexts, both past and present, the majority of all men have been subordinates. That subordination in an organizational context should universally have a strong feminine quality is therefore a questionable assumption.

Many women (biologically defined) practise sport, appreciate whisky and may be described as equally individualistic, aggressive and competitive as many men. Many men may be described as social, relaxed, friendly and team-players. Studies of all-female shopfloors suggest that women often swear and participate in aggressive and sexualized forms of behaviour (Collinson and Hearn, 1994 themselves refer to such research). One may, of course, say that they are 'masculine' or express 'masculine' behaviour, but the point of using this concept is presumably that it is, in a particular cultural context, more typical for and appealing to men than women. Otherwise, these concepts become too one-sidedly researcher-driven and too insensitive to cultural context, given the criteria that the cultural meanings of masculinity and femininity should be balanced in the way the researcher uses the terms.

One way of avoiding the premature imposition by the researcher of his or her understanding on social phenomena would be to adopt a more local emerging approach in which the people in the area being studied may define what is masculine or feminine for them. In a specific organizational context, for example, one may investigate to what extent a particular vocabulary or behaviour is seen by the natives as masculine or feminine or gender-neutral. Such interpretive research tries to avoid imposing pre-structured categories and follows carefully the meanings of the natives. This may be a painstaking enterprise - at least if one wants considerable depth in the meanings being studied. The interpretive powers of the concept masculine/feminine may be weakened or even lost. It is likely that there is some variety in what people see as masculine/feminine or as neutral in these terms. For most gender researchers the entire area of management may be seen as fused with masculine meanings, but for many blue-collar worker the polite, tidy and physically safe area of management and white-collar work may appear as feminine or as perhaps rather ungendered. Such confrontations between perspectives are valuable as a counterforce to elitist /a priori researcher ideas, but interesting interpretations often call for the use by the researcher of some core concepts as an aid and not just letting these float and vary with the meanings of various groups and individuals.

As in many other cases, finding a balance between the theoretical/analytical use of the core concepts for the sake of direction and interpretive depth, and being empirical/sensitive to cultural meanings of people in context of the study is important. Such a balance is never contradiction free, as a critical reading of any research on the subject matter will make obvious. We here come close to the poststructuralist (postmodern) critique of dominant research that assumes and - consequently finds - fixed and coherent meanings. Any attempt to freeze a specific masculine or feminine meaning may be an easy target for a deconstruction, in which the fragile nature of the ascribed meaning is exposed. The author uses here the description given by Alvesson and Billing (1997, p. 89) who briefly illustrate problems with using ideas on masculinity/ femininity. Stiver (1993) uses these concepts with respect to US public administration. She argues that its self-understanding, 'as reflected in its images of leadership, expertise and virtue, is culturally masculine (although its masculinity is as yet unacknowledged), but that it also reflects a significant element of femininity (although consciousness of its femininity has yet to dawn)' (p. 122). The approach taken may be said to be rather elitist, in the sense that the voices of the people in the field do not seem to have been considered. (The reader does not encounter any in the entire book text.) People in the area are viewed as ignorant about the cultural meanings gendering their organizational world (within as well as outside US public administration). It is likely that there is great variation among different groups about its masculine or feminine characteristics. If one continues Stivers', questionable treatment of US public administration as a unitary whole, its masculinity/femininity varies with the yardstick or object of comparison. From a traditional working-class horizon, much of it presumably appears as rather unmasculine. Compared with business life, often seen as more competitive and powerful, the public sector is generally also understood as unmasculine. Trying to adopt business management rhetoric may strengthen a superficial aura of masculinity, or may do the opposite -for some groups exposing its hollow character in terms of masculinity. From the viewpoint of a feminist (or an anti-masculinist, i.e., a critical student of masculinities), wanting to promote radical transformation, masculine domination emerges almost routinely as the most appropriate interpretation. If one considers the enormous variation within not just US public administration but also most specific organizations, it is likely that one may find many examples of culturally masculine as well as feminine meanings, not just contingent upon how one frames and positions the object being studied but also as a result of the enormous empirical variation.

Consequently, given the problems with the concepts of masculinities and femininities we think that particular caution is required when using them. In particular, the risk of reproducing stereotypes and of arbitrarily imposing masculinity or femininity must be considered. It seems that (almost) all jobs may be constructed as male or female, depending on which dimensions one emphasizes, the language used and how one chooses to reason (Leidner, 1991). This is the case not only for people being studied but also for researchers. Researchers may construct jobs and other phenomena quite freely according to what they choose to emphasize. Rather than feeling free to label all sorts of phenomena one believes appeal to men or are more typical for men than women in thinking, acting and valuing 'masculine', great care and restraint should be exercised. What is masculine for one group or person may not be for another. Many phenomena are not necessarily best interpreted as masculine or feminine. Nevertheless, these concepts are valuable interpretive tools and gender studies could not do without them. A cautious, ironic approach is therefore to be recommended. One should be careful in sorting out analytical use of the terms and empirical descriptions of cultural meanings among people being studied, and seek a balance between analytical definitions and theoretical reasoning on the one hand and sensitivity for cultural context on the other. When combined with careful listening to the meanings ascribed by the subjects being addressed and followed by cautious interpretative work and careful grounding, an interest in masculinities and femininities as aspects of workplace cultures, social practices and identities may be productive in gender studies.

Women and Work Inequality

Economic development is the main goal of the society. A country can achieve development to the fullest extent only if all the human resources in it are being utilized to its optimal level. This implies that both men and women must participate equally in the achievement of this goal. Thus women should be allowed to play an equally crucial role in the socio-economic development of a country like men. But both in the industrially developed and less developed countries, women are burdened with cumulative inequalities as a result of discriminatory socio-economic practices. The situation is much worse particularly in the case of rural women. Unfortunately, a major and often overlooked feature of third world agrarian systems, particularly in Africa and Asia, is the crucial role played by women in agricultural production. Hence research studies have tried to look into the fact as to why in spite of all the provisions made by the constitution for the development of women providing them equal opportunity and also the changes taking place all over the world in the name of modernization, we still find women not being equally looked at in all aspect. Thus, women and work have become a much research and debated area. Often the underlying assumption and arguments for women's employment is that economic independence is the pre-requisite for moving towards gender inequality. As a result of all these debated discussion this women question has of late attracted the attention of economists, sociologists, research scholars and many others and hence a deep analytical study of the socio-economic discrimination against women in jobs has become one of the burning topics of today all over the world and particularly in India (Arpathamurthy, 1990).

Why So Less Change at Top

The enormous findings about the under representation of women in the top decision-making position may seem surprising given the existence of a women movement for over twenty years. The legislation aimed at providing equal opportunities for women in some countries and given that United Nations made improvement in the status of women an explicit. In 1975 the United Nations launched the United Nations Decade for Women: Equality, Development and Peace (Richardson, 1999).

The experience of many women striving to hit the top levels in business is that they must work harder, often struggling with extraordinary demands on their personal lives, to earn the same recognition or success as men. A tightening labour market is opening up now chances of top women to go ahead. Women bosses are hot issue, a sensitive one and with the good reasons. The fact is that experience of them is already wide spread at certain levels and in certain sectors, and the equally indisputable fact is that there are lots more coming along. The future of management everywhere is to be a lot more females involved in it. (Richardson, 1999).

Research on the aspect of as to why so few or lesser number of women reaches the top shows mixed views. The optimist believes that in the past women were excluded from full participation in the labor force and education. Once they are given the opportunity to acquire the necessary credentials and experience backed by supportive legislature, they will inevitably move into positions of authority and power and this is a time (Richardson, 1999).

The pessimist argues that the situation is complex and resistant to change. They believe that the optimist give little attention to prejudice, male and female resistance to changing roles, the effects of competition for desirable positions, as to who will perform the many unpaid tasks that women have traditionally done. They felt simply allowing women into college and the workforce will not necessarily and result women moving into positions of authority (Richardson, 1999).

Gender Stereotypes. Researchers have found women being discriminated against men in the social and economic spheres. Backward mental attitudes resulting from blind adherence to tradition and the absence of education especially among rural women are partly to blame. Illiteracy, for example, does induce a mood of unhelpful resignation to one's lot and the person feels that the injustice suffered is pre-ordained and inescapable. In rural households, the feeling that women are born to suffer and have to live a life of self-abnegation is deep rooted. This scenario exists for the rural women where lack of proper education allows social discrimination among men and women to continue, but we find that similar scenario does not prevail among urban women. It is seen that urban women are living within a modern world and are also given freedom to have best of education in a higher level and in this respect there are no discrimination. The problem arises once she steps in to the world of work.

The empirical evidences suggest that gender inequality is not found at a low level in the occupational aspect. We find according to statistics that at lower level women are well represented in the job field. It is only when situation of being represented at the top level that the percentage of women lower down and this is something like 2.3 per cent in case of women managers compared to male which is around 97 per cent. Thus, this is an area of research where our interest lies, to look into the deep rooted cause for this low representation of women at top level. The question that is widely asked in this context is that, Is it because of gender inequality, social tradition and culture or mental attitudes of women in choosing their priorities between work and family or their performance ability forbids them to reach the top level in managerial jobs in which men mostly rule.

Socio-Economic Perspective of Women Managers

Although the percentage of employed women is increasing in most countries the number in management remains disproportionally low and the number holding executive positions remains negligible, almost everywhere. This pattern holds across oriental and occidental cultures across communist, socialist and capitalist systems and also among the developing countries. Evidence suggest that the under representation under the utilization and skewed distribution of women managers is neither coincidental nor random but rather a function of systemic cultural sanctions, educational barriers, legal restrictions and corporate practices. The single most outstanding statement to make in this regard is that women in management are very few (Caulking, 1977).

One of the most prominent themes to emerge is that women manager regardless of the country, in which they live and work, have similar experiences derived from their assigned status as women and such a situation is prevalent till today irrespective all other changes taking place this area has not seen much change in positive terms. Patriarchy and its masculinist value persist world wide, varying by country only in degree to which they dominate policy and legislation. These circumstances provide the background of values in which women managers have to function and create viable life style. Women face discrimination on basis of marital status and have to conform to masculine standards of behaviour to progress through managerial rank and also has to balance societal responsibilities of parenthood and work. The organizational atmosphere has not yet changed to the level where they can accommodate, women as members fully equal to men. The widely relevant obstacle to women in the management field is the stubborn assistance of most societies to recognizing housework and childcare as roles to be shared equally by women (Caulking, 1977).

Equal Opportunity for Women. The concept of equality of opportunity in employment, need to be viewed in the context of diversity of women's life situations in different section of the social segments. The process of class and gender differentiation is reflected in employment patterns. For certain classes employment is viewed as a survival strategy while for some it is a factor of mobility. On broad spectrum of women employment at one end are women working as casual labourers in unskilled and low paid jobs and at the other end are high status professional women workers. The later create an illusion about the idea of individual merit and that every one can do it. The idea of equality of opportunity nestled in the egalitarian framework of our constitution has remained an abstract principle in a society characterized by social and economic equality.

To quote Exter Boseroup, "the division of labor according to sex is often explained as a natural result of physiological and psychological differences between men and women. But apart from the obvious case of childbearing, there are extremely few convincing examples of sex division of labor being truly explicable in term of natural differences between men and women. This is apparent when the sex pattern of work in different parts of the world are compared. In different human communities, quite different tasks are labeled as male and female tasks".

In significant ways women experience in the labour market has differed from men as reflected in most revealing statistics of gender gap in education, employment, income and rights to own assets.

Recent research on the impact of development policies and strategies particularly on poorer section have destroyed the myth that the male breadwinners in the families support women. The proponents of equality did not find support with those who are arguing for special measures so that woman can overcome the handicaps that they have suffered for centuries and are better equipped. Those who argue for preferential treatment of women do emphasize that the move toward equality of opportunity cannot be made without acknowledging women's family responsibilities and supportive measures needed to release her time and energy.

Economic Development and Women Representation in Organizations. Economic development affects women's opportunity structure in general and their access to managerial positions in particular (Adler and Izraeli, 1988). In the labour market, owing to the expansion of the economy and technological advancement, new job positions, including managerial positions, will be open up to women especially when there is a shortage of qualified men. Thus, in countries with developed economy more opportunities are available for women to job positions with authority.

Until recently, a single theme dominated questions about women managers worldwide: the concern for understanding women's under-representation, under-utilization and skewed distribution among the levels of management. Only in the 1990s, has the question of global competitiveness and transnational efficacy begun to transform and complement these equity-based concerns. To appreciate the organizational reality faced by today's women managers worldwide, our understanding of the issues must expand to include the business dynamics of the 1990s and the 21st century.

The intensification of global competition has become a major influence compelling firms to view women managers as a competitive advantage rather than as a legislated necessity. Global competition challenges corporations to maximize the effectiveness of their human resources. The opportunity cost of prejudice of rejecting women and limiting selection to men is much higher than in previous economic environments. As A. Fisher wrote in Fortune in 1992, "The best reason for believing that more women will be in charge before long is that in a ferociously competitive global economy, no company can afford to waste valuable brainpower simply because its wearing a skirt."

The patriarchal ideology, based on the superior position of men, is evident in both government and the corporate world. The division of labour is often based on stereotypical gender roles. Management is still dominated by socio-economically forward class males, as reflected in the latest available statistics and depicted in the board representation of the corporate. Women are further from the centre of power because, historically, forward class women have had indirect access to economic, social and political power through their alliance with men from similar background.

Antal and Izraeli (1993) have suggested a number of predictors for women's progress into management in a cross-cultural setting. These predictors include level of female labour force participation, women's participation in higher education, economic structure, and women's political representation. To a large extent, these contextual factors are associated with the level of economic development in a country. Moreover, their career advancement (Deal and Stevenson, 1998; Orser, 1994; Schneier and Bartol, 1980; Strykowsha, 1995; Tharenou, Latimer, and Conroy, 1994).

A Theory of Globalization and its Impact on Women and Work

The impact of globalization on women and work varies from one country to another, and in particular differs between industrialized and developing countries. There are certain generalizations, however, that can be made about how globalization affects women in the workplace. In general, a theory of globalization and its impact on women and work suggests that globalization significantly expands opportunities for women in the workplace, but it does not remove barriers to advancement, cushion the impact of recessions, or ameliorate the predominance of low paying, menial jobs held by women.

Globalization of businesses leads to the rise of the transnational corporation generally, and in particular places greater emphasis on a certain type of management style that is based on characteristics perceived as women's strengths. The international business enterprise is often centered on relationship building, and is based on a structure that is less hierarchical and more circular or team-structured. Working in such an organization is perceived as easier for women, and one in which they can function more effectively than men. More management positions at higher compensation for women may result from globalization, the growth of the transnational company, and relationship-oriented management positions.

Globalization plays a definite role in increasing opportunities for women in the workplace. It does not, however, automatically solve problems of advancement to executive positions (known as the "glass ceiling") or the movement of women beyond low-paying and menial jobs. However there are most common beliefs held by companies about women in international management:

Women do not Want to be International Managers

- Women in dual-career marriages are poor candidates for overseas assignments.
- Foreigners' unwillingness to accept women as managers dooms women international managers as failure.

Promoting Women in Global Economy

Given the global competitive pressures business face, why don't companies assign more women internationally? They don't because managers and executives base decisions about assigning women overseas on myth instead of fact. Interviews with human resource vice-presidents and managers from many large North American companies revealed that firms resist assigning women overseas because they assume certain things about female managers characteristics and about the competitive conditions that women managers face when they go abroad. More than half the companies cited such beliefs as the reasons they hesitate to send women abroad, although many of the firms are quick to promote women into domestic management positions.

In one of the studies, which were conducted, to examine whether female managers' careers progress at the same rate as male managers' careers (Stroh, Brett, and Reilly, 1992). Given that the men and women in the study appeared indistinguishable with respect to work experience, education, functional area, and industry, we anticipated that the men and women's financial compensation would increase at approximately the same rate. In fact, the gap was significant. The male managers had increased their salaries by 65 per cent during the prior 5-year period, whereas the female managers had increased their salaries by only 54 per cent. Their self-reported rates of promotion were the same; however, on average, the women had relocated 2.3 times for their careers, whereas the men had relocated 2.7 times. In other words, the males' larger increases appeared to be related to their having been offered and/or accepted more relocations.

This male-female difference may not be due to career track but "mommy track" (Schwartz, 1989). Support for this possibility was available in empirical studies that indicate that women with children reduce their working hours in countries like Sweden and Norway, which support such a coping mechanism (Kalleberg and Rosenfeld, 1990), and their job involvement in countries where such support is lacking (Schwartz, 1989).

In general, marriage and parenting have negative effects (salary and promotions) on women in management and positive effects on men (Thatenou, Latimer, and Conroy, 1994). Getting to top requires enormous commitment to work and also putting in extraordinary long hours. By having proper work-family management women managers were found working 51 or more hours per week (Brett and Stroh, 1999).

Whatever, may be the cause of the escalation in managerial hours of work, no one disputes that the escalation is real. Just at the time when more and more women qualify for higher-level management positions, the job of balancing work-family becomes harder because of the expectations for long hours. The net result is that increasing numbers of women feel they must choose between making a commitment to their careers and having families. These women's choices not only pose problems for their own career development but also for the organization that have nurtured their careers.

Enterprises struggling to retain high-tech talent are increasingly offering flexible work schedules and other benefits, in part to appeal to female workers. But even that is not enough: Experts say that companies must go deeper and change their culture in order to keep women from leaving. A survey of more than 20,000 female employees found women wanted more flexible work schedules, but they also wanted guidance from senior managers on how to succeed, and they wanted to see proof that women could make it to senior posts in the company (Boyd, 2000).

Work-Family Management

In light of the dramatic social transformations occurring in the nature of family and worker demands, nearly all employees today need to make decisions on how to manage work and family roles. Managing the integration of work and family demands is a critical challenge facing most employees and an issue of growing importance in the management literature. Nearly half of managers in Fortune 500 companies are in dual career families (Brett, Stroh, Reilly, 1992).

Therefore, the management of work and family roles becomes an important issue.

The work-family conflict literature typically assesses the sources, processes and types of conflict between work and family roles and their consequences for attitudinal outcomes (Kossek, Noe and Demarr, 1999). Considerable work has focussed on the processes of role interaction between work and family, such a spillover, where attitudes and behaviours might carry over from one to another, often provoking competing (and conflicting) demands (Greenhaus and Beutell, 1985; Koppelamn, Greenhaus and Connolly, 1983). By mainly focussing on measuring and describing conflict, the work-family conflict literature overlooks the individual's influence on the selection of personal strategies for work-family role integration that may beget spillover and conflict in the first place (Kossek, Noe and Demarr, 1999).

The selection of personal strategies by the women managers to manage work-family roles is most of the time rooted in our socio-cultural context. In societies, that are high on power - distance women have the major responsibility to look after family needs. Men are supposed to be breadwinners and therefore they get priority over women in terms of career development. It is the women who have to sacrifice promotions because of family obligations. Thus, the social role of men and women in society shapes their responsibilities at home. The structural role in the organizations generates pressure most of the time on women managers as she finds a lot of social constraints in order to successfully perform her structural role. The family demands longer hours from women as compared to men. On the other hand men spent longer hours at workplace than that of family. This is likely to create lots of stress amongst career-oriented women managers who feel that family is the responsibility of both husband and wife and therefore there should be partnering and equal sharing of family obligations.

Managing Social and Structural Roles

The preceding discussion indicated that in work-family management the social and structural role of the individuals play a crucial role. Most of the times, the demands put forth by these roles are incompatible. This is likely to produce a good amount of stress in women managers. But before that it is necessary to understand the concept of role and the related concepts.

The concept of 'role' I the key concept in understanding the integration of the individual in a system. It is through the role that the individual interacts with, and gets (or does not get) integrated with the system (Pareek, 1976). Role is meant here any position a person holds in a system (home/organization) as defined by the expectations that different persons including himself/herself have from that position. As suggested by Katz and Kahn (1966) an organization can be defined as a system of roles. From the point of view of an individual, two role systems are important, the system of various roles an individual occupies and performs, and the system of various roles of which his role is a part, and in which his role is defined by other significant roles. The former is 'role space' and the latter 'role-set'.

Role space. Each individual occupies and plays several roles, i.e., father, son, husband, wife, daughter, daughter-in-law, mother, etc. All these roles make the role space of a male and a female. As the concept of role is central to the concept of an organization, the concept of self is central to the concept of role. The various roles occupied and performed by a person are patterned around the self. Role space, then, can be defined as the dynamic inter-relationship both between the self and the various roles an individual occupies and amongst these roles (Pareek, 1976).

Role set. The individual's role in an organization is defined by the expectations of significant role senders in that organization, including the individual himself. The expectations from the role by the individual himself are termed 'reflexive role expectation' by Kahn and Quinn (1970).

Role Stress

The term stress has been taken from engineering where it implies an inherent capacity to withstand stress. Interest in organizational stress has increased a great deal in recent years. There has been a spate of writings on managerial and executive stress (Cooper and Marshall, 1978; Cooper and Payne, 1978; Greenwood and Greenwood, 1979; Kahn et al. 1964; Marshall and Cooper, 1979; Selye, 1956; Wright, 1979; Yates, 1979).

Kahn et al. (1964) were the earliest to draw attention to organizational stress in general, and role stress in particular. Pareek (1983) says, "...there are inherent problems in the performance of a role, and therefore stress is inevitable" (p. 12).

In view of the two proposed concepts of role systems (role space and role set) role stress is used in the present study as discussed by Pareek (1976).

Role Space Conflicts. Five main role stresses or conflicts in the role space of an individual have been identified:

1. *Self-role distance.* This is the conflict between the self-concept and the expectations from the role as perceived by the role occupant. If a person occupies a role, which he may subsequently

find conflicting with his self-concept, he/she feels the stress.

2. *Intra-role conflict.* Since the individual learns to develop expectation as a result of his socialization and identification with significant others, it is quite likely that he/she sees some incompatibility between the two expectations from his own role.

3. *Role stagnation.* As the individual grows physically, he also grows in the role he occupies in an organization. With the advancement of the individual, his role changes and with this change in role, the need for his taking his new role becomes crucial. This is the problem of role growth. Role stagnation also includes stress related to career progression. Marshall and Cooper (1979) have commented in the American context. A lot of this is true for Asian countries, as Marshall and Cooper (1979) have commented career progression is perhaps a problem by its nature.

4. *Inter-role distance.* An individual occupies more than one role. There may be conflicts between two roles he occupies. Such inter-role conflicts are quite frequent in modern society when the individual is increasingly occupying multiple roles in various organizations and groups.

5. *Role boundness.* If an individual feels highly obligated to the expectations of significant role senders, and sacrifices his/her own interests, preferences, values, comforts, etc. he/she may be said to be role bounded. He/she may experience the conflict between his tendency to live as a person and live as a role.

Role Set Conflicts. An individual occupying a particular role may have some expectations from his role. Interacting with him (role senders) may have quite different expectations from him/her. Such incompatible expectations and other problems arising in the role set are called role set stress or conflicts. Some of them are:

1. *Role ambiguity.* When the individual is not clear about the various expectations people have from his/her role, he faces the conflict, which may be called role ambiguity. Role ambiguity may be due to lack of information available to the role occupant, or due to lack of understanding of the cases available to him/her. Kahn and Quinn (1970) have suggested that role ambiguity may be in relation to the activities, responsibilities, personal style and

norms. They have suggested three foci of role ambiguity: the expectations role sender holds for the role occupant, the expectations sent by the role sender to the role occupant and the expectations the role occupant receives and interprets in the light of prior information and experience. They have suggested that four different kinds of roles are likely to experience ambiguity: roles new to the organization, roles in expanding or contracting organizations, roles in organizations exposed to frequent changes in demand, and roles on process. Role ambiguity may result in various other conflicts.

2. *Role overload*. When the role occupant feels that there are too many expectations from the significant roles in his/her role set, he/she experiences 'role overload'. This term has been popularised by Kahn et al. (1964). They measured this stress by asking questions about the feeling of people whether they could possibly finish work given to them during the modified work day and whether they felt that amount of work they did might interfere with how well it was done. Most of the executive role occupants experience role overload. Kahn and Quinn (1970) have suggested some conditions under which role overload is likely to occur. According to them, role overload is likely to occur more in the absence of mechanism of role integration. In the absence of power of role occupants the large variations in the expected output and when delegation or assistance cannot procure more time. Marshall and Cooper (1979) talk about quantitative and qualitative overload. Quantitative refers to having 'too much to do' while qualitative means work that is 'too difficult'. French and Caplan (1973) while summarising the studies on quantitative and qualitative role overload writes that it produces atleast nine different symptoms of psychological and physical strain: job dissatisfaction, job tension, lower self-esteem, threat, embarrassment, high cholesterol levels, increased heart-rate, skin resistance and more smoking.

3. *Role isolation*. In a role set, the role occupant may feel that certain roles are psychologically near to him/her, while some other roles are at a distance. The main criterion of role-distance is frequency and ease of interaction. When linkages are strong the role-role distance will be low. In the absence of strong linkage, the role-role distance can therefore, be measured in terms of

existing and desired linkages. The gap between the desired and the existing linkages will indicate the amount of distance between the two roles.

4. *Role erosion*. A role occupant may feel that some functions, which s/he would like to perform, are being performed by some other role occupant. The stress felt may be called 'role erosion'. Role erosion is the subjective feeling of an individual that some important role expectations s/he has from his role do not match with the expectations other roles have from her/him.

5. *Role inadequacy*. Role inadequacy refers to two types of feelings: (a) that the role occupant does not have adequate resources to perform the role effectively, and (b) that s/he is not fully equipped (lacks internal resources) for effective performance of the role.

A person's role at work has been isolated as a main source of occupational stress, involving ambiguity (i.e., a lack of clarity about one's job), as well as responsibility for people and conflicts stemming from organizational boundaries.

A central pressure point that female managers often experience is their own and others' concept of the female executive, i.e., executive role expectation. According to Henning and Jardim (1977) male and female managers can both suffer from role stress if there is an incompatibility between their view of themselves and their definition of the executive role. The complication occurs specially for the female managers when her perception of the executive role is at variance with that of other managers. As Hennig and Jardim (1977, p. 71) suggest that 'it is here, in the bit between others' concept of a particular woman and their concept of the executive role, that the particular woman tends to lose her individuality and to become any woman'. Since the executive role, is usually perceived by both men and women as fundamentally a male role any individual woman manager is unlikely to be seen as adequately fitting or meeting the role requirements. Although an individual male manager can suffer from lack of role clarity and role conflict, he does so more on an idiosyncratic basis rather than because he is a man. The same cannot be said of women attempting to fulfill exclusively male roles.

Certainly, a proportion of female managers try to cope with this problem by becoming more like male managers. Women managers are also more susceptible to role stress due to the multiple role demands inherent in running a career and a home and family. It seems that time demands impose a tighter schedule on the personal lives of executive women than on men, the women being less able to relax at the end of the day. Moreover, Ritzer (1972) noted that it was the women in upper levels of the organization who tended to experience significantly greater amounts of 'internal strain', due to conflicting role demands on their time and energy. As more and more women enter management, they will also have to face the stresses and strains of maintaining their dual managerial roles—corporate manager and family manager.

Personality and Stress. One of the major issues in the area of stress research per se is the old question: Why are potentially stressful situations perceived as stressful by some individuals and non-stressful by others? When investigating stress in female managers, as with any occupational group, one has to be aware that we are still dealing with individuals who will have their own unique life histories, demographic variables (e.g., age, management level, marital status), experiences, behaviour patterns and personalities—all of which can be instrumental in determining individual responses to stress.

We will discuss two main variables in this regard: personality and sense of security/ insecurity. The sex stereotyped behaviour and personality attributes seemed to be a potential source of pressure on female managers. It is obvious that a great deal of sex-role learning takes place among women during the early phases of their lives, and that this can translate into an attitude of mind that creates difficulties later in working life. A number of internal blocks that women experience are derived from early sex stereotyping.

As women are frequently socialized not to be assertive, aggressive or to seek power or control, and since, as McClelland (1975) has suggested, the most successful male managers are the most assertive and have the most highly developed desire for power, women are grossly disadvantaged from the 'pink' cradle of birth.

On the one hand where men are socialized to be independent and career-oriented, women, on the other hand have been encouraged by their parents and peers (the toys and games they are given to play with as children, and the role-taking within the family) to be dependent and nurturing.

Whatever may be the differences, in principle, a person can be both masculine and feminine. The concept of androgyny (from the Greek *andro*, male and *gyne* , female) refers specifically to this blending of the behaviours and personality characteristics that have traditionally been thought of as masculine and feminine. By definition, then, the androgynous individual is someone who is both independent and tender, both aggressive and gentle, both assertive and yielding, both masculine and feminine, depending on the situational appropriateness of these various behaviours (Bem, 1977).

The Managerial Grid theory suggests that better managers are androgynous by advocating a combination of task-oriented (i.e., mostly masculine) and people oriented (i.e., mostly feminine) behaviour. A second reason offered in support of androgynous management is that androgyny is the best route to fulfillment in men's and women's personal lives and makes them happier people. A third reason offered for androgynous management is that it is particularly appropriate for the climate in which organizations currently operate (Powell, 1988

Gender Differences in Negotiation

Men and women conduct research studies to look into the causes for differences in outcome of negotiation. The differences in outcome are expected due to contextual factors of men and women. Through various sample studies it was found that men negotiated better than women did. Although the overall difference in outcome between men and women was small, none of the tested variables and sample eliminated this effect. Negotiations occur at and across all levels and types of organization. Negotiations may involve a formal process as in case where individuals and groups negotiate for contracts or for resolution of grievances. In broader sense however negotiation is concerned with individuals attempts to acquire organizational privilege and resources, which are not always tangible or distributed equitably in organizations. Negotiating is a fundamental skill that must be acquired by any individual, seeking to occupy a position of power, status and responsibility. As greater a number of women advance into upper level position in organization its increasingly important to have an understanding of and the outcome of negotiation. If men and women do differ in their negotiation abilities, an awareness of these differences could suggest training or other intervention designed to faster understanding and equality between sex (Stuhlmacher, 1999)

It is found that empirical studies results present a mixed picture of gender differences in negotiation outcome. Whereas theoretical perspectives propose that men receive better negotiation outcome due to perceptional. Behavioural and contextual gender differences. The perception about men and women are as follows:

1 The stereotypes suggest that women are less effective negotiators than men are. In addition to them, evidence suggests that women perceive themselves to be less entitled to rewards and compensation than men (Callahan-Levy and Messe 1979; Major and Konar, 1984).

2. Women consistently allocate less resource to themselves than men when determining their own compensation or dividing profit between themselves and others. Thus they may have the expectation of receiving profit in negotiation. To the extent that expectations lead to higher outcomes for negotiators. Women would be expected to be less successfully in negotiation by individual (Stuhlmacher, 1999).

Behaviour of Men and Women

Beyond differences in individual's perceptions of men and women some would argue that men and women receive different outcomes because of differences in their negotiation behaviours (Kimmel et.al, 1980) reports that women in their study made less use of distributive tactics such as threats, positional commitments and put-downs, showed less interest in bargaining task, spoke less and displayed more self doubt than did men (Schor, 1995).

A recent meta-analysis of gender differences in negotiators competitiveness (Walters Stuhlmacher and Meyer, 1998) found that women in fact exhibit significantly more cooperative behaviour than men. But the overall magnitude of this difference is quite small. Even if men and women possess different negotiating styles, it is unclear if the discrepancies affect the outcome of men and women. Some have associated co-operation with ineffectiveness while others have drawn opposite conclusions (Schor, 1995).

On one hand it is argued that cooperating allows one to be exploited by ones negotiation partners and thus it is not a good bargaining behaviour. Therefore, some suggest that behaviour differences of women are less effective in negotiation than men are. Three explanation for gender entitlement differences in outcome and rewards have received empirical support (Major, 1987).

One is that women differ from men in the types of outcome that are valued. Women are said to be more motivated maintaining relationship while competition and status motivate men.

The second explanation for gender differences in entitlement concerns the frame of reference used by women and men. Women have limited social comparison information that is, women compare themselves to less successful standards than men do. Inequity is thus perpetuated by lack of comparison information.

A third explanation concerns the value of men and women's performance. Women's performance may be devalued in comparison to men's performance. This is supported by finding that:

(a) Success by women tends to be attributed to external causes (Hansen and O' Leary,1985).

(b) Female performance is devalued relative to identical male performance (Nivea and Gutek, 1981).

(c) Women perceive that their own job related inputs as lower than men's (Major and Deaux, 1982).

In terms of negotiation both gender stereotypes and entitlements differences would be predicted to result in poorer negotiation settlements for women than for men. In short gender differences in negotiation behaviour may influence the negotiation outcome.

In contrast to the proceeding perspective that suggest percepiion that suggest perception of behaviour exert differences on negotiation outcomes. It is argues that contextual or situational differences between men and women influence negotiation outcomes. There is ample evidence that power is not distributed equally between men and women in society (Kanter,1977; Waston,1994).

Given gender differences in perception behaviour and situations all have been shown related to negotiation outcomes. As studies have found conflicting results in the area of gender and negotiation it is felt that this research area would profit from meta-analytical investigation. Given the rise of labour market participation for women is imperative that the organization explore the reasons behind work place inequalities in organizational resources between men and women. Considerable evidence suggest that women has less access to organization resources such as pay promotion and status than men (Kanter,1977; Waston,1994).

The negotiation outcomes may be a factor for creating glass ceiling for women in workplace. At every stage of their career women are less effective in gaining power position and status than men. Though women are one-half of the workforce it does not include the top level. Hence women and men's inequality in the workplace should be minimized and women should become more effective (Fireman, 1990).

Leadership Style of Women in Business

The current trend in the field of management today is for a more participatory type of leadership and this is considered as good news for the women professionals. As more women attain high level positions in business and government services, researchers and practitioners alike have pondered whether women have a distinct style. Most of the research describing the managerial style of female executives has been carried out in most of the industrialized countries (Adler and Izaraeli, 1994; Adler, 1996). Gender related management style has received scant attention and one finds little or no research on managers on either sex. There is limited agreement among most scholars on gender - related differences in leadership style in management. Some researchers find no male/ female differences (Donnell and Hall, 1980; Fagenson, 1990; Powell, 1993) while others find female managers in fact different (Grant, 1988).

Changing Ideas on Leadership

The general perception about leadership is that it is constructed with a masculine subtext. Dominant views on leadership are seen as difficult to integrate with femininity (Lipman-Blumen, 1992). An interest in moving away from more bureaucratic- technocratic modes of management to more personal-ideological forms means that issues of a more social, subjective and involving nature are increasingly being seen as crucial. It is quite likely that changes in management and organizational practices are grossly exaggerated in many accounts of the 'postmodern world', the 'knowledge-society', 'post-fordism', etc. (Alvesson, 1995; Thompson, 1993) as not only journalists and consultants but also many researchers want to concentrate on what may appear as novel or radically changing - and not pay serious attention to all the stuff that remains pretty much the same. Nevertheless, some changes in social practices take place and even more so at the 'meta-level' of mass media, books, conferences, debates and public opinion. At present, rational forms of control are 'out' and normative forms are 'in' (Barley and Kunda, 1992). Here, the popularity of adhocracies, corporate culture, flexible forms, decentralization, service management, quality, innovation, empowerment, networks, etc. provide space for constructions of management and leadership partly in less masculine ways than has traditionally been the case (Gherardi, 1995). Machine bureaucracy may be seen as the extreme example of a masculine organization that has lost some appeal even though it still dominates. Emotions are increasingly seen as significant in organizational practice as meaning, involvement and action to some extent replace rationality, cold calculation and separation of decision and execution (Alvesson and Berg, 1992). Themes like identity, cohesion, teams and social integration also often point in a 'non-masculine' direction. Of course, not only many of the themes which are unchanged, but also some new ones do not necessarily lend themselves very easily to an exploitation 'pro-feminine' terms. Charismatic leadership is one example of a concept that has attracted considerable interest during the last decade (Bryman, 1993). Most of the public figures who fit into this category are men, often with a clear masculine, even heroic aura.

This general interest in new idea's on leadership appears to have accompanied the interest in feminine leadership and/or women in management. The two streams partly overlap. The issue of changing forms of management / leadership provides a vehicle (one of many) for considering and facilitating career opportunities for women. If a more participatory, non-hierarchic, flexible and group-oriented style of management is viewed as increasing appropriate and this is formulated in feminine terms (or androgynous combining characteristics of the two genders), then women can be marketed as carriers of suitable orientations for occupying positions as managers-network orientation, a preference for participation, and so on. Lipman-Blumen (1992, p. 183), for example, believes that female leadership 'contains the seeds of connective leadership, a new integrative model of leadership more suited to the dramatically changing workplace of the twenty-first century'. Fondas (1997) also notes that contemporary writings on management prescribe qualities that are culturally associated with women - even though this linkage is seldom explicitly made. Alternatively, and minimally, the new criteria for management would at least open up the opportunity for females have better access to senior positions in organizations. The strong 'masculine' nature of traditional management/leadership would then lose some of its appeal and the work field would form a more open terrain in terms of genderedness of those moving into and within it. This last version does not say anything about women in general being specifically suitable - either in terms of having a specific 'essence' or a common set of traits, or that having these is the critical prerequisite for being a competent manager - but only that crucial gender obstacle for equal access to such jobs may be remove/ weakened.

There are reasons to be sceptical with regard to much of the talk about radical changes taking place in organizations leading to a substantial requirement for 'female skills' or female managers (Calás and Smircich, 1993). Behind the rhetoric are perhaps only superficial changes, which do not prevent some speeding-up of the increase of females in low-level at middle-level managerial jobs.

Style of Leadership—Women Compared to Men

The extensive research on women and leadership suggest two schools of thoughts. One that believes in no-difference. Here it is commonly concluded that 'in general, comparative research indicates that there are few differences in the leadership style of female and male designated leaders' (Bartol and Martin, cited in Eagly and Johnson, 1990). The other is the gender-stereotypical school. Here, some crucial differences are believed to exist. Feminine leadership is characterized by cooperativeness, collaboration between managers and subordinates and problem solving based on intuition and empathy (e.g., Helgesen, 1990; Loden, 1986). The first school is typically academic, heavily measurement-oriented and thus adhering to the variable perspective. The second is more strongly made up of practitioner-oriented authors, often journalists or consultants, typically relying on qualitative work and often of an anecdotal character. Some are more academic and derive ideas about women's way of managing from readings of literature on the psychology of women (e.g., Fletcher, 1994; Grant, 1988).

Let us start with similarity. Bayes (1987) has studied female and male managers in public administration. While some women exhibited a management style, which was open and participatory, other women favoured control in their management style. Men, too, varied in their management style in the degree of openness and participation they showed. The only area where some male and female respondents agreed that women were different from men was in the area of their dedication to work. Women were perceived to work harder, to take their work more seriously, or even too seriously, and to be less concerned with monetary rewards than with recognition when a good job was done. Bayes concluded that women in public bureaucracies do not manage by using a different leadership style, nor is any different leadership style reflected in the attitudes they express regarding organizational structure. Kovalainen (1990) also found no significant differences in a study of male and female Finnish bank managers.

Comprehensive research by others has come to the same conclusion. Bartol (1978, p. 806) summarizes her examination of different organizations as follows: 'In most cases, there are either no differences or relatively minor differences between male and female leaders on leadership style, whether the leaders are describing themselves or being described by their subordinates'. Powell (1988, p. 165) reaches the conclusion that female and male managers 'differ in some ways and at some times, but, for the most part, they do not differ'. As opposed to the above mentioned studies, a number of other writers maintain that there are clear differences between women and men in their management style. As a rule, this thesis is based on theoretical considerations and has been derived from assumptions about the character and the importance of gender socialization (see, for example, Grant, 1988; Lipman--Blumen, 1992). Some authors, such as Loden (1986) and Helgesen (1990), present empirical examples in support of their ideas about a distinct female style. Their studies do, however, express a journalistic rather than scientific ethos, and are methodologically weak.

While these authors promote a specific female style, Marshall (1984, p.13) has another point, namely to refute the thesis that 'women are different from men, therefore they will not become good managers'. On the basis of various investigations she concludes that women are very similar to men in their style of management. Marshall points out that the most frequently reported difference is that female managers score higher than men on the supportive side of management. Marshall concludes that the differences between women and men are very slight and that female qualities may be more in demand in the future in management positions. Women might perhaps become better managers than men, she thinks.

Eagly and Johnson (1990), in a review of the research, find that available (positivistic) academic studies show another picture than the 'no-difference' one that almost all other (academic) commentators have favoured. They refer to research findings indicating that women as a group can be described as friendly, pleasant, interested in other people, expressive and socially sensitive. Even though socialization and selection in organizations may mean that gender differences in managerial jobs are reduced or even non-existent, they believe that some level of sex difference in leadership style may follow from 'gender-role spillover'. In a meta-analysis of other studies they find that laboratory studies - mostly with students as research objects - typically show sex differences in leadership style, while studies of leadership in organizations do so to a lower degree. The explanation of the former may be that in laboratory settings, the rules about how one should behave are unclear, which means that people fall back on gender roles to provide guidance and therefore behave more gender-stereotypically than in other situations, or that the subjects are students rather than managers. In organizational settings, that is, studies of 'real' managers, those occupying these positions are selectively recruited and have typically adapted norms for appropriate behaviour. In addition, structural positions influence attitudes and behaviour (Kanter, 1977). Still, however, Eagly and Johnson (1990) found that women had a slightly more democratic leadership style than men.

In a research review of gender and leadership effectiveness Eagly et al (1995) found that on an aggregate level there were no differences in the effectiveness of female and male leaders. Scrutinizing the findings, however, they found conditions under which men fared better than women and vice versa; leadership roles defined in relatively masculine terms favoured male leaders and leadership roles defined in relatively feminine terms favoured female leaders' (p.137). They found that sex differences were significantly correlated with the congeniality of these roles for men and women. There were tendencies, albeit weak, for women to be more effective than men in business, education, and government or social service and for men, significantly, to be favoured leaders in military organizations. Or to put it differently, 'women fared poorly in settings in which leadership was defined in highly masculine terms, especially in military settings. Men fared slightly worse than women in settings in which leadership was defined in less masculine terms' (p. 140).

There is thus a trend also in some academic work to bring forward difference/gender stereotypical explanations. Earlier there was a strong support for the no-difference school. Butterfield and Powell (1981, p. 130), for example, concluded that 'it is now commonly believed that actual (leader sex) differences in the behaviour of real leaders are virtually non-existent'. Recently, authors summarizing the field have been more inclined to favour the idea that there are differences. Fagenson's (1993, p. 5). The summary of the research is that there is evidence suggesting that women managers "have a transformational, democratic, and/or "web" rather than hierarchical style of leadership and more satisfied subordinates than men managers. Still, the majority of the academic empirical work supports the no-or-little-difference thesis (as cited above). As we have stressed earlier, positivistic studies are much less reliable than they appear. It is very likely that measurements of leadership styles or behaviours do not catch the nuances and subtleties of processes and relations of leadership very well (Alvesson, 1996; Alvesson and Billing, 1997; Smircich and Morgan, 1982).

The change of emphasis in the literature on women and leadership to embrace the different, supposedly superior qualities of women as leaders may reflect certain 'actual' changes in 'objective' reality. Changes may follow from an increase in the number of female managers and a reduction of constraints in terms of expressing their own 'genuine' style - in case people should have a fixed orientation, installed early in life, independent of work experiences, situational conditions and learning. A trend involving demasculinization of the construction of management may also be significant here. Helgesen (1990) finds examples of an interest in feminine leadership also among the US armed forces. But the changing ideas about women and leadership may also reflect the spirit of the time in broader and less obvious respects, affecting research respondents as well as researchers and review authors. Redefinitions of managerial ideals in a more 'pro-female' direction may improve the self-confidence of the female managers. Writers on the topic of women and management may also feel that the case is no longer one of 'proving that women are people too' (Calás and Smircich, 1996), but that there is space for women's voices on the topic. This may mean that what was earlier seen as 'no differences or relatively minor differences' supporting the similarity idea today tends to be expressed as 'some differences' supporting the idea that women manage in a different way. To determine 'objectively'when 'no', 'insignificant', 'minor' or 'some' is the best word to describe a relationship is hardly possible. When the research area is summarized, it is not easy to sort out new results, new analysis, new emphasis in conclusions from the changed use of words.

Of course, ideas and cultural norms do not exist on their own, but also affect the feelings, thoughts and actions of people in organizations - ideas on female leadership and the practices of women managers may therefore interact.

There are also some more specific problems in sorting out how male and female managers may be compared. Managerial jobs differ tremendously. A complication is that many female 'managers' have positions of limited authority. The meaning of a 'manager' is often highly ambiguous and the title may tell us rather little - except about norms for classification. Sometimes the title just masks a position as 'glorified secretary' (Jacobs, 1992), although Jacobs himself found that this does not seem to be common or explain the rapid increase of women in managerial jobs. Survey studies may easily overlook the fact that classification hides diversity—what 'managers' really do and their 'real' social relationships to 'subordinates' may be very difficult to pinpoint - and such studies thus compare quite different phenomena. Another complication in drawing conclusions about sex and leadership is that the gender congeniality of leadership roles may be accompanied by different patterns. Eagly and Johnson (1990), for example, found that although male leaders were often more task oriented than females, the latter tended to be more so than males in a leadership role that was more congenial to women (e.g., head nurse). Establishing general, abstract correlations between sex and leadership may be a misleading or at least not very informative enterprise.

In one of the few cross cultural studies it was found that women leadership in four countries were more likely to focus on interaction facilitation than men who placed more emphasis upon goal setting. Several studies from United States of America and other countries reported that women apparently preferred a more participative style than men did. Although there has been much change in working world women still face the glass-ceiling in their climb and they are still bearing primary responsibility for home and family chores. These and other factors lead to a high level of stress among women than men. Women can help their own case by recognizing and exploiting their superiors abilities in interpersonal relationship and developing service-oriented business. Organizations can help women by providing better mentoring, guidance and training opportunities and by increasing their sensitivity to work in home conflicts (Powell, 1991).

To summarize, the person wanting a clear and simple answer to the question of whether women manage in a different way to men is bound to be frustrated, not only by the research available, but also by the complexity of the issue. On the whole, male and female managers do not seem to differ very much in leadership behaviour, according to the heavily US-dominated research in the area, but also according to a few non-US studies. There may be some, but not significant, differences in terms of women being more personnel and democratically oriented. It is possible that many women are more inclined to adopt a democratic style than some men. How can we account for any possible tendency in this direction? It may be 'natural' for them, in the light of childhood experiences, female socialization or later experiences in family or at work. But it may also be an expression of their weaker authority, given the traditional image of leadership as a masculine activity. Or it may be a consequence of the stereotypical expectations of other people, assuming that female managers are more 'soft'. Given the unfruitfulness of keeping these aspects fully apart, one should not necessarily aspire to reach a final conclusion. If there are cultural stereotypes / understandings about the way women 'are' in a particular sense, these may be self-fulfilling. The self is not developed in a social vacuum. We become men and women in the context of dominating masculinities and femininities and interactions partly guided by these cultural understandings.

One should also bear in mind that even if there should be some minor or moderate differences between the way in which male and female managers behave in a particular historical and cultural situation, this should not obscure the fact that there are wide variations within the two categories: some women managers may very well be seen as autocratic and there are male managers that can be described as democratic. This may be obvious, but is ignored by a lot of writings on the subject trying to compare 'men' and 'women' in order to establish whether or not the groups differ.

Sex Preferential Pattern of Employment

It has been recently demonstrated that sex-based preferential selection can have deleterious consequences for women's self-perceptions of competence (Heilman, Simon and Repper, 1987). Specifically, being selected for a leadership position on the basis of sex rather than merit was shown to have detrimental effects on women's regard for their accomplishments, desire to remain in a leadership role and views of their leadership skills. However, method of selection had no effect on men. A subsequent study replicated these findings and also shed light on the process underlying them (Heilman, Lucas and Kaplos, 1990). It demonstrated that sex-based preferential selection gave rise to negative perceptions of competence only when individuals lacked confidence in their ability to perform effectively and that men as well as women were adversely affected by preferential selection when they lacked such confidence (Powell, 1991).

The results of these investigations support the idea that preferential selection exacerbates doubts and insecurities individuals has about their ability to perform. Unlike merit-based selection, which affirms and individual's competence, preferential selection along a work-irreverent dimension is ambiguous with regard to competence information, allowing such doubts and fears to go unchecked. For women, who typically approach traditionally male roles, positions, or tasks with less confidence in their performance capability than do men (Heilman, 1983; Lenney, 1981; McMahon, 1982), this situation is particularly problematic. Because most high-level and important organizational positions (i.e., managerial positions) are traditionally considered male in character (Heilman, Block, Martell, and Simon, 1989; Powell and Butterfield, 1979, 1989; Schein, 1973, 1975), women who are selected to occupy such positions are especially vulnerable to the negative consequences of believing that they have been preferentially selected because of their sex (Powell, 1991).

Concern about the effects of sex-based preferential selection on women is not without basis. Many affirmative action programmes in today's organizations are perceived to be little more than preferential selection in not - too - subtle disguise. Whether or not this actually is the case is not a concern here. What is important to this discussion is the fact that if women perceived that being hired for traditionally male positions is due to their sex rather than to their credentials and qualifications, then they are in danger of suffering the negative self-perceptions of competence that have been documented in earlier research. This, no doubt, is an unintended result of affirmative action efforts, but is nonetheless one that is apt to have broad implications for behaviour in work settings. It already has been demonstrated that task selection decisions are influenced by such perceptions (Heilman, Rivero and Brett, 1991).

Further, Powell and Butterfield (1994) found that those women who believed them to be selected preferentially for traditionally male jobs do indeed experienced negative self-perceptions of competence as a result of the selection procedure, and this, in turn, are likely to affect how these women deal with others in the work setting. In particular, it should affect how they react to other women. For when minority status carries with it negatives connotations about the self, it can lead to a rejection of like others.

Separate and Unequal Career -Building Relationship

The mostly asked question among researchers in area of women in management is "Do women executives also have to be like one of the boys to get to the top"? The answer to this from research studies conclude to be no (Schor, 1997). During the past twenty years scholars and practitioners have been scrutinizing the challenges women face as they attempt to climb the corporate ladder. Men dominate executive positions in most of the organizations in India as well as abroad as yet. A very small percentage of women according to statistics are placed in top managerial level and this is as it shows on entire world viewpoint. But while other researchers are documenting that many women bumping into the now infamous glass ceiling, another critical question needed to be addressed is that : How do those few women who are at the top become successful in spite of the obstacles. Both men and women who have risen into the rare field ranks of senior management who have risen into the rarefied ranks of senior management credit the nature and quality of their relationships with other people as key elements. They see most of the beneficial relationship as those they have with their mentors and with people in the informal networks (Schor, 1995).

It is widely researched question, which tries to find out as to what women should do to get what they want. Are there a men's way and women's way of advancing to senior management? According to many findings the short answer to the above questions is "yes". With mentors and colleagues women executives' work harder at maintaining richer, broader relationship around work issues than men did. They were actively involved in building multiple relationship that meets the variety of career needs they perceive they have. The men were considerably less active in doing this (Schor, 1995).

Differences between executive women and men's relationships in organization parallels what psychologists have been reporting about male and female development. For men the emphasis has been on autonomy and individualization; for women on a process of growth with relationships. Men's identity has been defined by separateness, women's by attachments to others. In considering this we can better understand how career-building relationships in this study differ at their very core. The men and women of the cooperation can, as individuals, take some comfort in knowing they do not necessarily have to change. Men's modes of career advancement have worked for years. Women can actively engage their relationship building strengths by seeking development through mentoring, initiating and maintaining informal networks, building alliances and seeking support from friends and family (Schor, 1995).

What we can conclude from the success stories of the executive women and men in this study is as follows: It is however obvious to state that business hierarchy has only a few positions at the top, for men or for women. This truism reminds us that there are plenty of people of both sexes who will do all the right things and because of luck, fate or circumstances, still wont make it. Then there are also men whom we find managing to reach the top. What is fascinating in this context is to note that there were women executives who also made it to the top though they were few and this can increase if women continue to struggle and maintain a relationship that is lasting in the organization by being professionally close to both men and women who will in return reciprocate. (Schor, 1995).

The Present Investigation

The cultural values attached with the social role of a woman significantly affect her career choice. If we take the case of 'glass ceiling' (which refers to a transparent barrier that prevents the upward mobility of women in organizations) then it becomes clear that one main explanation for its existence is the traditional sex role stereotypes toward women (Nivea and Gutek, 1981; Norris and Wylie, 1995; Tabak, 1997). Conventionally managerial jobs have defined as largely a matter of instrumentality, autonomy and result-orientation (Alvesson and Billing, 1997) which fit the stereotypes of men rather than those of women. For that reason, male stereotypes (that focus on attributes such as independence, competitiveness, control and ambition) have predominated in the world of management. Given this women are perceived as lacking management skills and leadership abilities, and thus they are denied access to managerial positions.

Nevertheless, it should be noted that sex stereotypes are culturally based beliefs prescribing appropriate and inappropriate behaviours for the two genders. Against this backdrop the present study intends to examine the socio-cultural determinants of women leadership at the top in South-East Asian countries.

The literature in the preceding section yields a conceptual framework which is displayed in Fig. 1.1.

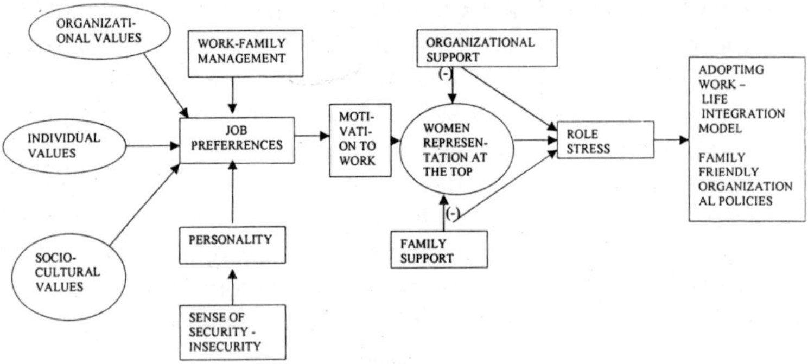

Figure 1.1 The Conceptual Framework

The focal point in Fig. 1.1 is the women representation at the top (Box 11). There are a host of factors responsible for it. One's preference for a job (Box 1) is likely to be influenced by one's own values (Box 2) and the socio-cultural values (Box 3). The assumption is that the culture of the society shapes the job preferences for men and women. If it is so, then, the path of career development (Box 4) for men and women will be different. The career development of women managers seem to be influenced primarily by one's motivation to work (Box 8) and secondly by work-family management (Box 5). Further, the personality (Box 6) alongwith sense of security/ insecurity (Box 7) seem to influence the career development of women managers.

But does this mean that if women are successful in planning her career her representation at the top is likely to increase (Box 11)? The present book is an effort to understand the factors responsible for it. Two broad categories of support mechanisms may positively influence it: (a) Organizational support (Box 9) and (b) Family support (Box 10). The author advocates that in order to increase women representation at the top efforts need to be put at individual level and at organizational level. At individual level change of mind-set is required and therefore if we use Work-Life Integration Model (Box 12) that will help to change our attitudes towards social role and help to enhance men and women's ability to successfully integrate the various aspects of their complex lives. At organizational level there is need to introduce and implement Family-Friendly

Policies (Box 13) so that the organizations are able to retain the talented women workforce. There is a need to marry the two (Boxes 12 and 13) in order to increase the women representation at the top. A complete mind-set change is required at individual as well as organizational level.

For keeping the presentation simple the feedback loops are not shown. In sum, in the present book the author has made an attempt to examine the socio-cultural determinants of women representation at the top in South-East Asian organizations.

References

Aaltio-Marjasola, I. (1994). Gender stereotypes as cultural products of the organization. *Scandinavian Journal of Management*, 10 (2), pp. 147-62.

Alpern, S. (1993).In the beginning: a history of women in management. In E.A. Fagenson (ed), Women in Management: Trends, Issues, and Challenges in Managerial Diversity. Thousand Oaks, CA: Sage.

Alvesson, M. (1993) Cultural perspectives on organizations. Cambridge: Cambridge University Press.

Alvesson, M. (1995). The meaning and meaninglessness of postmodernism: Some ironic Remarks. Organization Studies, 15(6), pp. 1047-1075.

Alvesson, M. (1996). Leadership studies: from procedure and abstraction to reflexivity and situation. Leadership Quarterly, 7(4), pp. 455-485.

Alvesson, M and Berg, P.O. (1992). Corporate culture and organizational symbolism. Berlin / New York: de Gruyter.

Aron, C.S. (1987). Ladies and gentlemen of the Civil Service: Middle class workers in Victorian America. New York: Oxford University Press.

Barley, S and Kunda, G. (1992).Design and devotion: surges of rational and normative Ideologies of control in managerial discourse. Administrative Science Quarterly, 37, pp. 363-399.

Bartol, K. (1978).The sex structuring of organizations: a search for possible causes. Academy of Management Review, (October) 3(2).

Baude, A. (1992). Kvinnans plats Pd jobbet. Stockholm: SNS Forlag.

Bayes, J. (1987). Do female managers in public bureaucracies manage with a different voice? Paper Presented at the Third international interdisciplinary Congress on Women, Dublin, 6-10 July.

Billing, Y.D. and Alvesson, M. (1994). Gender, managers and organizations. Berlin / New York: de Gruyter.

Blomqvist, M. (1994). Konshierarkier i gungning: kvinnor i kunskapsforetag. Uppsala: Acta Universitatis. Upsaliensis. Studia Sociologica Upsaliensia 39.

Borchorst, A. (1993). Arbejdsliv og familieliv i Europa. In S. Carlsen and J.E. Larsen (eds), Den Sudre Balance. Copenhagen: Ligestillingsrhdet.

Bradley, H. (1993).Across the great divide: the entry of men into 'women's jobs'.In C. Williams (ed), Doing 'Women's Work': Men in Nontraditional Occupations. Newbury Park, CA: Sage.

Bradley, H. (1994).Gendered jobs and social inequality. In The Polity Reader in Gender Studies. Cambridge: Polity Press.

Bryman, A. (1993). Charismatic leadership in business organizations: some neglected issues. Leadership Quarterly, 4, pp. 289-304.

Butterfield, D.A. and Powell, G.N. (1981). Effect of group performance, leader sex, and rater sex on ratings of leader behaviour. Organizational Behaviour and Human Performances, 28, pp. 129-141.

Calas, M. and Smircich, L. (1992a). Re-writing gender into organizational theorizing: directions from feminist perspectives. In M. Reed and M. Hughes (eds), Re-thinking Organization. New Directions in Organizational Theory and Analysis. London: Sage

Calas, M. and Smircich, L. (1992b). Feminist theories and the social consequences of organizational research. In A. Mills and P. Tancred (eds), Gendering Organizational Analysis. London: Sage.

Calas M and Smircich, L. (1993). Dangerous liaisons: the "feminine-in-management" meets globalization. Business Horizons, (March-April), pp. 73-83.

Calas M and Smircich, L. (1996). From the "woman's" point of view: feminist approaches to organization studies. In S. Clegg, C. Hardy and W. Nord (eds), Handbook of Organization Studies. London: Sage.

Collinson, D.(1988). Engineering humour: masculinity, joking and conflict in shop-floor relations.Organization Studies, 9(2), pp. 181-199.

Collinson, D. and Hearn, J. (1994). Naming men as men: implications for work, organization and Management. Gender, Work and Organization, 1(1), pp. 2-22.

Connell, R. (1987). Gender and power. Cambridge: Polity Press.

Connell, R. (1995). Masculinities. Cambridge: Polity Press.

Eagly, A. and Johnson, B. (1990). Gender and leadership style: a meta-analysis. Psychological Bulletin, 108(2), pp. 233-256.

Eagly, A, Karau, S. and Makhijani, M. (1995). Gender and the effectiveness of leaders: a mets-analysis. Psychological Bulletin, 117(1), pp. 125-145.

Ehn, B arid Lofgren, 0. (1982). Kulturanalys. Lund, Sweden: Liber.

Engels, F. (1972). The origins of the family, private property and the state. London: Laurence and Wishart.

Fagenson, E.A. (ed.) (1993). Women in management: Trends, issues, and challenges managerial diversity. Thousand Oaks, CA: Sage.

Ferguson, K. (1984). The feminist case against bureaucracy. Philadelphia: Temple University Press.

Fletcher, J. (1994). Castrating the female advantage: feminist standpoint research and management science. Journal of Management Inquiry, 3, pp. 74-82.

Fondas, N (1997). Feminization unveiled: management qualities in contemporary Writings. Academcy of Management Review, 22(1), pp. 257-282.

For South Asian Women Bias Begins Before Birth. http://www.siliconindia.com/women/

Frez, M. & Early, P.C. (1993). Culture, self-identity and work. Oxford: Oxford University Press.

Frost, P. (1987). Power, politics, and influence. In F. Jablin et al. (eds), Handbook of Organizational Communication. Newbury Park, CA: Sage.

Frost, P. et al. (eds) (1991). Refraining organizational culture. Newbury Park, CA: Sage.

Frost, P. et al. (eds) (1985). Organizational culture. Beverly Hills, CA: Sage.

Geertz,C.(1973). The interpretation of cultures. New York: Basic Books.

Gherardi, S. (1995). Gender, symbolism and organizational cultures. London: Sage.

Goransson, A. (1996). Kon sam analyskategori i den ekonomiska historien. In E. Borgstrom and A. Nordenstam (eds), Kvinnovetenskapens vadan ach varthan.Gothenburg: Lansarkivet.

Goransson, A. (1978). Den konsliga arbetsdelningen och dess strategiska konsekvenser. Sociologisk forskning, 15(3), pp. 51-81.

Gordon, F. and Strober, M.H. (eds) (1975). Bringing women into management. New York: McGraw-Hill.

Hall, E. (1993). Smiling, deferring, and flirting: Doing gender by giving 'good service'. Work and Occupations, 20(4), pp. 452-471.

Hirdmann, Y. (1988). Genussystemet: teoretiska reflexioner kring kvinnors sociala Under- ordning. Kvinnovetenskaplig tidskrift, 9(3), pp. 49-63.

Hollway, W. (1996).Masters and men in the transition from factory hands to sentimental workers. In D. Collinson and J. Hearn (eds.) Men as Managers, Managers as Men. London: Sage.

Illich, I. (1982). Gender. New York: Pantheon Books.

Jackall, R. (1988). Moral mazes: The world of corporate managers. New York: Oxford University Press.

Jacobs, J. (1992). Women's entry into management: Trends in earnings, authority, and Values among salaried managers. Administrative Science Quarterly, 37(2),pp. 282- 301.

Kerfoot, D. and Knights, D. (1996). The best is yet to come?: The quest for embodiment in Managerial work. In D. Collinson and J. Hearn (eds.), Men as Managers, Managers as Men. London: Sage.

Kessler-Harris, A., Lewis, J. and Wikander, U. (1995). Introduction. In U. Wikander et al. (eds), Protecting Women: Labor Legislation in Europe, the United States, and Australia, 1880-1920. Chicago: University of Chicago Press.

Kimmel, M. (1994). Masculinity as homophobia: fear, shame, and silence in the construction of gender identity. In H. Brod and M. Kaufman (eds.), Theorizing Masculinities. Thousand Oaks, CA:Sage.

Kirkham, L. and Loft, A. (1993). Gender and the construction of the professional Accountant. Accounting, Organizations and Society, 18(6), pp. 507-558.

Knights, P. and Morgan, G. (1991). Corporate strategy, organizations, and subjectivity: A Critique. Organization Studies, 12, pp. 251-273.

Kovalainen, A. (1990). How do male and female managers in banking view their work roles and their subordinates? Scandinavian Journal of Management, 6, pp. 143-159.

Leidner, R. (1991). Serving hamburgers and selling insurance: gender, work, and identity In interactive service jobs. Gender & Society, 5(2), pp. 154-177.

Lewis, J. and Rose, S.A. (1995). Let England blush: protective labor legislation. In U. Wikander et al. (eds), Protecting Women: Labor Legislation in Europe, the United States,and Australia, 1880-1 920. Chicago: University of Illinois Press.

Lipman-Blumen, J. (1992). Connective leadership: female leadership styles in the 21st- century workplace. Sociological Perspectives, 35(1), pp. 183-203.

Loden, M. (1986). Feminine leadership, or how to succeed in business without being one of the boys. New York: Time Books.

Lofgren, 0. (1977). Arbetsfordelning och konsroller i bondesamhallet. Kvinnovetenskap ligtidskrift, 3.

Loring, R. and Wells, T. (1972). Breakthrough: Women into management. New York: Van Nostrand-Reinhold.

Marshall, J. (1993b). Organizational communication from a feminist perspective. In S.Deetz (ed.), Communication Yearbook, Vol. 16. Newbury Park, CA: Sage.

Marshall, J. (1984). Women managers: Travellers in a male world. Chichester: Wiley.

Martin, J. (1992). The culture of organizations: Three perspectives. New York: Oxford University Press.

Meuser, M. (1996). Konsforhold og maskuliniteter: et videnssociologisk perspektiv. Dansk Sociologi, 73(3), pp. 7-30.

Mookerji, R.K. (1957). Women in Ancient India. In Tara Ali Baig (ed.)

Women of India (pp. 1-8). New Delhi: Ministry of Information and Broadcasting, Government of India.

Morgan, D. (1992). Discovering men. London: Routledge.

Nieva, V. and Gutek, B. (1980). Sex effects on evaluations. Academy of Management Review, 5, pp. 267-276.

Novarra, V. (1980). Women's work, men's work: The ambivalence of equality. London: Marion Boyars.

Ortner, S. (1984). Theory in anthropology since the sixties. Comparative Studies in Society and History, 26, pp. 126-166.

Panikkar, K.M. (1957). The middle period. In Tara Ali Baig (ed.) Women of India (pp.9-13). New Delhi: Ministry of Information and Broadcasting, Government of India.

Powell, GN. (1988). *Women and men in management*. Beverly Hills, CA: Sage.

Reskin, B. and Padavic, I. (1994). Women and men at work. Thousand Oaks, CA: Pine Forge Press.

Schmitt, S. (1995). All these forms of women's work which endanger public health and public welfare: Protective labour legislation in Germany, 1878-1914. In U. Wikander et al.(eds.), Protecting Women: Labour Legislation in Europe, The United States and Australia, 1880-1920. Chicago: University of Illinois Press.

Shorter, E. (1975). The making of the modern family. New York: Basic Books.

Smircich, L. (1983). Concepts of culture and organizational analysis. Administrative Science Quarterly, 28, pp. 339-358.

Smircich, L. and Morgan, G. (1982). Leadership: the management of meaning. The Journal of Applied Behavioural Science, 18(3), pp. 257-273.

Sommestad, L. (1992). Fran mejerska till mejerist: en studie av mejeriyrkets maskulinisering--sprocess. Lund, Sweden: Arkiv.

Stivers, C. (1993). Gender images in public administration. Newbury Park, CA: Sage.

Sundin, E. (1993). Ny teknik i gamla strukturer. Stockholm: Nerenius and Santérus.

Tewksbury, R. (1993). Male strippers: men objectifying men. In C. Williams (ed.), Doing Women's Work: Men in Nontraditional Occupations. Newbury Park, CA: Sage.

Thompson, A. M. and Wood, M.D. (1981). Management strategies for women, or now that I'm boss, how do I run this place? New York: Simon and Schuster.

Thompson, P. (1993). Fatal distraction. In J. Hassard and M. Parker (eds), Post modernism and Organizations. London: Sage

Wikander, U. (1991). Delat arbete, delad makt: om kvinnors underordning: och genom arbetet. Uppsala University: Research Report no. 28.

Williams, C. (ed.) (1993). Doing Women's Work: Men in Nontraditional Occupations. Newbury Park, CA: Sage.

2

Objectives and Hypotheses

An Overview

The number of women in the workplace has shot up considerably over the last five years. The extra Ladies' Special trains, special buses for women, crèche facilities for working women, takeout food joints and extension of other domestic services all over the country are a testament to this trend. In spite of these indications and statistics of the rising pool of employed women from the Government of India's Human Resources Ministry, few women have reached coveted top managerial and corporate decision-making positions.

Some Reflections on Women in Management

Many feel that the secondary status of women and the treatment they receive from the family spill over into the corporate world. The acculturation of the Indian women has been to be a home-maker and peace-keeper - to be a follower and a loyalist, but never to rock the boat or lead from the front. Just like the family, society and other fields, the world of business too is dominated by men; women are few and far between. Those who have proved outstanding and have made their mark are not looked at with the admiration they deserve; the pervasive assumption is that their success came at the cost of family peace. Even brain scientists have gone back to the laboratory drawing board and have come up with the news that neurological sex differences exist, i.e., that men and women are irrefutably different, like chalk and cheese. Sheela Vasanth, who started life as a school teacher, got into PR casually, and today heads the PR division of a multinational firm located in Bangalore. Says she, "Men also grow in steps. But, perhaps, it's more significant in the case of women since they generally have less opportunities and lower self-esteem. There ARE tangible differences in styles of functioning between the sexes." Today's organizations have more women in responsible, high-profile positions, but few have climbed all the way up. Men call women better managers. Women also call themselves better, more sincere and honest managers, yet the corporate echelons include only a handful of them. Do years of conditioning and lack of exposure affect their managerial performance?

Perveez Aggarwal, Director of Diners Business Service and a high-level executive in the travel and business centre services for the last 30 years, feels that the number of women executives has definitely multiplied in the last five years. "There is a greater awareness amongst families to give the same education and career-planning opportunities to both sons and daughters. They are climbing the corporate ladder slowly but surely"(Ghosh, 2000).

However, women are not visible in business associations or chambers of commerce because they simply have no time, after managing the home, children and other responsibilities. Dilnawaz Shroff, chairperson and managing director of the El Dorado Group of Companies in financial services, feels the number of women executives has increased, but there is still a long way to go. Few women who have already crashed the glass ceiling have created a pathway for the younger generation; more women leaders than men leaders are driven by a vision beyond economic goals. According to Lynn De Souza, President, Initiative Media India, the media buying house of one of India's leading advertising agencies, Lintas, "In creative pursuits people tend to be more open-minded. Once at the top, gender is not an issue." Though Reena Ramchandran, chairman and managing director of the public sector Hindustan Organic Chemical Ltd. warns, "Changes in mindset are taking place, but the change is not happening fast enough."

Nergis Wadia, Director of General Media Research Users Council, feels there is a great difference in the way men and women respond to their jobs. Men are driven by monetary rewards, and women look for environmental and social benefits. Having worked for 30 years as the head of the Inter Pub ad agency, Wadia recalls that in a staff of over 100 people, only a few were women and they cared more for their safety than the men. This was the only major difference.

Shroff has a staff of 150 reporting to her, 75 per cent of whom are women, mostly coming from Mumbai, Goa and Bangalore as the other offices are in smaller cities. She says her treatment of and expectation from men and women is the same. She observes that women are known to excel at developing relationships and working collectively.

Studies show that women managers tend to have a more inclusive style than their male counterparts, but there isn't enough information to call it a pattern in top female executives. In women's workshops and seminars that are generally attended only by women, it is proudly proclaimed that women are the superior sex and are better managers. Concurring, Aggarwal explains that this is because they have management qualities such as patience, tolerance, honesty, loyalty and communications skills. They are better team leaders because they have the experience of carrying the family with them in meeting objectives.

Wadia, however, refrains from making generalizations. She believes some women are very good managers in certain industries, which require customer services. On the other hand, men can handle stress much better than women and have a grasp of overall business perspectives. Since men and women bring different styles to work, the onus is on companies to maximize their effectiveness by giving them appropriate assignments.

There seems to be a new tokenism these days in deference to the post-feminist climate. While women still appear to be struggling, middle-level female professionals are being promoted over more deserving men simply because it is the politically correct thing to do, maintains Suresh Guptan, executive in charge at Tata Services (Ghosh, 2000).

Today, women have broken many stereotypes and have proved themselves equally if not more committed, says Shroff. What are the challenges facing today's managers in the wake of globalization and a liberal business environment? Aggarwal feels it's the competition - it is survival of the fittest. Excellence will command a higher premium with 'quality' as its hallmark, adds Wadia.

Aggarwal feels downsizing will not affect women who are competent, knowledgeable and reliable. They can use the opportunities for freelance assignments. People are known to earn more that way than at a job that binds them down. But still, women employees are considered more dispensable than their male counterparts, says Shroff.

A cross-section of men seem to think that if women work, kudos to them, but often in middle- and upper-class families, they get to keep the money - while the man's earnings go to his family's welfare. "If we persist in our old ways, we stand accused of chauvinism and sexism. If we stretch ourselves to take on new responsibilities without equal demands, we are overloaded and strained to the breaking point. But more dangerously, if we let go of our traditional masculine style completely, we find to our terror that we are becoming invisible, unsexy and unworthy in the eyes of most women," adds Jagdeep Kapoor, Chairman and Managing Director of Samsika Marketing. It was easy for Mom and Dad; roles came prepackaged, but nowadays women are asking too many questions. And getting too few answers. Like a precocious kid, she wants to know why everything is the way it is; and if you call her `baby', she will most likely get very offended. Anything you say will be used against you, if not right away, then down the line.

Katy Merchant, Vice President and General Manager of panel and media research at Indian Market Research Bureau (IMRB), says, "A man's role in society is that of the breadwinner. No confusion. A woman's role has been defined as mother, wife, daughter, sister - and now boss the woman plays multiple roles." Adds Lalita D. Gupte, Deputy Managing Director of Industrial Credit and Investment Corporation of India (ICICI), a lady to reckon with in financial circles: "A woman is two separate entities at home and at work. That does not mean that she is a split personality. It's just that one has to be different as a mother and a wife and as a serious executive."

While the debate goes on, women in India will continue to make their voices heard in the workplace. They are making significant strides in what is considered by the West as one of the most repressive cultures towards women. From prime minister to senior managers to astronauts, they have successfully multiplied their roles in the family, society and the workplace.

Hewlett-Packard's new CEO and President, Carly Fiorina, heads the list for the second time. At 45, she is the first female CEO of one of

America's largest corporations. For the power she wields, the responsibility she takes on, the challenges she faces, the innovations she brings to the workplace and the work she puts in, her pay packet is close to a whopping US$100 million!

Good enough, you find, for her husband to hang up his boots at AT&T, where he had met her 16 years ago. "Last year the couple decided that life is too short - and too chaotic - for dual careers." And so he and not she quit his job. And there are a couple of other husbands in the Fortune Top 50 list, who have given up their careers to either manage their wives' careers or take care of the home and the kids.

Enough evidence to show that women managers have arrived. What makes a woman manager tick? Does she have the required leadership qualities? Communication skills? Are they good listeners? What about their negotiating skills which are so crucial in any enterprise? Can they motivate their colleagues and resolve conflicts without creating earthquakes or shedding blood?

Obviously these are traits which cut across gender, and if given proper training, the right work environment, support systems at home if they have a family, and most of all, a fair opportunity to compete, women managers have shown that they can deliver, and excel too. Right at the very top.

To the level of an Indira Gandhi or a Margaret Thatcher. To find out what Thatcher brought to her job, let us look at what Dame Sheila Masters, whose credentials are as impressive - a Partner at KPMG, President of the UK Institute of Chartered Accountants, and a non-executive Director of the Court of the Bank of England - has to say about the former British prime minister.

Describing Thatcher as her role model, she says in the *Financial Times*, "What I admire about her is that she came through on sheer ability, guts, and political tenacity. She held on to power and ruled innovatively. Her certainty was one of her great qualities; she was always convinced of what she was doing. She never relied on her feminity, but she always looked immaculate. Even if you didn't like her style, she never seemed to have bad hair days like the rest of us".

Masters then goes on to describe her only meeting with Thatcher "where she frightened the life out of me... She was very aggressive. It was so terrible a meeting we all had to go to the pub afterwards, but she completely energised us."

What about Masters herself.. what kind of a manager is she? In her own words, she has a fierce reputation and cannot "tolerate fools... I have a huge workload, so I'm very ruthless with my time. I'm driven by the need for results and I'm a perfectionist, so I can't stand people prepared to work below their ability".

So what, one may well ask, these are not necessarily the traits of a woman manager. They could belong to any good and successful manager, and gender should have nothing to do with it. Precisely. Management, good management, is no longer the exclusive preserve of the male of the species. Though it used to be, once upon a time. And hence, the glass ceiling or the invisible and artificial barriers created by attitudinal and organisational prejudices, which are often put up to prevent women from reaching top management positions. The term itself was coined in the US in the 1970s, and despite the Masters of this world shattering it to reach where they are today, more and more women find themselves struggling to get over this invisible barrier in offices and enterprises across nations and cultures.

In one survey conducted on the glass ceiling by the popular 'Ask Annie' column of Fortune magazine, one junior woman manager wrote, "Is there a glass ceiling in my company? You bet, and my boss insists it is my job to keep it clean and shiny! No wonder so many women start their own businesses".

Yet another woman, a former stockbroker says, "the only female and the highest producer in my office" endured blatant discrimination from her manager and co-workers. After sending her manager on many a free trip for her outstanding performance, she finally got smart, resigned and "filtered over US$100 millions out of my office to other firms where I networked and made other friends. Talk about ultimate revenge.. it felt great. I then joined a woman's company where the only glass ceiling that exists is in my own head. Yes, we do have a choice."

But while an overwhelming number of women executives and managers have talked about the hampering of their career advancement by the glass ceiling there are senior women managers who have denied its very existence. Reena Ramachandran, Chairman and Managing Director of the public sector Hindustan Organic Chemicals, who has had several stints in the public sector in India, says she was never confronted by a glass ceiling. "If there was a glass ceiling I should have felt it, but I never felt any glass ceiling," she told in an interview.

Fiorina is another woman manager who had to take a lot of flak, especially from women, for saying, after she had got the coveted title of CEO at Hewlett-Packard, "I hope we're at a point that everyone has figured out that there is not a glass ceiling". Even after she had raised a storm over this statement, she stuck to her opinion. "Sure, there are barriers at companies that haven't woken up to competition. But at companies competing hard to win every day, there is not a glass ceiling."

But then Fiorina is different. Obviously she has gone beyond the gender divide in achieving. Small wonder then that she does not want to be a role model for women. She wants to be more than that. A role model for both women and men. Here's what the Fortune article says about her. "In her view, power flows to men and women alike who think of themselves as self-directed free agents."

Self directed... self motivated. These are among the crucial qualities which make a woman manager tick. Like Sulajja Motwani, the Joint Managaing Director of the Kinetic group, who likes to set goals for herself, whether it is in the number of jogging rounds she does in her morning workout, or the number of Kinetic vehicles the company sells during a given year.

But there are instances where all these qualities - ambition, motivation, long hours, dedication and excellence - are just not sufficient to see the woman through the glass ceiling. An International Labour Organisation study conducted in December 1997 on 'Women's progress in workforce' found that while women had made substantial progress in closing the gender gap in managerial and professional jobs, most female managers worldwide were still barred from the top positions, in both the private and public sectors and the government.

This study found that the hurdles that women aspiring to management jobs have to overcome can be "so formidable that they sometimes abandon efforts to make it to the top of large firms. Such women often take their energy and knowhow to smaller and more flexible companies, or set up their own businesses. In the United States a third of small and medium-sized companies are now run by women", says the report (Ghosh, 2000).

Many women on the 'mommy track' in the developed countries opt to take part-time or flexitime jobs. Others opt for shared jobs - two women doing the work of one and dividing the salary. But in countries such as India, where support services are still available within the home, the "mommy track" concept is yet to take off. Many women might be ready for it; but the employers are not.

There are no authentic figures available of women managers in India. But there is ample evidence to show that the scene is changing in India too, as it is in the rest of the world. The participation of 15 women executives at the southern region's contest for young managers conducted by the All-India Management Association in Bangalore in June exemplifies the transition.

But let's examine a source, which does have firm statistics. Like a 1998 Fortune 500 survey, which found that while women hold 40 per cent of all management positions in America, (in Europe the figure is between 20 and 30 per cent), American women held only 11 per cent of board seats in the top 500 companies. In Britain, women held only five per cent of board seats in the top 200 companies.

Says the Fortune article, "Despite China's two decades of formal commitment to sexual equality, there are no female business leaders of note. In Japan, the rigidity of the corporate culture keeps women out of the executive suite. The famed salaryman style can only exist with a full-time homemaker for support".

As for attitudes of the rest of the workforce, they remain much the same all over the world. When Sari Baldauf took her first senior management position at Nokia, and she visited the company's German operations, she found workers looking at her and saying: 'Fine, the secretary has come. Where is the boss?'

But women all over the world are battling against such attitudes and emerging victorious. Even in a country such as Japan where, at the workplace, women in junior management positions are expected to serve tea, a research survey conducted in July 1999 found that, for the first time ever, the number of female company presidents had crossed the 60,000 mark. But despite this increase, women CEOs in Japan are still very rare. Women headed 60,593 firms in June 1999, just 5 per cent of the country's 1.14 million companies.

But the survey established that women find it nearly impossible to rise to the top of larger and well established Japanese corporations, while having an easier time making gains in many smaller companies.

"Unlike female leaders on the career track in western nations, a majority of Japanese women are heading family-type firms," a spokesman of the Teikoku Data Bank, Japan's largest credit research agency, said. Despite the advance, women still face major hurdles when trying to move up the Japanese corporate ladder. Many companies push women to quit when they marry or when they reach their mid-30s, said the report.

Discrimination against women in business cuts across international boundaries. Take the case of Renata McGriff, who while raising money for her New York-based Internet start-up, did what any self-respecting entrepreneur does. She made the rounds of venture capital firms. But nobody took her seriously as she lacked business school training, and experience in running a company.

A Reuters report quoted her saying, "I went to a venture capital firm in New York that's well known, and they told me I should start a restaurant because I have such a good personality. When I got to the elevator, I cried. I was so broken."

Ultimately, McGriff used her savings and raised loans from family and friends to start Times Square Media and launched Times Square 2000 (http://www.timessquare2000.com). Despite the venture capital firms' no-confidence vote, McGriff's had no problem signing up partners. But the underlying tragedy of her success is that despite Internet companies attracting huge venture capital, women-owned businesses such as hers continue to get the wrong end of the stick from venture capital firms.

Move from venture capital to fishing and you find that discrimination against women takes various forms across careers. Like a royal decree handed down by King Jaime I, 750 years ago which gave exclusive fishing rights to men in the Spanish fishing village of El Palmar. After a five year period of judicial appeals and counter appeals, a group of women made history a couple of months ago when the Mayor, a woman of course - Rita Barbera - allowed them fishing rights.

But women are doing more than casting fishing nets. They are breaking rules and smashing barriers. And this is best demonstrated by an analysis of Fortune's Power 50 which found women managers storming the hitherto male bastion of finance and technology. More than half of the group turned out to be technology and finance wizards.

They include Joy Covey (No. 28 on the list), the finance-chief-cum-strategist at Amazon.com; marketer Jan Brandt (No. 39), "who built America Online into cyberspace's No. 1 brand"; and Dawn Lepore (No. 36), "the tech wizard behind the transformation of a bricks-and-mortar brokerage, Charles Schwab, into the category killer of online stock trading", says the magazine's cover story.

Other women who are flexing the financial muscle at top companies include the "straight talking and audacious" Debby Hopkins (No. 6), the new Chief Financial Officer (CFO) at Boeing and Dina Dublon who became the CFO of Chase Manhattan. "Now with Heidi Miller (No. 2) at Citigroup, two of the three largest US banks have female finance chiefs. At Barclays Global Investors, Patricia Dunn (No. 11) controls $675 billion in assets". Interestingly enough, a high powered career in management does not always require specialisation and qualifications from a B-school. In the Fortune list, only one out of three women had MBAs, and two had dropped out of high school! Flexibility is important, and, says the article, "many of these women inherited that trait from their mothers and developed it early on".

The survey also found that "the generalists win. In this volatile economy, the right stuff - for men and women - is versatility, not functional expertise or pedigree. Debbie Hopkins arrived at Boeing with neither an MBA nor any work experience in the aircraft industry. But her biggest asset was an ability to force change in change-resistant companies".

Combining kids and work is really tough, and one of the women is quoted as saying that half her friends from the Princeton and

Harvard B-Schools where she picked up her MBAs, have quit the business world to become full time wives and mothers.

But times are changing. As Dame Masters said in the FT article, "Opting for a serious career, I didn't particularly want children. It would have been very difficult then, though now it's possible for women to have both".

Such positive sentiment gives the woman the best of options... to be a warm and caring family woman at home and the efficient and no-nonsense boss in the office.

Are men from Mars and women from Venus in the boardroom, too?

What's Holding Women Back?

Fortune 1000 CEOs exhibit a striking degree of consensus as to the key factors preventing women from advancing to corporate leadership. A decisive 82 per cent point to lack of significant general management or line experience as the most crucial barrier. A second critical obstacle, according to two-thirds of CEOs, is that women have not been "in the pipeline" long enough; that is, until recently, the executive talent pool has included few women. No more than one-third of chief executives single out any other factor that might account for women's lack of advancement.

Senior women concur with male CEOs that women's lack of significant general management or line experience is a barrier to their ascendance on the corporate ladder, although they rank it third after gender stereotyping and exclusion from informal networks. The female executives in Catalyst's sample attest to the scarcity of senior women in line management: just 15 per cent are in general management or sales and marketing jobs, and more than 60 per cent hold staff positions.

The implication is clear. For the pipeline to contain a critical mass of women requires that significantly more women become plant managers, presidents of operating divisions and other senior line managers with profit and loss responsibility. Yet, because these are nontraditional roles for women and because few female role models exist, some women may be reluctant to put themselves forward for line management jobs. Companies also typically regard it as riskier to assign women to these positions. "There's a certain amount of reluctance on the part of any manufacturing company to ask some young woman to move to a remote location to work as a foreman," admits one Fortune 500 CEO. "And I think there's reluctance on the part of women to want to do that."

Executive women are far less likely than CEOs to agree that women have not been in the pipeline long enough for advancement, 29 per cent versus 64 per cent. This may in part reflect a difference in the way the two groups define "pipeline." Female executives may be thinking in terms of women's steadily growing share of corporate management positions generally, while CEOs may focus more heavily on women's lack of experience in core functions. As one Fortune 500 CEO puts it: "It's not that women haven't been in the pipeline long enough; it's what they have done while they are in the pipeline."

Although women executives and male CEOs may agree that women haven't been steering in the right direction to advance to senior positions, they beg to differ when it comes to the issue of gender itself. In any discussion of the "glass ceiling," it's impossible to avoid the issue of discrimination. Successful female executives in Catalyst's study identify male stereotyping and preconceptions of women as the number-one major obstacle to women's advancement to corporate leadership. They view exclusion from informal (read "old boy") networks as the next most serious deterrent. An inhospitable corporate culture also holds women back, say one-third of senior women. Male CEOs are far less likely to attribute women's scarcity in upper management to such cultural or attitudinal factors.

Despite the steady increase of women in corporate management in the past 25 years, six in ten Indian women still believe that women suffer discrimination in obtaining executive positions in business, according to the 1995 The Hindu Opinion Poll. In fact, more women hold this view than in 1970, when just half of women concurred. This increased perception of discrimination may reflect society's growing sensitivity to subtle forms of bias toward diverse groups of all kinds.

Some CEOs acknowledge that women face a challenge fitting into a traditional corporate culture and creating a comfort level with male managers. "I don't think it has anything to do with competency," says one chief executive. "I think it's just that our society has certain norms that have been built in-wives being uncomfortable with women working in the same office as their husbands, things of that nature."

Many female executives would agree that social norms have created a corporate environment that is not conducive to their presence. But most would disagree that it is simply a matter of time until the climate changes. They believe that companies committed to diversifying their leadership must take deliberate steps to change assumptions and behaviour. Company leaders must ensure that women have access to informal developmental opportunities and communication channels, as well as equal shots at "stretch" assignments such as serving on corporate-wide task forces, being part of start-up or turnaround operations, and gaining international experience.

The Backdrop

A vast literature has attempted to account for the lower involvement of women in management. Some studies have focussed on individual characteristics such as gender role and career choice while others have emphasized the organizational cultures, processes, and policies that subtly restricts women's opportunities of advancing up the organizational hierarchy (Alvesson and Billing, 1997; Powell and Butterfield, 1994; Stover, 1994). Although these studies have provided important insights into the mechanisms adopted by different management practices, which in turn affect women's access to positions of authority and leadership. For example, Steinhoff and Tanaka (1994) in their studies of Japanese managers found the emphasis on seniority and career continuity and the frequency of geographic transfers in Japanese organizations seriously limit career opportunities for women which seems to be quite true in Indian case too. Stephens and Greer (1995) also contended that, owing to cultural traditions and prevailing social mores, many Mexican employers continue to favour male executives over females in their hiring practices.

Aim of the Present Study

The cultural values attached with the social role of a woman significantly affect her career choice. If we take the case of 'glass ceiling' (which refers to a transparent barrier that prevents the upward mobility of women in organizations) then it becomes clear that one main explanation for its existence is the traditional sex role stereotypes toward women (Nivea & Gutek, 1981; Norris & Wylie, 1995; Tabak, 1997). Conventionally, managerial jobs have been defined as largely a matter of instrumentality, autonomy and result-orientation (Alvesson & Billing, 1997) which fit the stereotypes of men rather than those of women. For that reason, male stereotypes (that focus on attributes such as independence, competitiveness, control, and ambition) have predominated in the world of management. Given this, women are perceived as lacking management skills and leadership abilities, and thus they are denied access to managerial positions.

Nevertheless, it should be noted that sex stereotypes are culturally based beliefs prescribing appropriate and inappropriate behaviours for the two genders. Against this backdrop the present study aims to examine the socio-cultural determinants of women leadership at the top in Indian organizations.

Objectives and Hypotheses

Despite the importance of culture in shaping individual's career trajectory and work outcomes, only few studies linked women's representation in managerial jobs to cultural factors at the societal levels. The present study assumes that the socio-cultural factors does affect women's share in top managerial positions. Therefore, the first hypothesis is:

Hypothesis 1. Socio-cultural factors will have direct effect on women's share in managerial positions.

Further, the economic development generates the demand for female labour and increases women's educational attainment. The higher educational attainment of women in turn qualifies them to enter into the growing managerial and professional occupations (Charles,1992; Clark, 1991; Pampel and Kazuko, 1986). Additionally, economic development also leads to the evolution of a large and competitive labour market with hiring and promotion based mainly on individual's achievement. This in turn reduces the gender inequality in the workplace and facilitates women's entrance into managerial positions. The greater acceptance of egalitarian norms in advanced economies would also result in less gender inequality in the workplace with more rational and universalistic HR practices being adopted (Moore and Shackman, 1996; Ward and Pampel, 1985). In view of the above, the following hypothesis is proposed:

Hypothesis 2. Higher the level of economic development in a country greater will be the proportion of women in managerial positions.

In this study, we argue that national culture has important bearing on the constraints and opportunities for women managers in their career pursuit. Hofstede (1980), for example, pointed out that cultural values as the important elements of national culture impact upon organizations in a number of ways. In particular, cultural values reflect basic assumptions and traditions about the differential nature of men and women and the presumed role they could play within a society. The culturally presumed role of women may block their career choice and hinder them from entering positions of authority. Additionally, cultural values also permeate organizations by defining organizational processes, role structures, and role relations as culturally accepted (Lachman, Nedd, and Hinings, 1994). Therefore, it is postulated,

Hypothesis 3. Larger the power distance in a society lower will be the proportion of women in managerial positions.

The Interaction of Economic Development and National Culture

Although national culture and economic development seems to be independent, it is possible that they may act together to influence the dependent variable. In other words, the effect of some cultural values may be contingent upon the level of economic development of a country. For example, anti-discrimination and equal employment opportunity laws are likely to be enforced in more developed countries which may undermine the negative impacts of masculinity and higher power distance on women's economic role and status (Cannings and Lazonick, 1994). Similarly, egalitarian ideology prevails in advanced economies may overcome some cultural biases and traditional prejudices against women in management and leadership. Based on the above argument, the following non-dimensional hypothesis is proposed:

Hypothesis 4. There will be an interaction effect of economic development and national culture upon women's representation in management.

The research is of interest for several reasons. First, we want to argue for the importance of looking at socio-cultural factors to explain the share of women leadership in Indian organizations. Secondly, since managers control the bulk of power in organizations and largely determines a firm's human resources practices like recruitment, selection, placement, promotion, and compensation, the extent to which managerial positions are filled by women has important long term implications for women employees. Finally, the findings of the study will help us to establish linkages between national culture and organizational processes and practices that arguably act upon the constraints and opportunities women encounter in the workplace.

References

Alvesson, M. & Billing, Y.D. (1997). Understanding gender and organization. London: Sage Publications.

Cannings, K.&Lazonick, W.(1994). Equal employment opportunity and the "managerial women" in Japan. *Industrial Relations*, 33 (1), pp. 44-68.

Ghosh, A. (2000). Position of women in organization hierarchy. Term Paper under the Guidence of Prof. Sunita Singh-Sengupta at Indian Institute of Management Calcutta. India.

Hostede, G. (1980). Culture's consequences : International differences in work related values. Beverly Hills, CA : Sage.

htt: / /www.timessquare2000.com

Lachman, R.; Nedd, A & Hinings, B. (1994). Analyzing cross-national management and organizations : A theoretical framework. *Management Science*, 40 (1), pp. 40-45.

Moore, G. & Shackman, G. (1996). Gender and Authority : A cross-national study. *Social Science Quarterly*, 77(2), pp. 273-288.

Ward, K.B. & Pampel, F.C. (1985). Structural determinants of female labour force participation in developed nations, 1955-75. *Social Science Quarterly*, 66, pp. 654-667.

Charles M. (1992). Cross-national variation in occupational sex segregation. *American Sociological Review*, 57, pp. 483-502.

Clark, R. (1991). Contrasting perspectives on women's access to prestigious occupations : A cross-national investigation. *Social Science Quarterly*, 72, pp. 20-32.

Nivea, V.F. & Gutek B.A. (1981). Women and work: A psychological perspective. New York: Praeger.

Norris, J.M. & Wylie, A.M. (1995). Gender stereotyping of the managerial role among student in Canada and the United States. *Group and Organization Management*, 20, pp. 167-182.

Pampel, F.C. & Kazuko, T. (1996), Economic development and female labour force participation: A reconsideration. *Social Forces*, 64, pp. 599-619.

Powell, G.N. & Butterfield, D.A. (1994). Investigation the 'glass ceiling' phenomenon : An empirical study of actual promotions to top management. *Academy of Management Journal*, 37, pp.68-86.

Steinhoff, P.G. & Tanaka, K. (1994). Women managers in Japan. In N.J. Adler and D.N. Izradli (eds.) *Women Managers in a Global Economy* (pp. 79-100). MA : Blackwell.

Stephens, G.K. & Greer, C.R. (1995). Doing business in Mexico : Understanding cultural differences. *Organizational Dynamics*. 24 (1), pp. 39-55.

Stover, D.L. (1994). The horizontal distribution of female managers within organization. *Works and Occupations*, 21, pp. 385-402.

Tabak, F. (1997). Women's upward mobility in manufacturing organizations in istanbul: A glass ceiling initiative. *Sex Roles*, 36 (1/2), pp. 93-102.

Methodology

The present book examines the socio-cultural determinants of women representation at the top managerial positions. The glass ceiling commission concluded that the chief obstacle blocking women's corporate advancement is the prejudice and preconceptions that female executives are less able and effective than their male counterparts. Nevertheless, sex role stereotypes are culturally based beliefs prescribing appropriate and inappropriate behaviour for the two genders. The purpose of the present volume is to examine the impact of culture on the representation of women in management. The researcher deals the issues from individual as well as organizational perspective, both.

The Trend in India

Corporate India expects superior business results from its executives, and successful women recognize the need to deliver on those expectations. Many female managers believe that superior performance is particularly essential for women, who may need to over perform to prove their ability in a predominantly male business environment. On the other hand, some women say that gender bias has worked to their advantage. When colleagues have low expectations of a woman's ability to perform, they are easy to exceed. "There have been more than a few times that expectations of me have been extremely low," says a female vice president of a chemical company. "Knowing that I can do this with one hand tied behind my back, and then having people overly dazzled at the achievement, makes me kind of chuckle to myself."

Besides excellent job performance, it is noteworthy that the only career strategy considered critical to advancement by a majority of women executives is developing a style with which male managers are comfortable. Clearly, delivering superior business results, while necessary for executive success, is not sufficient—at least for women. And women often expect to bend further to reach the middle ground. "Women have to go 80 per cent of the way to make men comfortable with them," says a female corporate vice president of a consumer products company.

Women in corporate management often struggle with fitting into the organizational culture without losing a sense of their own identity. Some counsel "learning to play the game as men play it," including keeping one's personal life out of the office and taking up sports. Terry Savage, a Bangalore-based financial authority and director of that Corporation, advises: "Learn to play golf. I took it up two years ago, and now I know what they do. It's not about golf. It's about riding around in the cart and sitting around afterward and talking. I was always holding out, thinking, 'I'm different. I'm a woman, and I don't have to play the games.' Now I think that you can't set yourself aside and not socialize. It doesn't mean you have to be one of the guys. You can still be yourself. But it's nice to be able to be around them."

Other executive women emphasize that they have succeeded without compromising their personal style or identity. "In 1977, when I finished business school, women were coming in trying to be something that they weren't. They felt that they had to behave in a more masculine manner," says Fudge of Maxwell House. "One of the things I decided in my somewhat rebellious state was that if I felt like wearing a dress instead of a suit, that's what I was going to do. I decided I would be judged not by style, but by what I did in managing the business. That's the bottom line. Honestly, I think too many times we try to adapt, and we overadapt" (Ghosh, 2000).

Simultaneously, there is a growing understanding among women too that they don't need to be like men to succeed in the corporate world. To quote Shroff, ``increasingly, motherhood is being recognised as an excellent school for managers, demanding many of the same skills--organisation, pacing, the balancing of conflicting claims, guiding, monitoring and handling disturbances."

Another surprising trend. The earlier stereotypes of working mothers being neglectful of their families or making compromises with their jobs have disappeared. This change is actually evident only from the mid-to-late '90s. They credit this largely to the slow but definite transformation of the career of Indian husband, and, yes, even the mother-in-law, for whom successful working *bahus* have become a source of pride. And spare a cheer for the changing husband. ``Most of the women professionals felt that they could not have got where they had without their husband's support," says Pathfinders (Ghosh, 2000).

It lists four ways in which they received support: Encouragement to go out and pursue a demanding career, not making many demands and being understanding, offering both moral support and help in times of trouble and giving them freedom to do whatever they want without interference.

But proper support systems are still a problem. The study found that 40 per cent of women managers had left their full time jobs and gone in for a complete break from work till they were able to organize a support system, then returned to part time or full time jobs. Or switched to less time consuming options such as part time consultancy, flexi-time jobs or started their own ventures.

While supportive husbands are fine, they have their own jobs too. The majority of the respondents in all the studies lived in nuclear families, and relied heavily on support systems such as full time maids, crèches, daycare centres, friends and even neighbours to manage their lives.

Against this backdrop the author in this book have tried to emphasize the positive side of being women through the success stories of women managers and entrepreneurs. Like "all the happy families are alike and unhappy families have their own stories" all the successful women at work seemed to have same stories that we will see through different case studies. Altogether fifteen such cases that have been collected through different sources are produced here.

Case Studies

Case Study 1

Her slender frame, youthful looks and friendly smile, and above all, her 27 years, would make it difficult for anyone to take her seriously in her senior management position at the Rs. 800 crore Kinetic group of industries. **Sulajja Firodia Motwani**, Joint

Managing Director of the Kinetic group of industries spoke to **Business Line's** (Vol. 2,Issue. 4, November 1999) Rasheeda Bhagat. An excerpt from the article in THE HINDU BUSINESS LINE:

Though she is far from bossy, Sulajja Firodia Motwani, Joint Managing Director of the group, has made her staff know for sure who is the boss. Like the time when one of her senior colleagues, a man who had worked with her father, during a performance review meeting said she was like his daughter. "I told him very clearly: Look, I'm not like your daughter, and I'm never going to be your daughter. Let's get that straight. That is the equation. I'm here to listen to you and solve your problem and find out what caused it. But I'm not like your daughter. I'm your boss".

The man was obviously taken aback. "But then the equation was set. I never had a problem with him again". What kind of challenges did she face as a woman manager?

Did she face attitudinal problems with her male colleagues, who might have thought that management, like so many other areas, is a man's domain? Her first response is a sigh. "Everybody asks me that. The truth is that I've never looked at management as a gender issue. As for attitudinal problems, they might have had questions in their minds. But at work, I always mean business. I don't throw my weight around, and if I don't know, I say can you please show or explain this to me. I try to be very sincere about whatever I'm doing and go about doing it. I think it's a good way to do a job".

A "very active kid who was involved in every fight in the family", after completing a Commerce degree from Pune in 1990, Sulajja went ahead for an MBA from the Carnegie Melon University.

For the next four years she worked in California for Barra International, a leading investment technology company which does consulting, portfolio management and performance management.

She recalls with pride that she worked in finance, which is an area dominated by men. "And even where there are women you have the typical white, Caucasian women. I was the first non-American Asian woman and I enjoyed the fact that I was non-white, young, had an accent and was still able to do a good job. We sold very big projects and this stint gave me a lot of self-confidence. If there was anything I learnt about management, it was there."

But the young woman knew that she would always come back to the business where her father was Chairman, though her return to India was with a mandate from Barra to create and head their Indian operations. It was an exciting opportunity which ended in nine months when she decided to enter the family business in late 1996.

It was as a deliberate strategy that she joined as General Manager in the much smaller Jaya Hind Industries, a group company making welding machines. "I wanted to get to know the people in the group. Had I joined the bigger company directly, there would have been be all these factors about being the Chairman's daughter. I kept a low profile talking to people and sizing them up".

After a few months she joined Kinetic Motors where she chose the marketing role. For one thing, she considers marketing and finance her strengths. "The other reason was my father is a technocrat; he's very strong on technology. So it made sense that I should contribute in the business development side. So I took on the responsibility of planning and marketing in the Kinetic group".

She doesn't think that her youth, or her being her father's daughter, has been a disadvantage. "I think if you are sensitive towards people and respect their individuality, it goes a long way".

She does believe that women managers handle inter-personal relationships more sensitively. At the same time, they have to maintain a balance. As a manager, she can't stand her women employees whimpering or crying over something. "I tell my women colleagues, don't cry. Please never cry in the office. If you have a problem, keep quiet. If you need to cry, go to the loo and cry your heart out. But don't cry in front of your colleagues because then you are showing you are... kind of weak. You might get sympathy, but your professional respect will be gone".

Another crucial aspect of management, she feels, is to always mean business and not get into people's personal lives "even though you might want to help them out. Women bosses are better at human relationships because they are sincere and brought up to be considerate. Your mother tells you,`don't talk to your brother that way,' and you carry that along".

She's also found that women as managers are very conscientious.

"I was wondering why... then I realised that women are also mothers. A mother always teaches her child to be conscientious.. not steal, etc, and you tend to carry this.. a sense of correctness which a woman has, to the workplace. If there are more women managers, it would certainly improve the work culture. You certainly find less women involved in corruption or frauds."

"I also sort of decided that I'll never lose my temper on the job. When I get really upset, I keep quiet and let it pass. I don't think losing your temper or raising your voice can get anything done. I find that it is always better to be firm and keep your cool."

Sulajja's role model has been a woman manager at Barra. "Had I come straight from a business school into Kinetic, I would have been a very different manager. I learnt a lot from her. She had a purpose about everything she said or did, and I admired the sense of professionalism in her dealings. She would step back when things got off balance."

"If somebody did or said something which disturbed her, she would step back and tell him/her: Look, I really would like to talk to you about this, but I don't think this is a good time. Let's both go home, come back in the morning and talk about it. She would do that, and I tend to do that too."

She feels that the intense travelling she did - "not the kind I do here, which is a piece of cake because everything is taken care of, but the kind where you have to book your own flights, make your hotel reservations, rent the cars, check the maps, etc" - in her American assignment, has give her a lot of confidence to handle people and situations. "It toughens you up and prepares you. It makes you self confident and aware.. of both your strengths and weaknesses". Her response to the double bind syndrome of management is interesting. A very gender thing, this is an aspect of management where women bosses who are understanding are branded weak against a sympathetic male boss being considered 'humane'. The second equally unfair aspect is an autocratic male boss considered "business like" or efficient against the same quality in a woman boss being branded 'bitchy', with the woman manager freely being referred to as Hitler in the work place.

"It happens all the time. And not only that, if a man loses his temper they say: *Saab bahut gussa ho gaya*.. as though he is a victim. When a woman loses her temper she is seen as hyper or hysterical. These are very much there. The only way to deal with this syndrome is to be very professional about your work; be sweet, be polite, but firm. I've also found that over a period of time you learn to be perfect... or rather not cross the line between being sweet versus being soft. But ultimately you have to learn to be a professional, whether you're a guy or a woman".

She feels that a woman manager has a distinct advantage in that people around her have very low expectations from her to begin with. "Though unfortunate, it also means that you can really impress or make a mark and stand out. But over a period of time it stops being an advantage".

To the question whether colleagues are more co-operative and less rebellious with female compared to male bosses, she says, "This is true, but then you've got to be careful. If you play too much on the female factor, it will finally go against you. If you play too much on `Oh, can you please help me?' it will always go against you in the long run. If you make sense, men get up and listen to you because they have low expectations and there aren't too many women around."

She perceives the "listening skills" of a woman a distinct advantage in the managerial function. "Women are good listeners, and are open to criticism. And you'll find very few women who are egomaniacs. Women are not driven by ego, they are driven by other things. A lot of men are driven by ego, and I consider this a weakness. Ego makes you off balance and unidirectional."

She defines one of the "other things" which drive women managers as sincerity. "I do believe women are very sincere. They genuinely want to do a good job, whatever they might be doing. That's a very big strength. Because when you're sincere or have a sense of purpose, you'll always give your best. Women also tend to be honest."

About the disadvantages faced by women managers, Sulajja says, "You have to be much better than male managers to stand out and rise within an organisation. Secondly, there are the social factors. While you don't want to be like men, you have to be very professional and you should learn and define what professionalism means in your dictionary. You must learn to keep your cool, have a sense of balance and good communication skills, which are very critical."

She feels that women managers tend to be better communicators because they tend to be more expressive. "But this has to be balanced. You can be expressive in a very shrill, emotional kind of way or you can be expressive in a balanced way. Being communicative is a strength but women managers have to use it as a strength."

A major disadvantage is social factors like the family and the home. "These are factors which can pull you apart. If they don't pull you back, they pull you apart. Many women get pulled back and give up. But if you are strong and want to do something, and are really involved in your work, they really pull you apart. As a woman you would know that!"

"After work, when you go back home, you have this fight within you which is very difficult. No matter how supportive your family is. I come from a very supportive family..."

That comprises a husband, who heads the Kinetic Communications division, which has a tie up with Daewoo to make colour monitors. An engineer from Stanford, she met him in the US and got him to Pune. "I told him it really means a lot to me. He is a Sindhi from Hyderabad and I'm a Rajasthani, though people think we're Parsis. He has been very supportive".

There are no children yet. "Its not something I've written off as a possibility. It's been five years of marriage, but I'll have to be sure that I can do justice to both, and so far I've been able to manage work, and my husband and my own health and sense of well being". Ego clashes are averted, as he is not in the same company. "We're more like friends and so there are not too many social factors, which sort of pick holes in a relationship."

As a woman manager and an employer, Sulajja has viewed with concern the social constraints, which are stumbling blocks in the career of many women. "I've seen women having to leave after marriage. They have a kid, go on leave, and don't come back. So much potential is wasted and management's confidence in a woman as an employee gets shaken. That can change only as more and more women come in and take on a professional attitude that they have to work and manage the home too".

As a woman manager, she has to keep this factor in mind while employing women. Apart from trying to motivate such women to stay back, "I also tell them at least be very honest about it. If you think you'll be here only for a year or two, tell us when you join. But if you consider this a career, then don't give up. Factors will you pull you back, but if you seriously want a career, you can stay on. But its hard, and if I didn't have the kind of domestic environment which I did, it would be hard for me too. If I had a husband who expected me to cook and run the house, it would be difficult for me too".

Coming to the skills of a woman manager at the negotiating table, she says, "You can be very good if you know how to do it. Because other people don't expect you to drive hard bargains. So you can use it to your advantage. You have to learn that. I'm not very good at it! Because when you're being hard, you're always telling yourself that you should not be rude, which the guys don't feel. I think they are not worried about being rude. At business school, for a class on negotiating skills I got a remark that you are too concerned about your opponents' losses. That is emotional. So you have to kind of step back and put a wall, look at your interests and make it a hard deal".

Though she hasn't yet mastered this, she is confident she'll learn over a period of time. On another important aspect of management, conflict resolution, which is traditionally believed to be easier for a male manager because of the back-slapping and let's-have-a-drink routine, she says her position is different. "I'm in a different chair altogether; a chair with a different power... so you don't tread over other people's egos or self respect. But women managers can have their own equations for resolving conflicts."

"In the US, you can go out for a drink or lunch, but in India it is a different social context. But you can talk about it. It's really personal, not really gender based". Would male colleagues tend to take advantage of a woman manager who is very friendly or outgoing? "Yes. They feel they have a right to examine your personal life. Whereas you might feel that you're just making casual conversation. In the US nobody is bothered. When somebody asks how are you, you're expected to say fine or great. But if you say `Oh, I'm not feeling too good' people are surprised." Looking ahead, she says the major challenges before her pertain to the automobile sector being a very competitive industry. "Today, in this business, everything is important. You've got to be good in designing, R&D, logistics, dealing with hundreds or thousands of vendors, low cost manufacturing, distributing and advertising and marketing. It's a very complex industry and the dynamics are changing. Certainly there are a lot of things to do".

Another major professional challenge is to "always try for a better balance between personal and business life. But there is a dilemma and conflict in my mind. Being a workaholic, I love to work hard but then I also feel that I have to pay more attention to my health and family".

But she's candid enough to admit that this a balance she has not yet mastered. "I'm still pulled towards working hard. That's a dilemma which someday I hope to sort out", she says with a sigh.

Sulajja accepts stress as an integral part of business life. Her problem is not so much dealing with stress, as the "tendency to carry your work home. When I was in the US, I was a fairly sincere employee, liked my job, worked very hard but when I went home, that was it. Now when I go home, I carry the tension with me, and think about it while eating or driving. I haven't yet managed to make myself completely detached when I go home. But I'll have to learn. I'm at the front end of the business; responsible for the entire turnover. If I can't get the team to perform, then the company does not do too well. It's not like you're designing a product, or in accounting, or administration. You're the driver."

To a certain extent, restructuring of the group in the last three years, and bringing in professionals has helped. As for her achievements, she says she has contributed to Kinetic in the last three years, "but I wouldn't call it an achievement. I really love what I do and have definitely relieved my father of a very big responsibility".

After her entry, the group has introduced 'winds of change', something which has made her a symbol of change in the company. She thinks this is viewed positively. "People say the Chairman is very respected, but people are in awe of him... and he is aloof. But I'm seen as very open. Anybody can talk to me. After I came in, we got into new products. A lot of activities and a lot of new things have happened, from renovation of our dealerships to launching of new products.

"Kinetic has always been a strong manufacturing company but not a strong marketing company. I've tried to build a strong marketing team and give a strong marketing focus which people have definitely noticed. I will say I have contributed, but there is a lot more to do. But I would still call it a contribution and not achievement. What I did in Barra was achievement. It was like my own... I started as an assistant and grew to a manager. I'm proud of that."

She realises that she is "very fortunate to be my father's daughter" and getting a launch pad. "But I don't think that I have achieved anything yet of which I can feel proud", she says candidly. But the feeling of achievement is definitely a driving force, which makes her set targets; be it for jogging or at work.

As for her dream for the future, she wants the finance company to get more profit than the engineering company. "We're in a very competitive market. Today Kinetic is a Rs. 800 crore company and we're likely to become Rs. 1000 crore this year. I'd like Kinetic to be in the top 50 companies of the country."

Case Study 2

Lalita Gupte, Joint Managing Director and Chief Operating Officer, ICICI, recently appeared in Fortune's list of 50 most powerful women in business (http: / /www.naaritoday.com / news features/ womeninnews/archives1.html#2). On account of her outstanding abilities she has been entrusted this year with the responsibility of the group's international operations as well. For Lalita work is a passion, a commitment, a consciously chosen option. She is an unassuming and down to earth person, outside her workplace you meet her and you will find it hard to believe that this is the woman responsible for restructuring of a financial institute of ICICI's magnitude. She dislikes being put on a pedestal and feels there is nothing to it really. In her own words, "I am not a dreamer. But I have a vision. Everyone should have a vision to reach his / her goals. But at the same time, one has to be a realist."

Under her the focus of ICICI is on technology, finance, speed and people. Realising the importance of speed the company has made rapid strides in technological upgradation. Lalita Gupte's totally committed her company. She says, "My husband often jokes to me that if my skin were to be scraped off, you'd find ICICI and Gupte mingled together." She has been responsible for many an innovative schemes for employee's welfare. She has a firm faith in the potential of human capital and holds them valuable.

Success has not come without a price for Lalita says, When you aim to be a supermom, a superwife and a superexecutive at the same time, "you are forced to make a number of compromises. But by the end of the day, it all evens out. Especially when you realise that this is a way of life that you have consciously chosen and that you would cease to be yourself if you were to decide to drop out."

She attributes her success to the hard work, the right opportunity and the support structure at home, "My dad was a civil servant, who rose to the level of commerce secretary and cabinet secretary. My mother was a social worker. My parents were very encouraging. They always kept pushing us to do well in life. Husband Dileep Gupte is a retired naval officer. My in- laws have also given me a lot of space and are very understanding. My husband opted for early retirement, realising that both running behind our careers can make life miserable".

The most important factor for her success has been an equal - opportunity employer in ICICI , she says, "ICICI has always displayed more of a pro-woman bias than an anti-woman one. I have never encountered the glass ceiling here. I know it exists but I have never faced it."

According to Lalita women need to be given education as they influence family's decisions. For some people, a job is a job, a place that pays you for spending 8 hours of your working day there. And then there are people like Lalita Gupte, Joint Managing Director and Chief Operating Officer, ICICI, for whom work is a passion, a commitment, a consciously chosen option.

> We've all heard of those women who manage home and workplace and yet make the complex juggling seem like a cakewalk. Gupte is like that. Meet her outside her den in the ICICI Towers in Bandra, and you might even find it difficult to believe that this woman has been responsible for restructuring ICICI from a financial institution to a

consumer-banking corporation. The warmth, friendliness and affability that she brings to any interaction are more likely to remind you of a friend's mother.

Until three years ago, Gupte used to do the cooking at home. Nothing to it really, she says, dismissing, in her typical no-nonsense style, the incredulity that such a statement might evoke. "I liked doing it and the kids loved it too," she says, her manner indicating that all working women do it, why set me up on a pedestal.

This refreshing ability to sift the truth from the facts lies at the core of her success. That and her passion, her desire to excel and her integrity have been her companions on her journey from 1971 to today. In 1971, when the fresh-faced MMS student walked out of the Jamnalal Bajaj Institute of Management Studies to join ICICI, she scarcely imagined that thirty years later, she would head the financial institution she joined as an Officer.

But success has exacted its price. "When you aim to be a supermom, a superwife and a superexecutive at the same time," she clarifies, "you are forced to make a number of compromises. But by the end of the day, it all evens out. Especially when you realise that this is a way of life that you have consciously chosen and that you would cease to be yourself if you were to decide to drop out."

So the doubts and the guilt play on. The inadequacy and insecurity about oneself and one's relationships continue to knock down one's confidence. But Gupte has held her own. Gupte attributes the credit for her success to her support structures, her parents, husband and in-laws, who let her have the freedom to be the best she could be, without having to conform to a code of conduct for women. "They are my safety net. I doubt I could have achieved so much without them."

Another factor that has taken her where she is today is that ICICI has always been an equal opportunity employer. In fact, she says with a laugh, "ICICI has always displayed more of a pro-woman bias than an anti-woman one. I have never encountered the glass ceiling here. I know it exists but I have never faced it." It is a token for which Gupte is grateful and one that she has repaid in ample measure. Under her leadership, ICICI has made great strides.

Lalita Gupte's commitment to her company is complete. She

says, "My husband often jokes to me that if my skin were to be scraped off, you'd find ICICI and Gupte mingled together." While her inputs to the bottomline deserve appreciation, it is her contributions to the welfare of her employees, which are especially commendable. These contributions include sending employees all over India to see Fiza. That she holds them valuable is also seen from the fact that she personally supervises the health club and the toilets. The care and attention that is devoted to her home is also extended to the workplace.

Gupte's inputs recognise that employees don't work for their bread and butter alone. That employees need to feel wanted, feel part of an organisation that really cares for their well being. Having to look after all these things is very time-consuming. But Gupte has her reasons. "Business can wait. Business will come but pay attention to your people. They make your business. Your most important resource is your human capital. You can raise resources. You can buy technology. You cannot afford to lose your people. You have to make them feel wanted. You have to create an environment that facilitates this."

Strangely, it is a woman who can make an organisation feel more human. Gupte is tough as a businesswoman but she is soft as a person. "I am like a mother hen. I expect my people to work hard but I am fiercely protective of them."

> Joint MD and COO she may be in the office, but once she gets home she only answers to the call of wife and mother. Sundays are reserved for family and friends. On this day she cooks and gets in touch with friends from ICICI, friends of her husband, college and school friends too. Clearly, Gupte takes her friendships very seriously.

She takes her work home and strives to give her workplace a touch of home, but Gupte is adamant about making a clear distinction between home and the workplace. She admits that it is up to the individual to draw the line between home and the workplace. "It depends on the circumstances and your support systems. I was fortunate to have a supportive family. My job has been very exacting. If it hadn't been for my family, it would have been much more difficult."

She attributes her success to hard work, support and the right opportunity. Which is why she dismisses comments that the Law Ministry's recent order, stating that 20 per cent of all Board of Directors members should be women, is demeaning. "They are only trying to make up for lost time. Even after 50 years of Independence, not many women have the opportunities. An order like this can help to right the balance. There are more women getting out of MBA schools now. Perhaps in another ten years, we will see a more equitable distribution of the sexes in the corporate world. Right now there aren't too many women in the right places."

It is with a view to increasing that number that Gupte insists that we must ensure that women are given education and that they stay through school. After all, subtly or otherwise, women do influence family decisions on a number of issues. "Even in rural areas, women are taking initiatives in the panchayat," says Gupte. "Educating the woman will help ensure that more pro-women decisions are taken."

Remember what they said about speaking softly and carrying a big stick if you wanted to go far. Meet Lalita Gupte once and you'll know just what that means.

Case Study 3

Naina Lal Kidwai has ridden a flair for numbers to become India's most important investment banker in its most important investment bank in what may become its most important industry-information technology (http://www.naaritoday.com/newsfeatures/womeninnews/ archives 1.html#2). Her odyssey began in 1977, when she graduated from Delhi University with an economics degree. "I decided that acquiring more degrees was my best safeguard against gender discrimination," she said. So she did a chartered accountancy course in India, then in 1982 became the first female Indian citizen to graduate from Harvard Business School. Back in India, she rose through the ranks at ANZ Grindlays during the 1980s and joined Morgan Stanley in 1994 as head of investment banking, just as the country's infotech industry began to blossom. Things got off to a rocky start. In 1995 the company suffered a black eye when a domestic mutual fund it launched turned into a fiasco. But by 1999, JM Morgan Stanley was the No. 1 investment bank in India in terms of M&A, with deals worth nearly $700 million.

What's behind the astonishing turnaround? In large part,

Kidwai. She was the one who decided that Morgan should go full-speed ahead in IT, and it was her connections that helped the firm do so successfully. Though Kidwai is based in New Delhi, she spends much of her time shuttling to tech hotspots like Hyderabad and Bangalore to raise cash for Nasdaq-listed IT companies like Wipro and Infosys. Kidwai handles both accounts, drawing in lucrative deals like Wipro's forthcoming $200 million to $300 million ADR issue.

Morgan is now setting its sights on getting a piece of India's agonizingly slow, but potentially lucrative, privatization action. Again, Kidwai is leading the charge. Her current challenge: persuading foreign investors like British Airways to take a stake in state-owned Air India, perhaps the world's least-favourite airline.

Naina Lal Kidwai - the vice chairman of JM Morgan Stanley (India)—was recently included in the list of 50 most powerful women in international business. She has many firsts to her credit: she was the first Indian woman to join Harvard Business School and she is also the highest paid woman in banking—she was the first Indian employee to receive a salary of one crore rupees per annum.

Before joining JM Morgan Stanley Naina was Executive Director with ANZ Grindlays. It were Naina's decisions that helped Morgan Stanley to turnaround from a mutual fund fiasco and emerge the No. 1 investment bank in India in terms of M&A, with deals worth nearly $700 million. She was the one who decided that Morgan should go full-speed ahead in IT, and the IT advantage has paid rich dividends to the company.

Reacting to her inclusion in the list she says," Leadership is determined by performance and not by gender." She further adds, "The current status has come step by step from being a school leader, college presidentship to the corporate ladder". She is happy that Fortune has expanded its list and widened the research to include Asian women and feels more Indian women will now appear in the list in coming years

Case Study 4

Indra Nooyi has appeared as the 43rd rank in Fortune's list of 50 powerful women in business in USA (http://www.naaritoday.com/newsfeatures/womeninnews/archives1.html#2). She has emerged as the highest ranking Indian women in the USA. She is the president and the CFO of Pepsico one of the most successful consumer products companies in the world. She is responsible for Pepsico's acquisition of Tropicano and more recently of Quaker. Born in Chennai, Indra did her MBA from IIM, Calcutta. An achiever all the way, she has carved a niche for herself in a short span of time. Without Nooyi and her team, Pepsico would not acquire, divest, merge or spin-off any part of the $22 billion company.

At 43, after 22 years of corporate career, Nooyi still has the same bubbly enthusiasm about her work and perhaps that is the reason that Pepsi remains the choice of new generation the world over. She is a voracious reader and possesses the ability to finish a book in a day. At leisure she loves to strut at her guitar.

Nooyi was honored with "excellence in human capital management" award in New York in February this year.

Case Study 5

Dream merchants is how **Ms Sangeeta Talwar**, the 44-year-old managing director of Mattel Toys India, would like to describe her team (http://www.naaritoday.com /newsfeatures / womeninnews/archives.html). "We sell the dream world of Barbie, the adrenaline driving Hot Wheel cars and the nurturing comforts of the Fisher Price toys," she explains. It was perhaps her belief in the philosophy that "those who dare to dream have a whole world to win," compounded with the dream world of Mattel toys that managed her to lure her out of Nestle India after 20 invigorating years. Ms Talwar joined Mattel in April 2001, and her primary responsibility is to develop the overall strategy of the company and make Mattel the largest brand in the Indian toy market. "There is a tremendous opportunity to develop the toy market in India and I want Indian children to get exposure to the right kind of toys, ones that will help them understand the world around them better," says Ms Talwar.

The $6 billion Mattel is the largest brand in toys internationally and in India its turnover is around Rs 60 crore. Ever since she took over this year, Ms Talwar has worked hard to change the way Mattel India functions. First, she has linked Mattel India to the international systems and brought in all the sales, accounting and performance policy systems followed by the parent company. Secondly, she has tried to make the company much more responsive to change and delayered the sales team and encouraged team work within the organisation. "I have set the bar of excellence quite high and asked my team to think international and act local," says Ms Talwar.

> Ms Talwar believes that to be successful one has to have the essential five C's: concept, conviction, commitment, courage and compassion. Even as she graduated in Economics in 1976, Ms Talwar was very clear that she wanted to belong to the league of business managers. In 1979 when she completed her MBA from the Indian Institute of Management, Calcutta she had two lucrative offers: one from Nestle and the other from Smithkline Beecham. Since Smithkline had only Horlicks as the major brand, Ms Talwar opted for Nestle which had a plethora of brands in a number of segments. She believed that Nestle would have on offer much more exciting assignments with many leading brands.

In 1979, she joined Nestle and worked with the food products business. In those days the Maggi brand had met with huge success in south-east Asia and the Indian management was keen to bring it to India. Ms Talwar was instrumental in launching Maggi noodles and as the group product manager took the brand forward with a range of products like sauces and soups under the Maggi brand.

After her stint with marketing, Ms Talwar joined the sales team of Nestle as the regional sales manager , northern India. "Sales is an extremely challenging job because it requires execution of the strategies impeccably in the field," she says. To be a good sales manager one has to have the mental flexibility to deal with people who come from very different backgrounds, believes Ms Talwar. "A woman has to work much harder to get people to believe that what she is saying is actually going to work," she adds.

At Nestle, there was not a single day she can recall when she was bored with her work, primarily because the organisation had in store for her completely different assignments, one after the other.

After her experience with the sales team she had joined the human resource department and was directly responsible to share the vision of the company with its 3000 employees. At that juncture, Nestle India wanted to aggressively grow from a Rs 500 crore company to a Rs 2000 crore company in the next seven years and Ms Talwar's job was to change the HR policies and create leadership training programmes to make the staff partners in the company's progress.

After this two-year break from sales and marketing, she came back once again with much greater responsibilities as the executive vice-president, marketing. In 1996, she was seconded at the headquarters in Switzerland as strategic advisor and worked with other products like chocolates, confectionery and beverages. She was in Switzerland till 1999, away from her husband, though her daughter was with her. "I have been fortunate to have tremendous support from my family, my husband has always encouraged and respected the choice I have had to make. He has gone the extra mile to provide a best match between his profession, my work and our family," says Ms Talwar.

She cherishes a dream to travel across the globe with her family and other than travelling what excites her most during her leisure is socialising and reading. Ms Talwar believes in being "18 till I die" and her current job with all its colour and creativity has all ingredients to help her stay young at heart. "Mattel's offer helped me change my paradigm completely as this business is entirely focussed on the under 10 age group," she says.

Case Study 6

With a double Ph.D - in natural products chemistry and physical organic chemistry - heading the public sector Hindustan Organic Chemicals seems a natural assignment for **Reena Ramachandran**.

A senior woman manager who has done two fairly long stints in the public sector - from 1986 to 1992 she was in the ONGC - she does not wear her gender on her sleeve and was fortunate enough not to feel that she was shattering a glass ceiling.

In an interview to *Business Line's* Rasheeda Bhagat, she discussed the traits which had aided her in her career and called upon women managers to improve their professional visibility (Vol. 2, Issue. 4, November 1999).

From your two long stints in public sector what would you say are the main challenges that a woman manager faces?

As a person, I've never looked at my work from the gender perspective. Perhaps it is because right from the beginning, I was always a single girl in the class... whether it was M.Sc., doctorate or whatever. So I had already got used to studying/working with men.

But I do recognise that it may not be a similar situation for all women. Such issues do crop up, particularly when you change jobs and get into a new environment, where it is difficult even for men to adjust. But it becomes doubly difficult for a woman; apart from the need to deal with the new environment as a manager, the elements of being a woman, of proving herself, become even more challenging.

I love taking on new assignments and challenges. In a new assignment its always having to prove yourself; in terms of job content and as a manager and a leader. The higher you go up the ladder in management, the more you have to prove this.

And a man doesn't have to do it?

I'm not making this observation as a discrimination against women. But it is purely a number game. If the critical number of women managers goes up, the issues may become less complex. But so long as the disparity in terms of numbers remains, women will stand out and be conspicuous.

However, much you desire, you just can't wish this away. It is a practical reality. Ultimately we have to examine certain perceptions about women, which, even though gradually fading away, still remain. These pertain to their ability to move out, travel frequently, to be away from home, take on new responsibilities which might need longer office hours, which means being available to the management and the administration when required.

So what are these perceptions?

Generally the perception among employers is that women will not be able to do all this. Therefore they do not even make an offer. In that process women tend to lose out. That, to my mind, is more damaging to a woman's career. It is very important that a woman manager remove this perception. The only way you can remove it is in the beginning to even volunteer, to be a little proactive and demonstrate your professional ability. You cannot imagine that everybody knows that you can perform.

How can a woman improve her professional visibility?

By being proactive and talking about it. Now, this improving of professional visibility is required not only within the work system but beyond the work environment, when connected with professional interests outside office hours. That would improve her professional visibility even more.

Not running back home from the office!

Exactly. Making yourself available, making your presence felt, spending a little extra time to be in the milieu where professional people meet, interacting and discussing common concerns and day to day current developments in the profession. These things stand out and show her ability. But for all this, extra time, effort and deliberate action are required.

Do you see such an effort being made by your fellow women managers?

Yes, they are now doing it. Now you see a lot more women in management institutions and management associations and in the committees too. This is a good way to spread awareness. I'm not saying its happening everywhere. But a trend is developing. Also, in industry associations and the federations of chambers, there is a different wing for women, which is different from the ladies wing. This is a wing for professional women managers, or business women who are themselves entrepreneurs, to form small groups and hold meetings and discussions.

To answer your question, things are happening, but the actual number is very small.

You yourself have been there and watched many women managers perform... some even under you at junior levels. Do you think there is anything which distinguishes a woman's style of management? Is she more matter of fact, more businesslike or whatever? What are her advantages or disadvantages, for after all you cannot escape your gender?

I would say even amongst women, such things vary, just like they do amongst men. I wouldn't like to generalise that a woman manager has particular traits. A woman manager ten years ago was operating in an environment very different from today where there are lot more women in the workplace. So the psychology, environment and lifestyle have changed. Therefore her style of functioning has changed too.

What style of management do you adopt?

Down to earth. Absolutely down to earth. And practical, which is by demonstration. Setting a personal example. If I expect something from the staff, I need to do that first myself. Secondly in all my work, people have essentially been the centrestage of my management. Because ultimately an organisation or enterprise has no existence without people. So I've always believed that you can get success only if you take the people along with you.

What the Americans call the 'colleagual' approach?

Absolutely. Because nobody can succeed individually. So I've been fortunate to have excellent colleagues and subordinates who have made things happen.

How do men view a woman manager initially? It must have been a cultural shock, because we're talking about a period 20 years ago.

I didn't feel it. If it was a cultural shock then I should have felt it. Because you did shatter a glass ceiling... I never felt that there was a glass ceiling. I don't believe in a glass ceiling. I never felt that there was a shock.

You never felt that there were people in the organisation who were prejudiced against or resented a woman boss?

No. I believe that first of all you should not expect anything. In a new environment, when I take on a new assignment, my expectation is zero. I should be in a position to give first and the rest will automatically happen. So I must perform the function for which I'm hired to the best level possible. And how do you assess the best? Through the bottomline.. through results and this should get reflected in my actions.

And you cannot achieve unless you have the support of people. I never have to wonder when I take a new assignment, whether people are accepting me or adopting me or how they feel.

So you start off with the single main objective of delivering?

Absolutely. I'm a self-motivated person. I don't depend on

anybody else to motivate me and that is a strength which probably makes me do things in a more pro-active manner.

Do you think self-motivation is a gender-based or a more individualistic concept?

It has nothing to do with gender. There have been excellent professional men who have been self-motivated.. very hard working.

A woman's Emotional Quotient is supposed to be much higher than a man's. Do you think a woman manager scores in interpersonal relationships?

People have observed ... I can't assess myself. But I do get feedback of people saying she is a bundle of patience. When you deal with people you have to start with patience.

Do you think the role of a mother prepares a woman for this?

Perhaps. You definitely have that small little thing in the corner of the heart which makes a woman get possibly the best out of people without creating earthquakes and without too many hiccups. But sometimes you feel that this system may not work in all situations.

You may require a very harsh method of doing things if things do not happen the easy way. There is no single prescription you can describe or which a textbook can give you that in any given situation you can do this or that.

Can you give an example?

There are several management techniques and these are more people-related. One is the motivational method and the second is the harsher method, where we have to make use of the administrative ammunition and machinery at our disposal. I've used those too quite a lot. I've noticed that in the same company, you have to adopt different measures with different units or divisions. Because culturally the people are so different in this country. In a unit in the north, people react very differently to situations than people in the south, where people tend to be more emotional or sensitive. In each environment you have to follow a different technique.

Do you think such techniques can be taught in management schools?

No. I've never undergone any management course.

What about books.. there are so many books on management?

They are good. I like reading management books. That's in fact my extra-curricular activity and it certainly gives a lot of insight because, after all, in life as you go along and deal with various types of managerial assignments, you do make mistakes. Nobody can claim that everything a person does is right. In hindsight, one often thinks it could have been done in a different way.

By learning through the experience of others narrated in the books, one learns of different ways to manage a situation. But life and the actual doing of things teaches you something which can never really be described in a book. If you can learn from experience, that is a great achievement. But the worst scenario is to keep repeating your mistakes. So if you are very sensitive to your performance and results you'll learn not to repeat mistakes.

What about integrity?

I attach a lot of importance to it.

Do women tend to be more honest than men.. or to put the question differently, is it more difficult to corrupt a woman than a man?

Yes, both are true. But of course there have been exceptions which have been published. But sometimes, in some environments, it can even go against you.

In impeding ones' growth?

It can. So one should be able to strike an excellent balance of keeping your integrity and values and also perform within the system.

Is it possible to do that?

It's not impossible.

Without treading on toes?

Oh yes.

And they leave you alone.. whoever your bosses are, including the politicians?

I couldn't care less. Ultimately, you have to strike a balance, and I've survived for so long! It's one's intrinsic strength which takes one forward.

You said women tend to be more patient and understanding. Do you think male subordinates tend to take a woman manager for a ride because of these qualities?

But why should I blame the subordinates? In management, the first responsibility is that of a leader.. the person who is managing. If the person is a good manager, irrespective of gender, he/she should know how to manage the subordinates. If the subordinates are taking the manager for a ride, I don't think he/she is doing his/her job.

One of the most important traits of management is that you should manage people; below you, above you and around you!

In management jargon there is this thing called the double bind syndrome. An autocratic male boss means business; but for a woman they say power has gone to her head and call her a Hitler or even a bitch. On the other hand, if a woman is humane and understanding, she is perceived weak; a male manager doing that is a great human being. Your comments.

This has been widely researched, specially in the American context. This is an integral part of socially accepted norms and the culture we have been brought up in. We cannot change the culture overnight. So, even with the best of intentions if she doesn't take care of these aspects, there is a possibility of her being misunderstood.

I always tell my women colleagues that this aspect may seem to be innocuous but is very important. A lot of problems at the work place, and at home, can be handled very effectively if you handle this aspect of how to conduct yourself in the office.

You can't say I'll deal the way I want.. wear the dress I want or deal with a client the way I want. It doesn't work like that. It may not hit you immediately but it hits you at some point. But if one is firm.. some of these aspects can be positive. One needs to make the best of the positive aspects of both the trends and strike a good balance in the way you conduct yourself.

Do you think a dress code is important for a woman manager?

Very important.

The way she dresses, carries herself and even behaves?

Absolutely important. And the higher you go, these aspects

become even more important because everybody watches you as a symbol.

So where do you draw the line between being friendly and bossy?

It's judgement. You can't get an instant formula. There are instances when I've planned to do certain things but changed the course of action. The most important area which is a big gap for women is information management. This is a weak area.

Why and how?

Because they get busy.. managing both the office and the home. Outside information accessibility is very limited for them. Even in the office, because they are smaller in numbers, they tend to converse among themselves. And the kind of information which is very vital for their career growth, for equipping themselves as better candidates, for moving up and such crucial things, will be missed by them because they don't know what is happening around them.

Such information is very critical for their career growth. Professional information; you may have documents and libraries but that is only one part. There is unpublished information which one gets to know only by mingling with people.. talking to them. What I mentioned earlier about professional visibility.

I know cases of women who are not happy in the set up in which they're working and looking for an opportunity but don't know how to go about it. They don't know the options they have in another organisation.

You feel men are smarter and quicker in this?

Yes. I feel the media is an excellent source of information for professionally equipping yourself. Sometimes you don't have enough time to go through newspapers/magazines. You need a systematic collection of information and documenting. It helps you a lot. I have used it a lot.

I'm sure in your career you must have encountered irritating situations where you've wanted to scream and fire somebody. How have you managed? Have you allowed yourself to fly off the handle or tackled it more calmly?

Irritating situations arise even at home, where they can be more damaging! But I never lose my temper. I always analyse that maybe something needs to be done on my part to solve the problem. There can be conflicts between two parties on things like promotion which can lead to irritation. Where there are human beings, there will be diversity. Things are always seen from an individual's perspective. What is happening to ME? What is happening to MY career? What am I getting from it?

If a person has not performed, one should ask why. I spend a lot of time listening to people. My doors are always open; anybody can always walk in. As the head of HOC, I think I'm working for different segments of people and in their interest. And an enterprise will do well when all of them get together to deliver the goods. No individual can succeed alone.

So I should listen to what bothers them. That is the fundamental principle. I meet them in groups or as individuals and listen to them. Often I find just listening sorts out a lot of problems. There could be a background.. historic or family reasons. The person's psychology has to be analysed. Of course dark horses or mischief mongers have to be tackled. It involves planning.. strategy and working in a system.

But in a PSU, your hands must be tied.

Not really. A lot of things which bother people are based on wrong information or rumours. So it's important to talk to them. No point in saying I'll use the official machinery to deal with them. I don't go after people; it's not a good strategy. I work for people and not against them.

I suppose the top person giving them a hearing itself solves half the problem.

That's exactly what I meant.

Psychological therapy?

Yes, but the problem is that as you move up the ladder, time is the main thing. There are too many things to do and you think this is not a priority. But for me people and issues connected with them are always the first priority. Ultimately all people are good. Some perform better; the strength lies in working through their strengths. A lot of it rests with the leadership. In the public sector it becomes a little more complicated because there is the government and the political system.

How have you managed with political interference?

No politician has ever interfered with me. Absolutely not. Ultimately its all about the strength of the individual. There are chief executives themselves

Who want to be pliant?

Yes.

What has been the fundamental challenge of your career?

Showing results. But every time things may not turn out the way you planned because of factors extraneous to the organisation. The greatest challenge is how do you manage and perform in difficult situations in a highly competitive business environment and I've enjoyed that challenge greatly.

How are things with HOC? It has been making losses for the last two years.

Yes, but this year things are looking up. We have taken steps to tackle the situation and in the current year things are different.

Do you find it easy to admit that you've made a mistake, in dealing with either people or situations?

Oh yes. I begin with the premise that everybody is a gentleman till he proves otherwise.. I'm sorry I'm using the word gentleman!

How do you deal with complaints of sexual harassment? Do you get many of them?

Not really. When you have me sitting here, the problem gets less because they know it will be heard better than with a male boss. I encourage women to bring it to my attention because solidarity is very important.

But how do you solve the problem?

First of all I don't like bringing any external pressure to help women. They must learn to help themselves. I tell them `you be strong first.' Confidence building, strengthening the women executives and the staff to raise and discuss the problem and taking everybody along with you, are crucial. The man then knows that there are 50 people behind you. Legislation may not help. Many of the women do not even know what are the legal provisions. Strengthening the woman is very important.

You mentioned in the beginning that you haven't shattered any glass ceiling. Do you believe that it exists at all?

Must be... because a lot of women have said it exists.

But how come you never felt it?

Because I never perceived myself in that way. I suppose I got used to working with men. I never had any inhibitions with travelling or meeting the evening requirements of work like late office hours. I've in fact overdone on the work front. I was very conscious and sensitive. At certain stages in my life I've even compromised on my domestic requirements.

Do you think the personal life of a woman manager takes more of a beating than a man's?

Oh, yes, surely; it's a price one has to pay. I have compromised but I've never harboured negative feelings like I shouldn't have done it. I did it because I felt that was the way to do it. I've never regretted my actions.

Do you think support from the home front is important?

Very much, and I got it. But being one of four daughters, I was raised as an individual more than a girl. The home environment also helps a woman. Growing up in a different social environment and then expecting that to change at the work place cannot happen.

What more would you want to achieve?

The sky is the limit.

What is your dream for the future?

I have great interest in women's issues; building self-confidence in women, evolving strategies and giving some practical tips. I'd like to work with a wide cross section of women employees and give them self-confidence. When I came here there were no women executives. Now there are 10. Apart from striving to excel in the professional area, of course.

How much bigger can you become?

I'm not big in any case, and for professional excellence, there is no limit. There is so much to learn.

Case Study 7

Apsara Ramabhadran, Senior Marketing Associate, Cognizant Technology Solutions India Limited spoke to Deepika Davidar about work and the work atmosphere in India (Vol. 2, Issue 4, November 1999).

She began her working career in the US before moving to India a year ago. She joined Cognizant Technology Solutions as a Senior Marketing Associate. She is candid in her comparisons of the working culture in the US and India and feels that productivity in the Indian workplace would increase if people learn to be direct about their expectations.

What are your qualifications?

I did my degree in Mechanical Engineering from Crescent College. I then worked for a year as a service engineer with Unipro. I wanted to go to the States to do an MS in Mechanical Engineering but at that time, there were some problems with the GRE. Finally, one of my friends advised me to try for an MBA so I did that and got admission in the University of Texas. I majored in Information Systems so that's how I moved from Engineering to Information Technology.

And you began your career in the States?

Well, I did an internship with Merrill Lynch but my first job after I graduated was with the brokerage firm Charles Schwab and Co. I basically liaisoned between the IT department and the business departments. In Charles Schwab, I did the Series 7 and 63 exams which qualified me to be a registered representative of a stock exchange. Charles Schwab has an online trading software and I had to handle customer enquiries and customer support. The software was also outsourced to another company and I would teach people how to work with the software, check if modifications were needed and provide training to peers.

Was it exciting?

Definitely! The work atmosphere was charged. The people I worked with were so energetic. There was always a free flow of ideas, no one hoarded information. The amazing thing was that the management encouraged people at all levels to come up with new ideas.

In fact, at least once a month (if not more) everyone was given a time slot with the senior-most person in the company. During this time, you could make a presentation about something you thought viable within the company. You know, Charles Schwab were pioneers in the field of Web-based trading. And the idea came from a junior employee.

Management support made all the difference... Yes. I think there was a perfect combination of fun and work and that made the environment a very productive one to be in. We all had a feeling of 'I belong here'. Everyone felt that they had to do everything they could to make the company better.

I worked with Pacific Exchange a while later. It's a stock exchange on the West Coast and I worked there as a Business Systems Analyst. The environment was not as vibrant as Charles Schwab was, but the management was as encouraging. They encouraged all employees to come up with good ideas and would implement them if they were viable.

Are frank opinions always welcome?

In the US, yes; here, in India, sometimes no. In the States, they appreciate honesty and forthrightness. Your feedback is not held against you. Here, in some companies, if you give an honest opinion, you can shelve your career.

What about this trend of employees working round-the clock?

It's crazy. The sad thing is that here it's expected of you. No one appreciates the fact that you're staying overtime to help the company. If I were a manager, I would say I had goofed in my estimate of a job if my team had to work overtime consistently to complete it. If people are given an 8-hour working day, it's unfair to expect them to work 12 hours everyday. But I also have to add that often, employees are staying late just to impress the boss. They may be sending e-mail, surfing the Net or just warming their seat. But they're seen 'working' late because the boss likes that. It earns them a promotion... looks like it. Pleasing your boss seems to be the way to top. It's so wrong.

Promotions should be completely merit-based.

Did you find this 'people-pleaser' attitude in the States?

No, at least not where I worked. Maybe it's to do with our culture. We're so used to listening to and looking up to other figures in our lives... our parents, teachers, spouses... we end up being subservient and shy.

How do you think employees should be treated?

I firmly believe in giving my team members maximum freedom. I detest micro-management. This philosophy of constantly looking over someone's shoulder while they're working is just not on as far as I'm concerned. I believe you should value people's time. Everyone has a life of their own and work is not their be-all. Trust the people you work with not to waste time when they're on the job. I don't want daily or weekly worksheets. Status reports to let me know where the job is at are fine. Otherwise I'm all for the hands-free approach.

And how would you define your role?

Obviously, I'm here to help and give the team direction. A good team leader must be approachable. If anyone on my team needs help, I'm here. I believe in being straightforward. Tell me what's wrong, and we can both try and work towards a solution. But I also trust my team to do the job and do it well. I want to see people grow in confidence and be really productive at their work. It's crucial to have a personal rapport with the team you work with. You have to know what their personal aspirations are and find a way to meet them. Give them sufficient training to fulfil what they want to do.

And this encourages commitment to the company?

Definitely. Herb Kelleher, Chairman of South West Airlines, once said, "We hire for attitude, we train them for skills". That's great business philosophy. You have to hire people with the right attitude and train them into the job. Crucial to the success of this philosophy is knowing exactly why you're hiring that person. And telling him or her exactly what's expected of them.

As a woman, have you ever been discriminated against at work?

Not in the States. Here, I find that men, in general, cannot take directions from women. Then again, I haven't quite figured out if that's a gender thing or if my outspokenness makes them uncomfortable! But I do feel that if you want to make it to the top in India, as a woman, you have to be really pushy.

Of course, discrimination or harassment is not necessarily physical. It could be someone making a comment that you're not comfortable with. I find that happens but it seems to be part of the work atmosphere and no one questions it.

Do you feel Indian working women walk a tightrope between work and family demands?

In many cases, yes. I have a very supportive family, so I have no problems on that count. But a lot of others have wondered why I work. My job involves travelling, and they can't understand why I don't slow down and just stay at home. I hear all these statements that begin with 'Women must...' and 'Women should...'. Unless you're a very strong person it's difficult to stand up to that kind of pressure.

I find that in our society its generally considered derogatory for a man to help out at home. The same man will go abroad and run a home efficiently or share household work, but once he returns he slips back into his societal role. Once men start treating women as equals at home, that attitude will flow into the workplace.

Is it that much harder for a woman to exercise authority? Do junior employees resent a woman being tough?

I don't see it at my workplace. I definitely think this is a problem outside. You just have to look at the way men react to women drivers to prove that! In the workplace, you would come across the odd man who thinks you're too conceited or arrogant if you express a sensible opinion, but by and large this doesn't happen to me. I think a smart, ambitious, junior employee would work hard irrespective of the gender of his or her boss. I don't think team leaders are judged on the basis of their gender.

Does it help to have a mentor?

Well, in the States, I did find superiors taking a personal interest in employees. Ideally, your mentor should be your immediate manager. I found career aspirations were taken very seriously over there and senior managers would give you direction and advice.

Here, I don't see much of that happening but that could be because the company is so large. Its easier to establish personal rapport when companies or teams are small.

When you come to the negotiating table, what special skills do you bring?

Better communication skills. Especially in a business like ours where many of our clients are overseas. I'm comfortable with both Indian and American culture and therefore able to put our foreign clients at ease. Talking to them at par makes a lot of difference. Anyone can have technical and business knowhow. It's important to train people to communicate clearly.

Case Study 8

Preethi Nair was born to the Nair family in Kerala, South India. She says ...All I can say about that is I came wrapped in a lot of hopes and dreams. Shortly after, we came to London (http://www.gypsymasala.com / author.html). First I was a singer. Walked everywhere with my microphone hairbrush. Then, I was a fashion designer. Snipped at everything in sight; saris, bed sheets, curtains.... In the late 70's, my Red Doll was The Fashion Diva, wearing all the latest creations. Unfortunately, her career was cut short due to the loss of her left eye after an accident with my tailor scissors. Undeterred, I packed her up along with my other belongings and went to discover the world (the first trip by myself to the local newsagents at aged 7). Then, I became a foreign correspondent. Cutting out the newspaper, modifying only slightly, putting together a newsletter which I posted to my neighbours, threatening them with more products unless they supported me in my endeavour (some would say that nothing has changed that much).

Crossing the land to Adulthood, I became a Management Consultant (not just like that, but I only have a few lines). You probably saw me somewhere in London on the Metropolitan line, going to work. The final stages of frustration of my 9-7 existence became apparent as I battled with the characters of Gypsy Masala on my journey, mumbling things to them, writing out their thoughts on scraps of paper which I would thrust into my handbag as I reached my stop. The other bemused commuters dismissed me as yet another loony who could not take the pace. Pieces of paper on which I dreamt eventually became my book and yes, my ego is still waiting for someone to read it on the underground whilst I sit opposite them. Essentially though, I wrote the book not only to sell millions but because I really want you to feel the magic of just dreaming and believing.

Preethi Nair, the author publisher of Gypsy Masala was among eight individuals who won the 'Young Achiever' prize at London's annual Asian Women of Achievement awards in May this year. She was born in Kerala but shifted to London at the age of two years.

Preethi studied Law and Economics at Cardiff University and had a stint of work with the European Commission for four years at Spain. Later when she returned to London she obtained a Masters Degree in International Relations from Warwick University.

A management consultant by profession, Preethi, interestingly wrote the book in bits and pieces while commuting to work along the London's Metropolitan line, in the wee hours of mornings and on weekends. After receiving a few rejections from publishers, Preethi decided to publish and promote her own book under a pseudonym. She had an unflinching faith in her story that she could not allow anyone to play with it.

Incredibly the book did well and emerged as the number one book in many of the stores in London. Preethi managed the entire campaign by herself and came out a winner by overcoming her worst fears about rejection. "Gypsy Masala" in the author's words "is a story about dreams about going to wherever your heart may want to take you. It is about daring, daring to believe that there is something more, daring to face your fears." She says, "I have learnt an awful lot through doing this but above all, it has strengthened my conviction that anything is possible if you believe hard enough." Wise beyond her years Preeti feels very strongly about children being treated unjustly and about people bickering over petty things. She loves meeting people, reads a lot, does cooking and practices Yoga. She believes in looking at the beauty of life and being thankful for everything life has given.

Case Study 9

In a field of conservative, gray-suited men, **Tarjani Vakil** stands out both for her brilliantly hued saris and as the highest-ranking woman banker in Asia (http://www.saliltripathi.com /

articlesAsiaInc/Oct94AsiaInc.html).

She is the chairperson of Bombay-based Exim Bank, which handles foreign trade, export marketing and consulting. It has earned continuous applause from international financial journals for excellent performance and profitability. Vakil, 57, is conscious of her image as a role model for young women managers. She spoke recently at an international conference in Baroda, India, and later with Asia, Inc.'s Salil Tripathi, on women's role in wealth generation:

The major challenge before corporate Asia is a shift in mind-set that can usher in true equality for women. There is absolutely no doubt that women's potential as managers and professional workers is being underutilized in the region. In Asia, female participation in the workforce varies from 11 per cent in Pakistan to 47 per cent in Thailand and Vietnam. The undercounting of our contribution— by excluding household work from national accounting systems— continues. While political gains have been significant and educational opportunities expanded, they aren't enough.

Despite equal-pay legislation in many countries, differentials persist. The female-to-male wage ratio varies from 70 per cent in the U.S. and Sweden to 51 per cent in Japan and less than that in many Asian countries. And women's representation in administrative and managerial positions is pitiful—as low as 0.8 per cent throughout the 1980s in the Philippines, despite a woman president, and 1.5 per cent in Sri Lanka even though it was the first country to elect a woman prime minister. Ironically, several Asian countries— including India, Pakistan, Sri Lanka, Bangladesh and the Philippines—have been led by women. But the ground-level reality is far different. In 1991 only 20 per cent of management positions in Hong Kong were held by women. That figure was much worse for Malaysia (12 per cent) and Japan (3 per cent).

The greatest change in the global economy is the shift from the manufacturing sector to the service sector. The latter now accounts for as much as 65 per cent of gross domestic product in developed countries and up to 55 per cent in the countries of South and East Asia. That's good news for women. The service sector generally has been more women-friendly. Gender-branding increasingly is becoming an anachronism. But even as women transcend stereotypical images, male managers' attitudes tend to be gender-biased. A masculine management style by women is construed as "aggressive" while the adoption of an interactive style is viewed as "ineffective."

At Exim Bank, half the officers are women. It has been rated by Euromoney magazine on several occasions as one of the top Asian banks for productivity in terms of profit per employee. Surely that would not have happened if women managers were nurturers, emotional, unassertive or irrational. Sometimes I feel like a Sherpa climbing Mount Everest to clear a path for upward mobility.

Some companies now support working women with facilities like day-care centres, flexi-time and maternity and paternity benefits. Yet much more needs to be done. The examples of Singapore and Malaysia come to mind. These countries offer tax deductions and rebates according to the number of children. In fact Singapore's tax laws favour college-educated working mothers.

A 1993 United Nations human development report points out that no country in the world treats its women as well as its men. However, no one should take solace from the fact that this is a global phenomenon. Societies in the new world order cannot afford to ignore 50 per cent of their human capital and talent.

Case Study 10

T.S. Ushari tryst with technology began when she was seven years old and curious about the world around. To satisfy her urge for knowledge, this chief technology officer at Digital Global Soft read every volume of popular scientific encyclopaedia- " How things work."

This natural affinity for Science and Technology led Usha to be the first woman to get admission to the bachelor of technology course at the Jawaharlal Nehru Technical University. After graduation (winning a gold medal), Usha went to complete her masters in business administration from the IIM, Bangalore.

Armed with B- Tech and MBA, her first job was at Bharat Heavy Electricals, where for four years she was responsible for areas such as, strategic planning and systems Engineering. This was followed by a stint at NIIT, where she worked as a consultant, with their corporate services group. After eight years, Usha shifted to Ashok Leyland Infotech.

She has been involved with business development activities in multiple geographies including US, Europe and Asia Pacific. Prior to joining Digital, Usha was vice president—Enterprise Application Services—Wipro Technologies. Bangalore remains her favourite place to work, with Silicon Valley a close second.

Usha's main areas of interest are customer relationship management and enterprise resource planning. " More than the nuts and bolts of technology, we need to look at how it can benefit the end user, " she says. Organizations need to understand the functioning of their customer thoroughly, before beginning work on a solution for them. They should work towards providing a product which delivers in the least time at the lowest possible cost. In India, some companies begin their work without a clue about how their client works, she feels.

Companies, she explains, often donot know the fundamental difference between a contact and the concept of customer relationship management. The key to be successful, according to her, is by constantly updating your knowledge. Even top managers and executives need to update themselves, otherwise they will find themselves sidelined by the younger employees, who can absorb new thoughts and ideas faster, she added.

Usha has a novel way of spending time with her two children. Its not the usual weekends for children only. Instead, she wakes up at 3 am everyday and finishes her work before they wake up. " If one of my children has exams then I get home early from work, or if an important meeting is scheduled I may get home a few hours late," she explains. In her spare time, Usha listens to classical music (both western and eastern) and is also a closet poet (*The Economic Times*, Kolkata edition, Thursday, 21 February 2002).

Case Study 11

Subhalakshmi Panse epitomizes the new generation public sector banker: a banker comfortable with the use of information technology. Subhalakshmi is the deputy general manager (DGM) in Information Technology at the Bank of Maharashtra (BOM). She entered the banking sector without any definite intention of making a career in it. She had just topped the Pune University's MSc course in embryology, saw an advertisement for recruitment of officers by the BOM, for which she applied, got through and began learning the ropes.

Seven-eight years later, she made up her mind that banking was her chosen career and she must therefore get qualifications that set her off, doing a diploma course in business management, followed by a masters in management sciences with finance as a major. Her real breakthrough came when she took a year's sabbatical, in 1997, went to US and did a full-fledged MBA from Drexel University in Philadelphia. "I majored in bank management, doing a two year course in my year's sabbatical. Doing that was like getting a fast forward view since technology was already pervasive in banking in the USA," she replied.

That was her invitation into technology, which she believes is critical to make informed decisions as a decision support system. " You can see that the banking industry in the US is reaping the benefits of technology," she said. Remember, this was in the late 1990's when PSU banks had just begun their computerization programmes and so the "first forward view" of the use of technology in banking sector was a real eye-opener. Especially the uses it could be put to for customer service, with private and foreign banks having just begun to turn on the heat. On return to the BOM, her first challenge was the Y2K bug. Although the PSU banks had not imbibed so much technology in their working till then, nevertheless it needed attention. " We successfully faced the challenge, especially since cost is always an important aspect in India." But it is her core banking background which has really helped, she believes.

"It is because I have a banking background and am not just a pure technology person, that we were able to draw up realistic and achievable plans," she said. With convergence the name of everyone's game, Panse believes there should be consolidation in the banking industry too, which will make bigger banks, requiring business process re-engineering and a change in the way banking is done. In such an era, it is necessary to have multiple skills, giving the individual a global perspective in a globalised economy.

The 48-year-old Subhalakshmi believes, her science background has helped been better than an Economics or Commerce especially since she has now gone towards technology. "The science background trains your analytical skills, making technology absorption easier," said the Bank of Maharashtra's only woman DGM (*The Economic Times*, Kolkata edition, Thursday, 28 February 2002).

***Case Study* 12**

Shanti Subbaraman, networking is her forte. Creating new products and executing them from start to end is what she's best at. Given a choice, she'd grow organic food. An electrical engineer from IIT, Madras and an MS in Computer Science from the University of Cregon, Shanti started her career with DEC, in the US more than a decade back. After three years in trouble shooting network and artificial intelligence, she returned to India to start up DEC's export business here. In 1992, she joined Wipro as product development head of a group of 50. However she was rather disappointed with the way the products fared in the global market. Her other areas of specialization were in remote access servers and terminal servers.

With a head full of product ideas, Shanti quit Wipro and set up Aarohi Communications in October 2000, with four others. A start up focussing on storage networking, Aarohi is headquartered in San Jose, USA. It is also one of the few to write standards on this space. When she's not signing deals or cracking product ideas, she's spending time with her seven-year-old and three-year-old sons. This ebullient mother has volunteered to counsel on careers and teach physics at her elder son's school. She opines that we put too much focus on Computer Science. Environment Science and BioScience are going to be the in-things for the next decade.

Her passion is music. With a percussionist husband, her senior from IIT and a couple of friends, she has formed a band, which jams out once in a while. For someone who was never goal oriented, the designation founder and managing director is just incidental. And the secret of success is very simple. " Be happy in whatever you do. Success comes automatically, you don't have to chase it," she says (*The Economic Times*, Kolkata edition, 29th November 2001, Page 5).

***Case Study* 13**

Success does not depend on age. It is achieved through hard work. Look at **Prema Desikan**. She is sixty. Her example is an inspiration to thousands of entrepreneurs and thousands of others aspiring to be entrepreneurs all over Tamil Nadu (http://www.smallindustryindia.com/ ssiindia /wmncase.htm). Socially relevant work had always attracted Smt. Desikan. It was natural for her to think of helping women folk. What better way then to orient them towards employment and self-help. The latter virtually became a synonym for entrepreneurship. A deep urge of gender upliftment pushed her to start an industrial career by setting up Palmrosa plant in early nineties. But she could not do it due to lack of desired support to obtain land. She, however, examined alternatives and finally decided to manufacture plastic articles. This was a well thought of decision wherein she had done extensive surveys on the potential areas of marketing the end products, manufacturing techniques, material characteristics, economies of scale, cost and management data, manpower requirement, etc. What followed is the story of determination and success. From running a plastic unit with facilities to make wide ranging components for various end uses, Prema Desikan is now organizing short term training courses for women who are now having their own units. Simply a graduate with some training in manufacturing techniques in plastic industries from CIPET (Central Institute of Plastics Engineering & Technology), a premier institution of Government of India in Chennai, Prema recalls; "The initial activity generated satisfactory response from the end users, particularly from reputed companies. Good customer relations were established. Besides providing employment to 20 persons. Including 15 women. But, un-precedent recession in the industry has considerably affected the unit, which also suffered due to delay in realization of money due from customers, as also the accumulating bank interest. The machinery thus remained idle for a long time. Consequently the overhead costs could not be recovered.

But, even this adverse situation also could not stop Prema, who was determined to convert her imagination into reality in the small industries sector. She adds: "Undeterred by these developments, I vigorously pursued with organizations like Department of Commerce and Industry, Government of Tamil Nadu, National Small Industries Corporation, Small Industries Service Institute, Southern Railway, Integral Coach Factory, etc. in finalizing the registration as approved vendor and thereby procurement of orders. Supply of articles like packing rings, nylon bushes, cable ties, fish tails etc., made on a trial basis for these sources, have been accepted as they conformed to quality standards. These items are meant for safety and hence quality is of paramount importance".

Smt. Desikan has now established a tie-up with CIPET, Chennai, in plastic development, which provided her all possible help. This motivated her not to compromise on quality, even if the deal yields reduced profit. This has been applauded by various agencies.

The Tamil Nadu Government honoured her in 1995 as the best Women Entrepreneur. The print and electronic media provided her with an opportunity to express her thoughts. In her first talk on All India Radio, she expressed the importance of self-reliance among women and advised women to come out and contributed towards the creation of a healthy industrial climate. This advice was heeded by quite a few people, especially women, who contacted Smt. Desikan for guidance to start small industries.

The brave lady now has plans to build her organization in such a manner as to provide in-house facilities like training in processing, maintenance, finance and administration, etc. to develop entrepreneurial skill. Today, Smt. Prema Desikan is not only a known name among the successful entrepreneurs of Tamil Nadu, but she the distinction of creating an industrial atmosphere in the State that produces quite a sizeable number of successful entrepreneurs. This is obviously more valuable than any product manufactured in the industry.

Case Study 14

Who is **Sunanda**? The question may well be asked though she has created a path of success in the field of women entrepreneurship in Andhra Pradesh. It goes to her credit that the people who live in Vasanthapuri Colony in Malkajgiri area of Hyderabad know very well that the government is providing assistance in the form of loan under PMRY Scheme. That loan is being utilized properly by many persons as shown amply by the hard work of the promising entrepreneur, Smt. K. Sunanda Reddy (http://www.smallindustryindia. com/ssiindia /wmncase . htm). From selling Sarees from her house, she has grown to being an owner of Shri Balaji Food Products within a short span of eight years. She now has a monthly turnover of Rs. 60,000 to 70,000 supplying her food products to reputed Star Hotels like Ramada Manohar, Viceroy Hotel, Taj Residency and Kamat Lingapur, besides many cinema halls.

Shri Balaji Food Products, under the direction of the 34-year-old housewife-turned entrepreneur, is not only feeding thousands of people daily in Hyderabad but also providing full time employment to seven persons, including 3 women. This fulfils the PMRY Scheme's target of employment generation.

But how was it made possible? Actually, it is a three dimensional story. It is about the hard work and firm determination of Sunanda, assistance from Government of India, thorough its popular PMRY Scheme and training-cum-guidance provided by the Office of Development Commissioner (SSI) through its field office. Small Industries Service Institute (SISI), Hyderabad. All the three joined hands to fulfill the dream of producing quality potato chips. In due course, CFTRI Regional Center, Hyderabad and DIC (District Industries Center) of Ranga Reddy District, along with the officials of Vysa Bank, also extended their co-operation to Sunanda. These combined efforts resulted in the opening of M/s Shri Balaji Food Products in January, 1999 creating employment for eight families and supplying quality potato chips to thousands of Hyderabadis and visitors to the city.

Talking about her future plans, Smt. Sunanda states: "Two to three years ago, when I launched M/s Shri Balaji Food Products, supported by PMRY with Rs. 90,100 loan, people were not aware of my quality potato chips. So the market response was really slow. But now the time is ripe for it catch on in a major way. With the success in potato chips business. I am now planning to start manufacturing of papads also in near future".

Disclosing the secret of her success, she further states, "After selling sarees successfully, I decided to join the one-month Entrepreneurship Development Programme on Food Processing Industries organized by SISI, Hyderabad. Just after completion of my training. I conducted market survey with the help of my husband and under the guidance from the officers of SISI, Hyderabad. Finally, I decided to start potato chips manufacturing unit. I was advised to approach CFTRI Regional Center at Hyderabad for collecting information provided by CFTRI, Hyderabad".

Looking fresh from her success, Sunanda smiles and adds, "with the support of the project report I applied for PMRY loan at DIC of Ranga Reddy District from where my project was recommended to Vysa Bank, Malkajgiri branch. Meanwhile, I had also attended a one-week training programme conducted for the selected candidates under PMRY Scheme. Thereafter, I obtained provisional registration of my unit in the name of Shri Balaji Food Products at DIC, Ranga Reddy District. By this time, a lone of Rs. 90,100 was sanctioned by Vysa Bank after thorough examination of my project. With the help of the loan, I purchased the required equipments. After getting all the machinery I prepared a team of seven hard working women and men and then started manufacturing and selling potato chips from January, 1999."

In her entrepreneurial field, where men still dominate. Smt. Sunanda feels that these government schemes are capable enough to provide employment and guidance support to an entrepreneur so that she may stand and grow independently and effectively as it happened in her case. Though Sunanda carved a niche for herself in this profession, she never forgets repaying her loan to the bank, moving one more step forward Women's Empowerment.

Case Study 15

Indra K. Varma, a polymer scientist at the Indian Institute of Technology (IIT) in Delhi. A doctorate in chemistry from the Glasgow University in the UK, she was also awarded the D.Sc. by the same university. She joined IIT in 1966 as lecturer in the department of chemistry and became a professor in 1977. From 1997 to 2000 she was head of the Centre for Polymer Science and Engineering.

Indra has published more than 275 papers in reputed scientific journals besides being the principal investigator in 11 projects sponsored by CSIR, ISRO, UNDP, DST, DNES, MHRD, DRDO and NIST (US). She has made significant contributions in the field of polymers and her specialisation is the synthesis of polymers. Indra has four patents to her credit in the field.

One of her most outstanding achievements came in 1979, when she went to the US for two-and-a-half years to work in the National Aeronautics and Space Administration (NASA) laboratory in California on a special project. Says Indra, "NASA was interested in developing a material which doesn't burn in air." So Indra got down to developing the flame-resistant polymides. For this breakthrough project she received seven certificates of recognition and cash award from NASA.

Taking off into Space

In 1995, the space centre again invited her for eight months to work on a project involving electrically conducting polymers. "I was overwhelmed at seeing the shuttle from such close quarter," she says. But the job assigned to her was more than just marvelling at the space shuttle. She played a pivotal role in developing a thermal stable polymer that would not burn in the air when the spacecraft travelled at a tearing speed in the atmosphere.

The scientist is not aware how many of her patents are still in use. As other scientists were also involved in the projects the patents have become the property of NASA. The patents in the joint names of Indra and other scientists are: Phosphorous Containing Bisimide Resins (Indra K. Varma, G.M. Fohlen and J.A. Parker—June 1981), Phosphor Containing Imide Resins (Indra K. Varma, G.M. Fohlen and J.A. Parker—July 1983), Elastomer Modified Phosphorous Containing Imide Resins (Indra K. Varma, G.M.Fohlen and J.A. Parker, December 1983), and Phosphorus Containing Imide Resins (Indra K. Varma, G.M. Fohlen and J.A. Parker, January 1985).

Besides certificates of excellence from NASA, Indra is also the recipient of Dupont International Award for Polymer Characterisation by Thermal Analysis (1987). She has co-authored a number of books notable among them being **Recent Trends in Polymers and Composites, Thermosetting Resins -- Properties and Synthetic Polymers** as also a book for the undergraduate students of Indira Gandhi Open University and a class XI NCERT book of Chemistry (1977).

"Polymers have a wide array of applications both in domestic and industrial life. In the house they are useful in the form of plastic combs, buckets, bags, jugs and jars. Industrially they have played a key role in the development of spaceship, aircrafts, and in the electronic and construction industry," says Indra, who was also a visiting professor at the department of polymer technology at Sweden's Royal Institute of Technology last year.

She says the consumption of polymers in India is low as compared to the rest of the world. During the last 10 years global demand for polymers grew from 67 million tonnes in 1989 to 108 million tonnes in 2000. "There is no alternative or substitute to polymers. Researchers must concentrate on improving the quality of production and making it more efficient. The other two areas of focus must be the safe disposal of waste and recycling of plastic. These are our areas of emphasis at the IIT," she adds.

Inspired Research

Understandably Indra gives all credit to the IIT for her progress that has given her the opportunity to do her research on polymers. Some of her significant contributions in the area include the synthesis and characterisation of thermally-stable polymers, modification of synthetic and natural polymers and structure property relationship in polymers. Under her tutelage at the Centre for Polymer Science & Engineering at the IIT, 37 students have been awarded Ph.D. degrees and five students are currently working towards their doctorate on topics such as flame-resistant polymers, thermal stable polymers and adhesive from proteins.

However, in the initial years, the going wasn't easy for the eminent scientist. After her return from the Glasgow University, she applied for a research officer's job but the organisation turned her away saying that such specialised jobs were not meant for women. "At that time, the mindset of people in the industry was male-centric. Only men were expected to do serious scientific work," says Indra who later got a job in Centre for Scientific and Industrial Research (CSIR), Allahabad, before joining IIT in 1966.

"Over the years," she says, "there has been a seachange in attitudes. There has never been any gender-bias in IIT. In fact, my male colleagues have been positively encouraging." One of her now-retired colleagues was her husband Dr. Dharmendra Varma who was professor at the department of textile technology. Both her son and daughter have done their B.Tech from IIT and are now working in leading companies.

For a working women, managing both the family and a demanding profession can be a daunting task. But, says Indra, "You should have a determination that you will not fail either at the domestic front or in office. That's what's kept me going. And I can assure you today my family is both supportive and proud of me."

Indra has virtuous plans after retirement in October 2002. "Plastic waste management is one area where I would like to work in the future because this is an issue which is of concern to all of us today," says Indra who now occupies the Reliance Chair at the IIT.

Despite the fact that women are less in number in the field of science and technology as compared to men, their contribution is no less significant. Says Indra, "See the number of women in these fields and then see their contribution. If you work out the ratio it would equal or even be higher than that of men. That's because women usually don't have many distractions and are more focused if they go for higher studies."

So why talk of socialite evenings. Women like Indra are better role models for the younger generation of aspiring girls both in schools and colleges. (http://www.the-south-asian.com/june2002)

Breaking Down Barriers to Women's Success

WOMEN IN MANAGEMENT is a tale of two worlds - one Western and the other Eastern. Two worlds that have different cultural contexts and yet share common experience and also share an agenda for an evolution in Management now. Corporations were created by men, for men; and to start with, women had 'no business' to be in business.

In the West, primarily led by the US, and closely followed by Northern Europe, statistics show how women have increasingly flooded the job market and have now reached a critical mass in the range of 30 to 50 per cent in almost every white-collar profession, including business, especially in the 'cutting edge industries of the future'. A generation of women that entered management in the Seventies and the Eighties is now ready to break the 'giass ceiling' to the top (some of them have already done it) in the new millennium. And those who were fed up with the barrier started successful businesses on their own - at an entrepreneurship rate which is twice as fast as that of men. These are not merely trends but indicators of an evolution, which by the early part of the next millennium should have completely integrated women into the mainstream - management included.

Women in the other world, Asia, have relatively a long way to go before they reach such magnificent numbers (Sangeeta Mansur, 1999). A survey by Rose Mary Wentling (Ghosh, 2000) of women managers reveals obstacles to women's advancement and few steps employers can take to help qualified women move up. In our Indian context women still make up about 9 per cent of a loosely defined demographic category of executives, administrators and managers.

But only a small number of those women occupy top positions in major Indian companies.

More women will be seeking management positions because of their increased participation in the labour force, affirmative action programmes and expanded access to educational opportunities. During the next 10 years, women will make up a large segment of the available management talent, representing a resource that is often greatly underused. By tapping into this resource, companies can broaden their managerial base and, thus, their competitive edge. In fact, companies that do not remove obstacles to women's advancement are risking damage to their own growth.

Although advancement opportunities for women have increased substantially in recent years, there are still many barriers. One question remains unanswered: Why do so few women reach senior-level management positions? To try to find an answer, the question can be broken into three parts:

1. Are women now in the mid-level management positions aspiring to become senior-level managers?
2. If so, are they aware of obstacles they will encounter and the sacrifices required to reach the top ranks of management?
3. Do they know what actions they must take to obtain senior-level management positions?

The Challenges

Work seems to follow along traditional gender lines. Men do the agricultural and mechanical work, and women do the house work. In the communist revolutions, women again played an equal role. They fought alongside the men and both shared equally the tasks and jobs of daily living. After the revolutions ended, men invariably became more equal than women.

Why does this happen? Why does society begin on an equal footing and then get divided into male domination and female submission? This takes place because of three reasons: One, the way gender inequalities have evolved over the past one million years; two, the institutionalisation of this inequality; and three, the psychological differences between the genders (Sangeeta Mansur, 1999).

Can women ever take their rightful place in society and workplace? Things are changing mainly because an increasing number of women are not only working outside the home, but are also occupying positions that have so far been exclusively in the male domain. As Alvin Toffler says, "we are now shifting away from an economy based on muscle-power to one heavily based on mind-power-and that eliminates a crucial disadvantage for women" (Sangeeta Mansur, 1999).

Organizations have a few things to learn, too. Areas needing attention include revision of working hours, compensation packages (not just a driver's allowance, but perhaps a maid allowance, for instance), daycare facilities and emotional health support systems. Perhaps then the government find that it will no longer be necessary to legislate women into corporate boardrooms.

Women managers reach the top the hard way - it is toil, a struggle, a constant juggling of roles, a tightrope walk to maintain a balance between home and career. With all the old roles and new roles - mixing, matching, prioritizing to excel - few have reached the peak.

The Bombay Management Association has 150 women executives on its rolls, but only a handful occupy positions that matter. How are women executives facing the challenges of the coming century? Have the economic reforms, globalization and other policy shifts affected them in any way? Have women been the victims of downsizing, and how have they responded to the liquidity crunch? What strategies have they adopted for survival and growth? Has their gender come in the way? These are some of the issues hotly debated at different forums.

Measures

The data were collected with the help of a structured schedule. Before finalising the schedule the author conducted a pilot survey on 20 senior, middle and junior level managers who came to attend my Management Development Programme on "Women in Management and Leadership" (2000) at Indian Institute of Management Calcutta, India. The respondents were provided a host of open-ended questions.

1. Why do you work?
2. Why have you joined the profession in which you are?

3. What were the deciding factors while selecting the nature of job?
4. Do you have any career goals? If yes, what sort of career planning do you do?
5. What are the things you take into account while preparing your career path?
6. What obstacles do you experience in realising your career goals?
7. To what extent your organization promotes employee-friendly environment?
8. Do you feel the culture of your organization is masculine? If yes, why?
9. What difference do you feel while interacting with your male and female colleagues?
10. How will you characterise a male and a female manager?
11. Have you experienced or heard any sort of discrimination at the work place?
12. Do you get equal opportunities while receiving rewards?
13. Do you believe that to reach at top you need to be aggressive?
14. Do you agree that success goes with men?
15. Why do inequalities exist at work place?
16. Does your organization have equal opportunity policy? Is it implemented? If yes, in which areas?

The information received on the above questions helped in identifying the variables and operationalizing those variables.

Two separate questionnaires were framed which were a combination of, Likert type scales and open-ended items. The first questionnaire was designed to examine micro-level issues pertaining to the research theme. Hence the variables taken into account were in **Questionnaire - 1:**

1. **Organizational Culture Attitude Scale**. A 13-item scale was developed to measure the attitude of the respondents regarding the prevailing culture in the organization. The respondents were

asked to judge each statement on a 4-point scale by choosing any one of the alternatives. The scores ranged from 1-4. The internal consistency of the items was found to be very high as the alpha coefficient was .81.

2. **Belief and Practices.** A 19-item scale was used to examine the belief and practices prevalent in our culture. The respondents were asked to rate each statement on the dimension of agreeableness using the same 4-point scale. The scores ranged from **Strongly Agree (4), Agree (3)** through **Disagree (2)** to **Strongly Disagree (1).** Thus, the scores ranged from 1-4. The alpha coefficient was .83.

3. **The Values Grid.** The scale developed by Super and modified by Sinha (1990) was used in the present study to understand the values that the respondents satisfy or want to satisfy through their work activities. The respondents were provided a list of 21 statements and were asked to read each statement and judge its chances of realization through work activities on a 4-point scale where 1 means **Little or None, 2** means **Some, 3** means **Quite a Lot** and **4** means **A Great Deal**. The reliability of the scale was .91.

4. **Work-Family Interface.** Work and Family are two important aspects of any employee's life. Success or failure in any aspect has its affect on the other. Therefore, six items were used to measure different aspects of work-family interface. The respondents expressed their views on a 4-point scale where **Great Extent** meant **4, Some Extent** meant 3, **Little Extent** meant 2 and **Not at All** meant 1. The scores thus ranged from 1-4 on each dimension. Apart from these the respondents were requested to report the number of hours they spent at home and at workplace.

5. **Culture, Social Role and Self-Concept.** The dimension was measured by two different kinds of instruments. To understand the social role of men and women in a culture the respondents were provided open - ended items to express their views regarding:

   (a) What do you think about women's role in our culture?

   (b) What is men's role in a culture like India?

Further, Who Am I Test was used to explain how the men and women perceived their self-concept.

6. **Superior Subordinate Relationship:** A six-item scale was used in the present study to examine the superior -subordinate relationship at the work place. The respondents were asked the nature of support that they are likely to receive when they need and the chances of its availability. For illustrations,

   (a) How often you talk personal things to your superior?

   Quite often **Sometimes** **Rarely** **Never**

   (b) How often are they available?

   Rarely **Sometimes** **Generally** **Quite Often**

The responses were obtained on this four point scale which helped to get a score on each dimensions by multiplying the score of (a* b). The six dimensions were:

(i) Support for personal problem,

(ii) Support for job related problems,

(iii) Support for family related problems, and

(iv) Support in need, and

(v) Openness in relationship.

A few open-ended items were used. For illustration, a single item was used to examine the extent to which superior expects return of the favours that they do.

Further,

Whom do you consider to be a good mentor? Please provide reasons for it:

(a) A Male Manager

(b) A Female Manager

The scores ranged from 1-4. The alpha co-efficient was reported to be .70.

7. **Your Time Management**. An important aspect of an employee's life is how he/she distributes his/her total 24 hours among the

important activities that he/she performs. Therefore, the investigator became interested in understanding how do respondents plan their time for different activities ideally and actually. The scale used by Sinha (1990) has been used for the purpose. The respondents were asked to indicate the time that they spend on different activities or would like to spend on different activities. The differential - score of the ideal and actual number of hours (Ideal number of hours minus the actual number of hours) provided the score in order to understand the time management done by the respondents.

8. **Organizational Role Stress** : The Organizational role stress scale prepared by Pareek (1983) was used with slight modification in the present study. The scale measured 10 dimensions of organizational role stress:

   (a) Inter Role Distance

   (b) Role Stress

   (c) Role Expectation Conflict

   (d) Role Erosion

   (e) Role Overload

   (f) Role Isolation

   (g) Personal Inadequacy

   (h) Self Role Distance

   (i) Role Ambiguity

   (j) Role Inadequacy

The first five dimensions had five items each and the last five dimensions had four items each. Thus there were all together 45 items.

The respondents were asked to read each statement and indicate in the space against the corresponding number in the answer sheet how often do they experience the feeling expressed in the statement in relation to their role in the organization. The respondents rated each statement on a four-point scale where,

4 meant, If you **Always** feel this way

3 meant, If you **Frequently** feel this way

2 meant, If you **Occasionally** feel this way

1 meant, If you **Never or Rarely**

The scale had a reliability value of .95

9. **Security-Insecurity Scale.** The perception of security and insecurity has a bearing on how people perceive themselves and others. Therefore the security-insecurity scale initially used by Singh-Sengupta (2000a) was extended and used in the present research. The scale had 18 items and the respondents were asked to judge the items on a 4-point scale where a score of **1** was to be given for Never True, 2 for **Sometimes True, 3** for **Often True** and **4** for **Always True**. The scale had the reliability value of .85. The maximum score was 4 and minimum score 1 on each item.

10. **Your Preferences.** The scale developed by Khandwala (1984) was used in the present study to understand the motivational need of the respondents. The scale measured 8 motivation needs: Hedonism / Materialism, Career success, pioneering motivation and power and authority, self-actualization, affiliation, altruism and security.

The respondents were provided 10 hypothetical situations and then asked to respond in one of the 8 ways. The 8 ways were these motivation needs which were operationalized differently according to the context in which the respondents had to respond. The respondents were given the instructions' Please indicate as truthfully as you can whether you agree or disagree with each of the following sentences. If you **Agree Strongly** with a statement write 4 beside it in the left hand margin. If you **Agree** with it **But Only Moderately** write 3. If you **Disagree** with it **Strongly** write 1. If you **Disagree** with it **But Only Moderately** write 2. Please indicate what you prefer even if this is different from what you actually do. The reliability value of the scale was found to be .97.

11. **Women and Overseas Assignment:** The most common belief held by companies in international management is that women do not want foreign assignments because of their dual - career marriages. A single item was used to empirically examine the fact in Asian context. The respondents were asked: How often

international companies are ready to recruit women managers for overseas assignments? The responses were obtained on a 4-point scale of **Quite Often (4), Sometimes (3) Rarely (2) and Never (1).** The score ranged from 1-4.

12. **BEM Sex Role Inventory (BSRI).** The scale developed by BEM (1977) was used to examine the perception of once own identity. The respondents were provided a list of 60 adjectives, which they were asked to use in order to describe themselves on a 4-point scale. The anchorage's ranged from **Usually True (4), Occasionally True (3), through Sometimes True (2) to Never True (1).** The respondents were requested not to leave any characteristics unmarked. The BSRI measured masculine personality, feminine personality and neutral characteristics. Each dimension had 20 adjectives each. These sixty adjectives were intermixed in such a way to form a single list of characteristics. The average or mean number of points assigned by each persons to the masculine attributes constitutes his or her masculinity score, the average or mean number of points assigned by each person to the feminine attributes constitutes his or her femininity score. Using the median masculinity and femininity score as the cut off points the person is then classified as either Masculine (High Masculine: Low Feminine), Feminine (High Feminine: Low Masculine), Androgynous (High Masculine: High feminine) or Undifferentiated (Low Masculine: Low Feminine).

Background Variables. A list of eighteen items was used to gather the background information of the respondents. The items were related with age, sex, marital status, educational background, father's occupation, position in the organization, length of service, number of companies worked, number of promotions received, size of the company, present salary, past salary, etc.

Questionnaire - 2

The focus of the study was to examine the factors, which is likely to affect the low representation of women at the top. The assumptions were that the cultural values attached with the social role of women significantly affect her career choice. The emphasis was to examine the importance of socio-cultural factors determining the share of women leadership in Asian Organizations. Further the study aimed at investigating the organizational processes and practices that arguable act upon the constraints and opportunity women encounter in the work place. The responses on such issues were collected with the help of open-ended items. The schedule had altogether 23 such open-ended items, which the respondents had to respond.

Background Variables. A list of eighteen items was used to gather the background information of the respondents. The items were related with age, sex, marital status, educational background, father's occupation, position in the organization, length of service, number of companies worked, number of promotions received, size of the company, present salary, past salary, etc.

Sample

Hundred twenty-nine male and seventy-one female managers working in South - East Asian Countries (India, Bangladesh, Nepal, Sri Lanka and Korea) participated in the study. Out of which 32 respondents were from Sri Lanka, 20 from Nepal, 20 from Bangladesh, 15 from Korea and the majority 113 were from India. Convenient sampling was used to collect the data. The average age of the male respondents were 39.94 and of female respondents 38.12 years. More than 80 per cent in both the samples reported to be married. Both the categories of respondents seemed to have the educational qualifications of graduation and post-graduation.

The family background of the respondents revealed that the majority comes from service class (72.9 per cent in the case of male respondents and 64.5 per cent in the case of female respondents). Further, the findings indicated that in the case of male respondents 2.3 per cent reported their father's occupation to be agriculture and 15.5 per cent told it to be business against 1.3 per cent and 25.0 per cent reported by female respondents respectively. A small number of respondents (9.3 per cent in the case of male managers and 9.2 per cent in the case of female managers) did not respond to it. The distribution of respondents in the case of male sample seemed to be: (1) Senior Managers (38.8 per cent), (2) Middle Managers (54.2per cent) and (3) Junior Managers (7.0). In the case of female sample it was as (1) Senior Managers (23.7 per cent) (2) Middle Managers (60.5 per cent) and (3) Junior Managers (15.8 per cent). The majority in both the cases seemed to belong to large organizations (74.4 per cent in the case of male respondents and 71.0 per cent in the case of female respondents).

The male respondents seemed to draw on average a salary of Rs. 20840.75 per month and female respondents a salary of Rs. 29769.63 per month. The respondents in the case of male sample were found to have 15.63 years of service with on average 2.81 promotions and in the female sample it seemed to be 10.80 and 2.49 respectively.

Setting for the Research

The multi-national, national and private houses operating in India, Bangladesh, Sri Lanka, Nepal and Korea provided the setting for the present research. A wide range of organizations belonging to manufacturing, work and service organizations constituted the settings for the research. The list of the companies is given in Appendix-1.

Procedure

The purpose of the study was to understand the socio-cultural determinants of the low representation of women in Asian organizations therefore an effort was made to get the responses from a wide variety of organizations ranging from IT Consultancy Firms, Financial Consultancy Firms, Banking to hard core manufacturing organizations. Our interest was not to examine the organizational differences but to have a holistic understanding of the research issue.

The questionnaires were mailed to the contact persons in Bangladesh, Nepal and Sri Lanka. They took the responsibility to mail me back the filled in questionnaires. To collect the data from Indian organizations the author prepared first a list of the organizations, which she wanted to include in her sample. Next, the Managing Director of the companies was approached to seek the permission. The data were collected from June 2000-January 2001.

References

Deepika Davidar (1999). The Difference. *Praxis Business Line's Journal on Management*, 2 (4), November Issue.

Ghosh, A. (2000). Position of women in organization hierarchy. Term Paper under the Guidance of Prof. Sunita Singh-Sengupta at Indian Institute of Management Calcutta, India.

htt:p//www.narritoday.com/news features/womeninnews/archives1.htm#2

htt:p//www.narritoday.com/news features/womeninnews/archives.html

htt:p//www.gypsymasala.com/author/html

htt:p//www.salitripathi.com/articlesAsialnc/Oct94Asialnc.html

htt:p//www.smallindustryindia.com/ssiindia/wmncase.html

http://www.the-south-asian.com.june2002.

Rasheeda Bhagat (1999). A Conversation *Praxis Business Line's Journal on Management*, 2(4), November Issue.

Rasheeda Bhagat (1999). Next Step. *Praxis Business Line's Journal on Management*, 2(4), November Issue.

Sangeeta Mansur (1999). The New World. Praxis Business Line's Journal on Management, 2(4), November Issue.

The Economic Times, Kolkata edition, Thursday, 21 February 2002.

The Economic Times, Kolkata edition, Thursday, 28 February 2002.

The Economic Times, Kolkata edition, Thursday, 29th February 2001, Page 5.

The Hindu Business Line, Monday 07, 2001.

The Economic Times, Kolkata edition, Thursday, 29th November, 2001.

4

Results

The volume is based on an exhaustive empirical survey in South - East Asian countries. The central issue underlying this research was to examine the factors contributing to low representation of the women at the top in Asian organizations. The author used a multi - prong method for the purpose.

Two separate questionnaires were used (the details are given in chapter - III). The results will be discussed under different sub-headings.

Secondary Source Information

Male and Female Workforce. The percentage of economically active population is presented in Table 4.1.

Table 4.1
Percentage of Economically Active Population

Countries	*Male % of economically active population*		*Female % of economically active population*	
	1980	1993	1980	1993
INDIA	44.5	45.8	35.3	40.9
BANGLADESH	43.0	9.5	2.3	2.0
NEPAL	33.4	38.3	12.0	17.5
KOREA	30.6	36.7	14.3	22.5
SRI LANKA	39.7	34.3	14.7	18.1

Source: Human Development Index, 1998.

Table 4.1 showed that the percentage of female workforce has increased over a period of time in India, Bangladesh, Nepal, Korea and Sri Lanka.

Women in Management. The distribution of women in different occupation are presented in Table 4.2.

Table 4.2
Distribution of Women Workforce in Different Occupations

Countries	*Labour Force*	*Administrators/ Managers*	*Professional and Technical*	*Service Sector*	*GDP %US*
INDIA	34	2.3	20.5	11	902
BANGLA-DESH	42	4.9	34.7	11	767
NEPAL	40	-	-	2	763
KOREA	40	4.2	45.0	59	8,388
SRI LANKA	36	17.6	30.7	21	1,452

Source: Human Development Index, 1999
World Bank Development Report, 1998.

Table 4.2 suggested that as compared to other profession women's share in top managerial positions is quite low.

Intercorrelations Amongst the Socio-Cultural and Economic Factors. Intercorrelations were computed among the variables explaining socio-cultural and economic reasons for women representation at the top in the organizations. The coefficients of correlations are entered in Table 4.3.

Table 4.3
Intercorrelations Amongst the Variables for Socio-Cultural and Economic Indicators of Women Representation at the Top in the Organizations

Social Factors	GDI	HDI	GEM	IDV	MAS	PDI	GNP
GDI	-	.97**	.73**	.58**	-.08	-.51**	.68**

(Contd....)

(Contd....)

HDI	-	.65**	.50**	-.05	-.46**	.65**
GEM VALUE		-	.67**	-.16	-.62**	.66**
Cultural Factors						
IDV			-	.07	-.68**	.67**
MAS				-	.06	.06
PDI					-	-.56**
Economic Factors						
GNP						-

Note. N=50. ** Correlation is significant at the .01 level.

The results (Table 4.3) indicated that individualistic societies, which are high on human development index, provide greater opportunities for women to enter the managerial positions. In other words, it provides equal opportunities to women. Interestingly, all the three social indicators were reported to be related with the PDI scores negatively ($p < 0.05$ level). This suggests societies, which practices and believes in high power distance between males and females will provide unequal opportunities for the females. Masculinity was found to be negatively related to all the factors, except individualism (though insignificantly). Expectedly, individualistic countries contributed positively to GNP per capita income and negatively to the PDI scores. To add, PDI scores and GNP per capita income was reported to have negative relationship. This substantiates hypotheses 2 and 4.

The one-way ANOVA indicated countrywise significant differences in the means of the variables with respect to individualism ($F = 3.86$, $df = 47$, $p < 0.01$ level), power distance ($F = 2.06$, $df = 47$, $p < 0.05$ level), gender - disparity index ($F = 4.52$, $df = 47$, $p < 0.001$ level), human development index ($F = 3.86$, $df = 47$, $p < 0.01$ level) and GNP per capita income ($F = 2.06$, $df = 47$, $p < 0.01$ level).

Empirical Survey

An in-depth empirical survey was carried out. Two different

schedules were developed and administered on different samples: One examined the various micro-level issues related to low representation of women at the top in the organizations, and second investigated the macro-level issues.

National Culture and Women Representation at the Top

(a) **Social Values.** A nineteen-item scale was used to examine the social values of the respondents in terms of their belief and practices. The obtained data were factor analyzed. Four factors emerged out of it:

1. Collective Orientation (Eigen Value = 3.22; Pct. of Variance Explained = 16.95).
2. Reactive Culture (Eigen Value = 2.73; Pct. of Variance Explained = 14.370).
3. Emphasis on Normative Behaviour (Eigen Value = 2.22; Pct. of Variance Explained = 1.51).
4. Believe in Proactive Culture (Eigen Value = 1.51; Pct. of Variance Explained = 7.94).

The factors along with the description of the items and its loading are put in Annexure 1.

The obtained mean scores of the factors for male and female respondents are graphically portrayed in Fig. 4.1.

The Perception of Social Values by Male and Female Managers

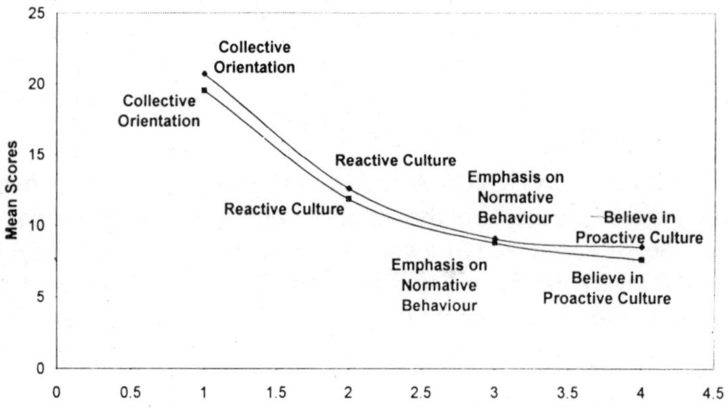

Figure 4.1

The findings (as exhibited in Fig. 4.1) disclosed that as compared to women managers men managers seemed to hold strong social values. On all the four factors the mean scores reported by women managers seemed to be low. The ANOVA suggested that the two level of respondents differed significantly on collective orientation ($p <. 0.05$ level) and believe in proactive culture ($p <.001$ level).

(b) **Self Concept and Men and Women Managers.** The respondents were asked to write 10 statements regarding how do they perceive themselves and then were asked to rank them. The content analyses of the items and their ranking indicated very interesting findings. The men managers perceived themselves first as an ambitious man then as an executive and then as a man.

While women managers perceived herself as an executive and a women simultaneously. Then she perceived herself as a mother.

This clearly indicates the impact of culture on the perception of self as, both, the men and women managers perceived themselves against their social role. Structural role as a construal of self seemed to be stronger in the case of men managers. The gyroscopic "I" was perceived more as a part of the self by the male managers than that of the female managers.

Women and Overseas Assignment. A single item was used to examine the issue that how frequently foreign companies are ready to recruit women managers for overseas assignments. The findings are exhibited in Fig. 4.2.

Women and Overseas Assignment

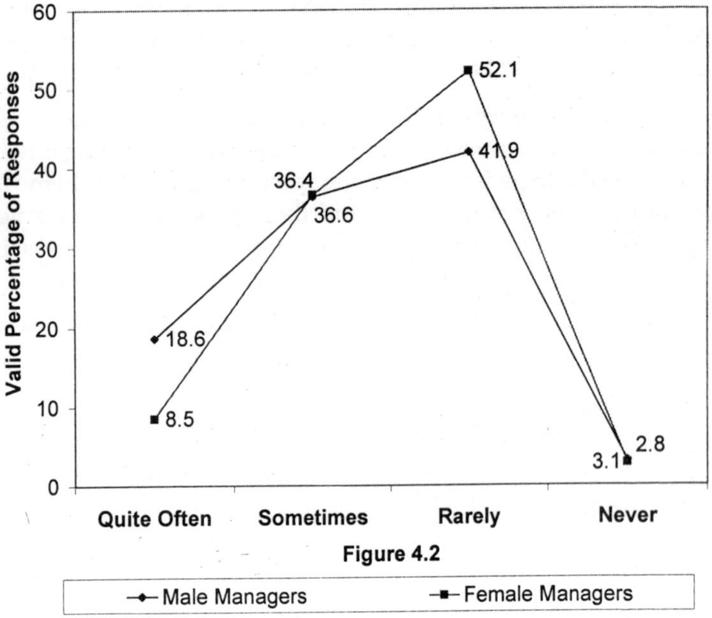

Figure 4.2

Fig. 4.2 suggested that both the levels of respondents expressed their views that international companies rarely recruit managers for overseas assignments. The reported mean score was 2.61 in the case of male respondents and 2.31 in the case of female respondents. The mean differences were not found to be significant ($p > .05$) which clearly indicated an agreement in their views.

Masculinity, Femininity and Work

Culture and Sex Role Perception. Sex role perception plays an important role in shaping the behaviour of the individuals, which is likely to have spill over in to organizational behaviour. The respondents were asked to express their views regarding women's and men's role in the culture of the society. The obtained responses were content analyzed and reported in Table 4.4.

Table 4.4
Culture and Sex Role Perception by Men and Women Managers

Role Perception	*Percentage of Responses*	
	Male Respondents (N= 129)	*Female Respondents (N = 71)*
Role of Women		
1. Dual Role	25.85	37.98
2 Educate and nourish the children	35.37	33.54
3. Educate the new generation with cultural heritage	38.78	28.48
Role of Men		
1. Bread winner	39.88	46.15
2. Authoritative	44.17	39.11
3. Develop the country	15.95	14.74

Table 4.4 revealed that the male managers perceived the role of women to be to educate the new generation with cultural heritage and educate and nourish the children. Dual role of women received comparatively low attention of the male respondents. On the contrary, female managers perceived dual role most. Educate the new generation with cultural heritage received comparatively low attention than that of educate and nourish the children. Further, the role of men was perceived to be authoritative which clearly shows the prevalence of power -distance in our society. The Asian societies are patriarchal, and therefore, men's role is perceived that of breadwinner (to earn for the family), authoritative (dominating) in nature and are responsible for the economic role to develop the country and not society which falls within the duty of women.

Perception of Organizational Culture. A thirteen -item scale was used to examine the perception of organizational culture by male and female managers. The factor analyses provided two factors:

1. Men Favoured Organizational Culture (Eigen Value = 3.50; Pct. of Variance Explained = 26.93) and
2. Work Motivation (Eigen Value = 2.45; Pct. of Variance Explained = 18.87).

The factors along with its loading and item description are given in Annexure - 2. The obtained mean scores of the respondents perception of men favoured organizational culture are graphically displayed in Fig. 4.3.

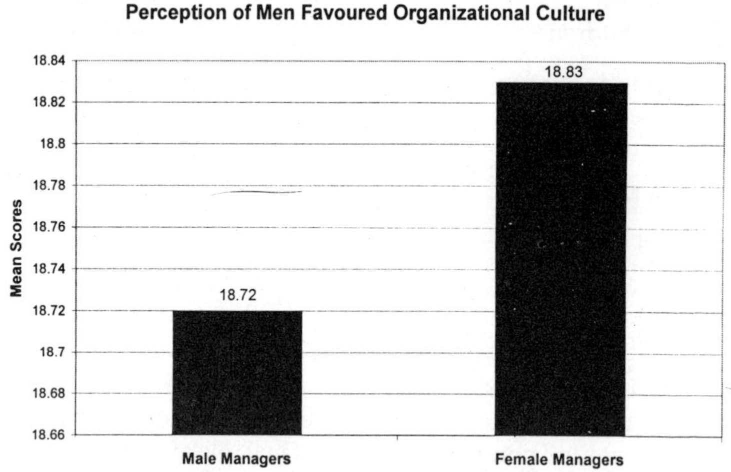

Figure 4.3

Fig. 4.3 showed that as compared to women managers men managers seemed to believe in men favoured organizational culture. The difference in the opinion (as reported by ANOVA) was found to be highly significant ($p < .0001$ level). The second factor talked about the motivation to work and the two levels of respondents more or less agreed on the dimension work motivation ($p > 0.05$ level).

The findings further indicated that both men and women managers of the sample agreed that women value working in a friendly atmosphere than what men do (Xs = 2.74 and 2.82 respectively). There seemed to be an agreement in their views ($p > 0.05$ level).

Job Preferences. The job preferences of men and women managers were examined with the help of two items: One directly asked, why have you joined the profession in which you are? And the second was framed to tap the individual's need behind joining a profession. Table 4.5 contains the findings.

Table 4.5

Valid Percentages Regarding Job Preferences as Reported by Male and Female Managers

Job Preferences	*Valid Percentage of Responses* *Male Respondents (N = 129)*	*Female Respondents (N = 71)*
1 Why have you joined the profession in which you are?		
(a) Financial need	34.05	27.9
(b) Economic independence	27.9	48.94
(c) Make use of educational achievements	36.45	32.76
(d) For the benefit of the society	1.6	2.8
2. People join a profession to realise their need for:		
(a) Power and authority	3.9	8.5
(b) Serve the society and humanity	5.4	5.6
(c) Economic pressure	29.7	38.0
(d) Career aspirations	61	47.9

Table 4.5 disclosed that the male respondents attached greater importance to make use of educational achievement and financial need as the reasons to explain why they have joined the profession in which they are, whereas, the female respondents attached greater importance to economic independence and then to make use of educational achievements. Table 4.5 further revealed that the male

respondents felt career aspiration to be the most dominant need which they want to realize by joining a profession. The female managers reported something different. For them economic pressure as well as career aspiration seemed to carry equal weightage.

The Value Grid. Job preferences seem to be influenced by the individual values that one wants to realise through his / her work activities. A 21-item scale was used to examine the value grid of male and female managers. Factor analyses were computed to have sharp categories of values that the managers want to realise at workplace. Four factors emerged out of it. To put them,

1. Inner Happiness (Eigen Value = 3.52; Pct. of Variance Explained = 16.75)
2. Work Values (Eigen Value = 3.23; Pct. of Variance Explained = 15.36)
3. Work Centric Caring Relationship (Eigen Value = 2.89; Pct. of Variance Explained = 13.78), and
4. Variety at Work (Eigen value = 2.51; Pct. of Variance Explained = 11.92).

The factor along with its loading and item description is given in Annexure-3. Fig. 4.4 depicts the factor mean scores as reported by men and women managers.

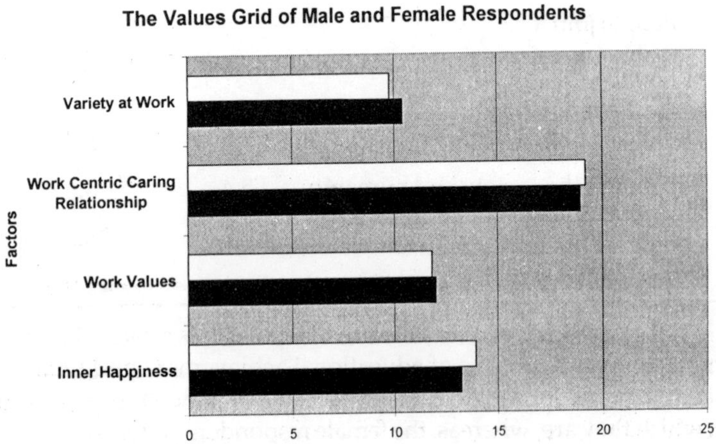

Figure 4.4

It is interesting to note (as Fig. 4.4 shows) that, both men and women managers, attached greater importance to work centric caring relationship as compared to other values. Further, the later preferred it more to the former. Variety at work was valued least amongst all the four categories of values by both the categories of respondents. To add, male managers were found to attach greater importance to work values than that of female managers, whereas, female managers reported to value inner happiness more than that of male managers. There seemed to be an agreement in the views of the two levels of respondents as the reported F-scores were found to be insignificant ($p > 0.05$ level).

Do Women Have a Different Career Path?

The efforts were made to examine the importance attached to career by men and women managers. The career progression of male managers was found to be greater than the career progression of female managers.

The findings further showed that as compared to female respondents the male respondents felt that they have made significant contribution to the occupational status that they possess. Fig.4.5 makes it clearer.

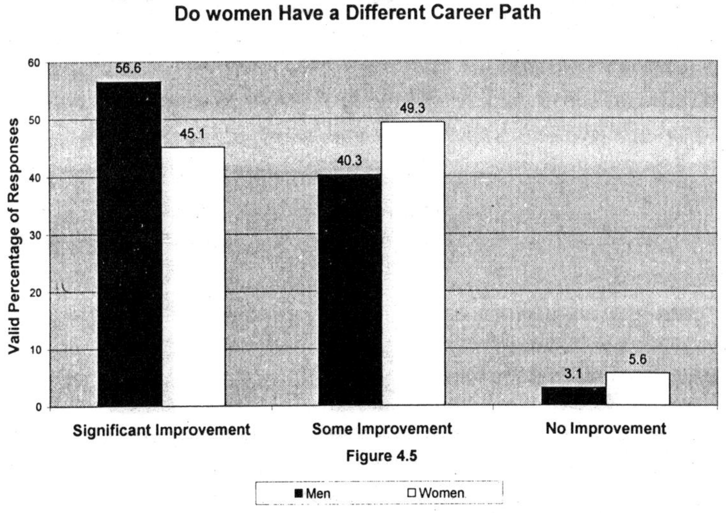

Figure 4.5

Fig. 4.5 displayed that the perception of men managers centred mostly around significant contribution whereas it seemed to be some improvement in the case of women managers. There seemed to be an agreement in the views of the two categories of respondents ($p > 0.05$ level).

To probe the issue further the respondents were asked to rate, which is more important for a male and a female member: career, family or both. The obtained percentage of responses were portrayed in Fig. 4.6.

The Importance of Career and Family for Male and Female Managers

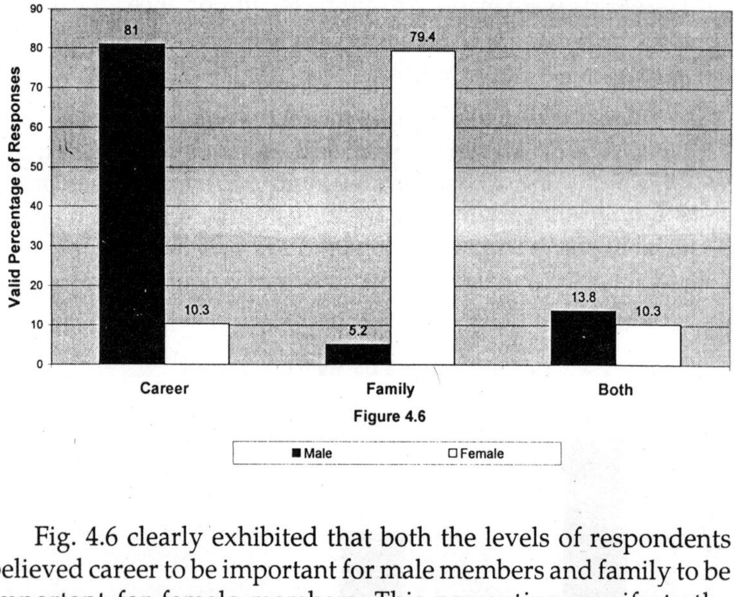

Figure 4.6

Fig. 4.6 clearly exhibited that both the levels of respondents believed career to be important for male members and family to be important for female members. This perception manifests the influence of social role.

Motivation to Work

Table 4.6

Mean and SD Scores of the Variables Related to Work Motivation as Reported by Male and Female Managers

Variables	*Male Managers*	*Female Managers*
1. Hedonism/ Materialism	2.89	3.06
2. Career Success	3.07	3.18
3. Pioneering Motivation	2.79	3.00
4. Power and Authority	2.52	2.63
5. Self Actualization	2.85	3.10
6. Affiliation	2.98	3.17
7. Altruism	2.81	2.98
8. Security	2.52	2.57

Note. Male Managers = 129; Female Managers = 71.

Table 4.6 revealed that almost similar trend in the motivational need of both the categories of respondents, except one. Self-actualization was reported to be significantly high ($p < 0.05$ level) in the case of female managers. There seemed to be an agreement in the views of the respondents as no significant differences were revealed by the analysis of variance.

Personality Characteristics and Men and Women Managers

Personality Profile. Bem Sex Role Inventory (BSRI) was used to examine the personality profile of men and women managers. The average or mean number of points assigned by each person to the masculine attributes constitutes his or her masculinity score, the average or mean number of points assigned by each person to the feminine attributes constitutes his or her femininity scores. The purpose of the investigation was to examine the personality profile of male and female managers, therefore, the mean scores were taken into account. The results indicated women managers to be androgynous, as they seemed to be high on both masculinity as well as femininity scores. However, the male managers were found to more masculinity oriented in their approach (high on masculinity scores and low on femininity scores. An agreement in the views of the respondents were noticed by the analysis of variance ($p>.05$ level).

Perception of Security / Insecurity. The scale measuring this dimension had 18 items. In order to have more focused results the items were factor analyzed. Four factors emerged out of this analysis. To put them,

1. Self - Orientation (Eigen Value = 2.65; Pct. of Variance Explained = 14.71).
2. Other - Orientation (Eigen Value = 2.60; Pct. of Variance Explained = 14.43).
3. Implacable Behaviour (Eigen Value = 2.55; Pct. of Variance Explained = 14.18).
4. Low Confidence (Eigen Value = 1.52; Pct. of Variance Explained = 8.45).

The factor along with its loading and item description are given in Annexure - 4. The descriptive statistics of the factors are presented in Table 4.7

Table 4.7

Mean and SD Scores of the Factors Related to Security-Insecurity Dimension as Perceived by Male and Female Managers

Dimensions	*Male Managers*		*Female Managers*	
	Mean Scores	*SD Scores*	*Mean Scores*	*SD Scores*
1. Self-Orientation	13.06	4.00	13.53	3.24
2. Other Orientation	8.41	3.25	7.84	2.43
3. Implacable	12.25	4.31	11.08	3.19
4. Low Confidence	6.57	2.28	6.78	1.83

Note. Male Managers = 129; Female Managers = 71.

Quite interestingly the findings indicated (as quoted in Table

4.7) almost a similar trend for both, men and women managers barring one - implacable behaviour, where the male managers scored higher than the women managers ($p < 0.05$ level). No significant differences were found ($p > 0.05$ level) on rest of the three factors.

Work-Family Management

A host of factors examined the work-family interfaces. To name them, centrality of family life, centrality of work life, family support, career vis-à-vis family commitment, hours devoted at workplace and in family and participation in household chores. The descriptive statistics of the above mentioned variables are given in Table 4.8

Table 4.8
Mean and SD Scores of Work-Family Interface as Reported by Male and Female Managers

Variables	*Male Managers (N = 129)*		*Female Managers (N = 71)*	
	Mean Scores	*SD Scores*	*Mean Scores*	*SD Scores*
1. Centrality of family	3.75	0.47	3.77	0.64
2. Centrality of work	3.76	0.46	3.56	0.53
3. Family support	3.60	0.68	3.69	0.57
4. Men to sacrifice promotion	2.91	0.69	2.42	0.84
5. Women to sacrifice promotion	3.50	0.69	3.58	0.67
6. Number of hours spent at workplace	8.98	2.47	8.86	1.87
7. Number of hours spent at home	9.98	4.25	11.51	3.19
8. Participation in household chores	3.22	0.78	3.67	0.65

Table 4.8 indicated that both the men and women managers perceived family to be central in their lives as the reported mean scores were quite high (Xs = 3.75 and 3.77 respectively on a 4-point scale). The centrality of work was found to be higher in the case of male managers than that of female managers. Both the categories of

respondents strongly agreed that family support is necessary to achieve career goals, however, the female respondents seemed to give it greater weightage as compared to her male counterparts. Women mostly sacrifice promotion because of family commitments seemed to be the common perception. Further, the results highlighted that the men managers spent slightly more time at workplace than what the women managers spent. To add, the women managers spent much more time at home than what the men managers did. This gives us the indication that family still seems to be the responsibility of women, even though the male managers told to participate in household chores.

The ANOVA disclosed significant differences in the opinion of male and female respondents with respect to centrality of work (F - scores = 8.12, df = 1/198, $p < 0.01$ level), men sacrificing promotion because of family commitment (F - scores = 19.31, df = 1/198, $p < 0.0001$ level), number of hours spent at home (F - scores = 7.04, df = 1/198, $p < 0.01$ level) and participation in household chores (F - scores = 17.77, df = 1/198, $p < 0.0001$ level).

The significant differences in the mean scores can be better visualized from Fig. 4.7, 4.8 4. 9 and 4.10.

Centrality of Work in Women and Men Managers' Lives

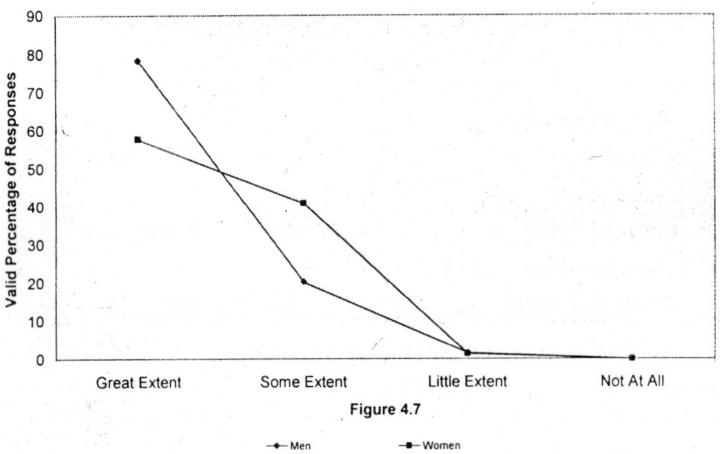

Figure 4.7

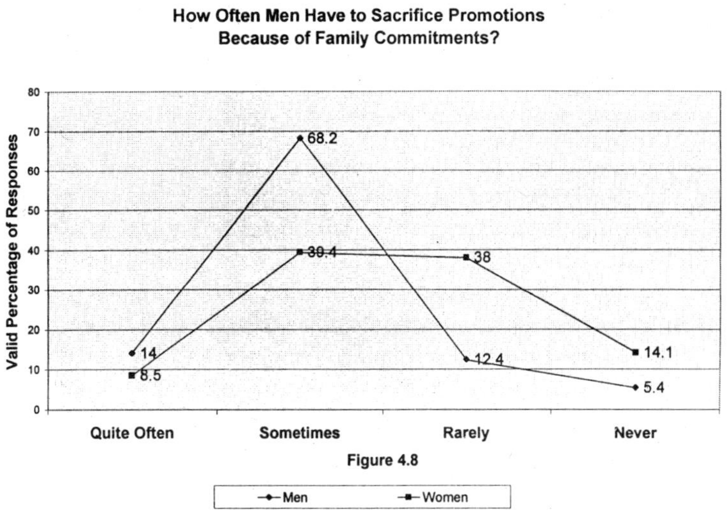

Figure 4.8

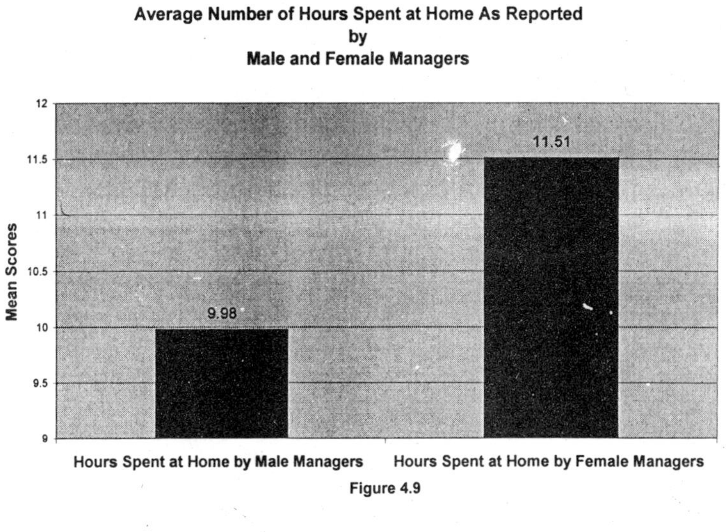

Figure 4.9

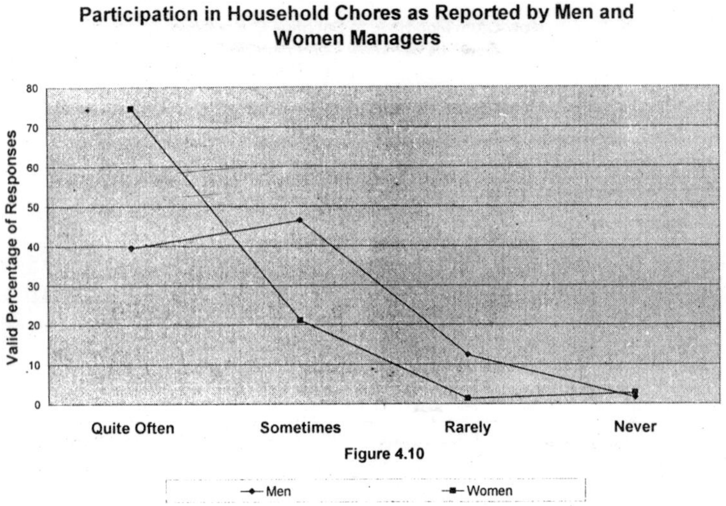

Figure 4.10

Your Time Management. The successful time management helps in using our time more constructively. Therefore, the author became interested in understanding the distribution of time in various activities by male and female respondents. The respondents were asked to judge each activity in terms of ideal number of hours and actual number of hours. The d-score between the two (ideal minus actual) provided an index to understand the distribution of time by the two categories of respondents. The mean and SD scores obtained on these d-scores are reported in Table 4.9.

Table 4.9
Mean and SD Scores for d-Scores (Ideal Hours - Actual Hours) on Time Management as Reported by the Two Levels of Respondents

Dimensions	*Male Managers (N=129)*		*Female Managers (N=71)*	
	Mean Scores	*SD Scores*	*Mean Scores*	*SD Scores*
1. Reading and studying	0.35	1.35	0.41	1.47
2. Working	-1.50	2.37	-2.12	2.79

(Contd...)

(Contd...)

3. Family and home	0.26	1.41	-0.25	1.74
4. Social	0.25	0.82	-2.63	0.95
5. Community Service	0.27	0.82	0.53	1.56
6. Leisure	0.16	1.49	-0.15	1.33
7. Other activities (e.g. sleeping, personal care, etc.)	-0.71	2.22	-1.10	3.25

The male respondents (as indicated in Table 4.9) seemed to spend more time in activities like working, leisure and sleeping, personal care, etc., whereas, the female counterparts were found to spend much time on social, leisure, family, work and other activities. The results clearly showed that in the case of female respondents family and related activities consumed most of her time.

Further, the analysis of variance revealed that the two categories of respondents differed significantly on the amount of time spent at family and home ($p < 0.05$ level) and social activities ($p < 0.01$ level).

Role Stress

The Organizational Role Stress scale measured ten dimensions of role stress that an individual experiences in the organizational context. The obtained mean scores of the responses on the different dimensions are entered in Table 4.10

Table 4. 10
Mean and SD Scores of Male and Female Managers on Organizational Role Stress Scale

Dimensions	*Male Managers (N=129)*		*Female Managers (N=71)*	
	Mean Scores	*SD Scores*	*Mean Scores*	*SD Scores*
1. Role Ambiguity	5.65	2.57	5.59	1.86
2. Role Erosion	10.22	3.97	9.70	3.46
3. Role Expectation Conflict	8.54	3.42	8.44	2.97
4. Role Isolation	7.02	2.64	7.14	2.79

(Contd...)

(Contd...)

5.	Resource Inadequacy	6.83	2.93	6.79	2.35
6.	Role Overload	8.56	3.63	8.87	3.50
7.	Role Stagnation	9.01	3.67	9.13	3.32
8.	Self-Role Distance	6.70	3.00	6.17	2.17
9.	Personal Inadequacy	6.97	3.00	6.87	2.61
10.	Inter-Role Distance	10.03	3.81	9.73	3.64

Table 4.10 indicated that the male managers experienced role erosion to a greater extent whereas female managers experienced inter-role distance maximally. There seemed to be an agreement in the views of two categories of respondents as the reported F-scores were not significant (p >.05 level) on any dimension of the ORS scale.

Fig.4.11 graphically portrays the different types of role stress experienced by men and women managers.

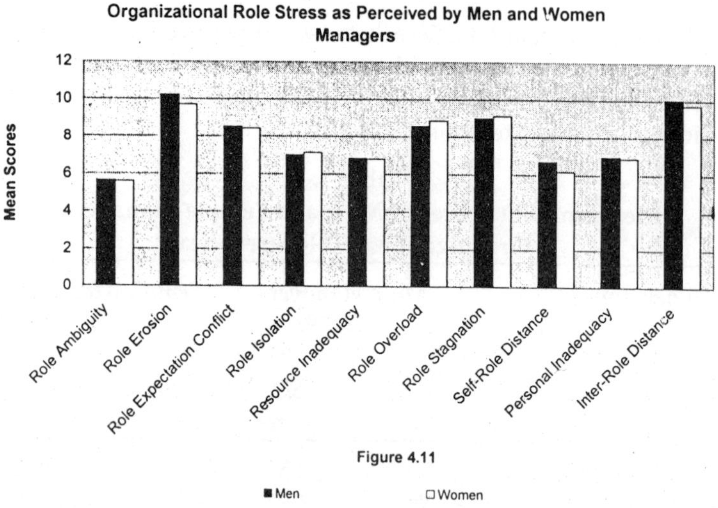

Figure 4.11

Supportive Relationship at Workplace

The prevalence of supportive relationship at workplace was examined. The study focussed on five major areas of support, i.e., support for personal problems, support for job related problems, support for family related problems, support in need and openness in relationship. The score on each dimension was calculated by multiplying the score indicating one's effort to seek the support by the availability of the support system. The mean and SD scores were computed and presented in Table 4.11

Table 4.11
Mean and SD Scores Pertaining to the Availability of Supportive Relationship at Workplace

Dimensions	*Male Managers (N=129)*		*Female Managers (N=71)*	
	Mean Scores	*SD Scores*	*Mean Scores*	*SD Scores*
1 Support for personal problems	7.27	3.41	6.80	3.64
2. Support for job-related problems	10.21	3:37	9.78	3.63
3. Support for family-related problems	8.52	4.52	8.73	3.85
4. Support in need	10.03	4.43	9.77	4.83
5. Openness in relationship	9.56	5.67	8.91	4.66

Table 4.11 disclosed that both the levels of respondents perceived the availability of supportive relationship at workplace mostly when they felt the need and when they had job-related problems. In both these cases male managers perceived the supportive relationship to be more as compared to the female managers. Women managers sought more support for family-related problems than that of her male counter-parts, whereas, male managers sought support for personal problems more than that of his female counterparts - women seemed to be a bit hesitant which may be one of the reasons why the male managers perceived openness in relationship to be more as compared to his female counterparts.

There seemed to be an agreement in the views of male and female managers that participated in study ($p > .05$ level).

Relationship is a reciprocal process, therefore, it is quite natural that the superior who helps his/her juniors will also expect return. The respondents were thus asked with the help of a single item to rate the chances of such expectation to occur. They were further asked to explain the different sorts of return that the superior expects with the help of an open-ended item. The results indicated that, both, the categories of respondents perceived that the superior expects return sometimes, as the reported mean score was 2.52 (on a 4-point scale) in the either case. There seemed to be an agreement in the views of two categories of respondents ($p > .05$ level).

Further, the content analyses of the responses collected on the nature of return that the superior expects, as expressed by the male and female managers seemed to be mostly to supervise the juniors and keep him well informed about the work atmosphere, collect information (administrative) which he / she may require for the work that is to be done and help him in a new assignment by contributing through sincere, hard and innovative work. The expectation to contribute to a new assignment seemed to be more from male managers and to submit information about work from female managers.

A Good Mentor: Male or Female Manager

After examining the supportive relationship at workplace the author became interested in knowing the views of the respondents as who do they consider being a good mentor: male or female. The obtained percentage of responses are graphically presented in Figure 4.12

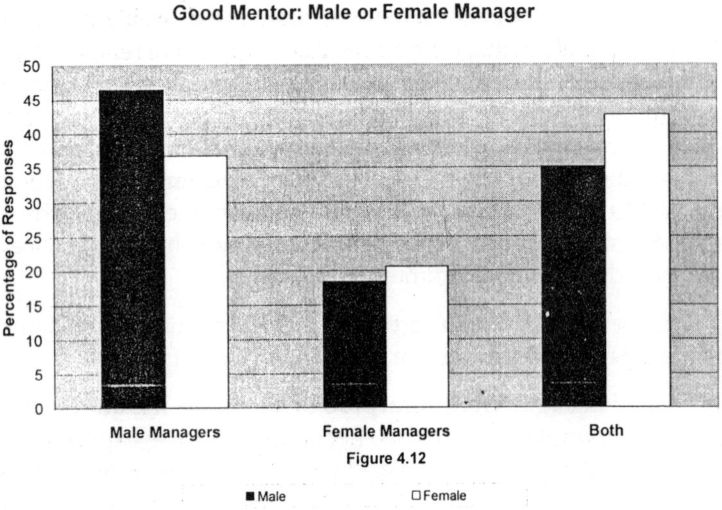

Figure 4.12

Fig. 4.12 exhibited that both the level of respondents perceived male managers to be a good mentor. Interestingly, a good number of respondents in both the categories expressed it to be both.

Who is an Effective Leader?

The related question which comes to mind is do the perception of an effective leader differs with respect to sex. The content analyses of the responses revealed that both, male and female managers perceived an effective leader to be charismatic and assertive on the one hand and on the other hand be aware of the world competitive development and try to be innovative so that the organization grows. The female respondents attached greater importance to being co-operative than that of male managers. The male managers attached greater importance to management of work as compared to their female counterparts.

Linking National Culture with Organizational Policies

The second questionnaire was used for this purpose. The obtained results will be discussed under separate headings:

(1) The Society

The Asian societies are patriarchal in nature that grants more power to men as compared to women. Men are supposed to be the breadwinner whereas women to look after family. The similar perception was exhibited in the views of the respondents when they were asked to share their views about the role of men and women in one's culture. The findings are graphically portrayed in Figures 4.13a.b

Fig. 4.13a revealed that men were perceived as authoritative more by men managers as compared to women managers. The women respondents perceived the role of men to be that of breadwinner.

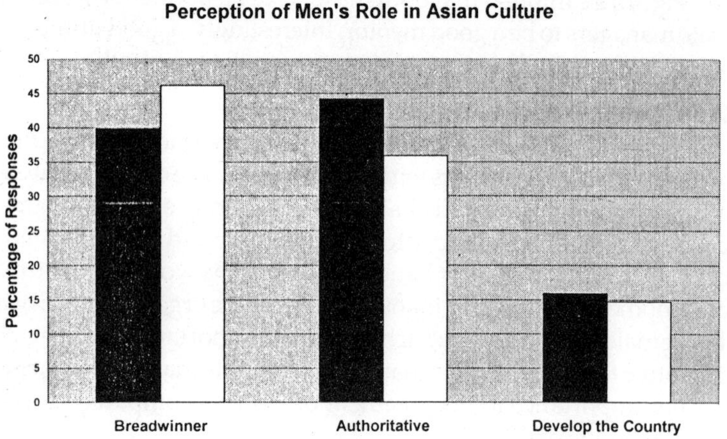

Figure 4.13a

Figure 4.13b

Fig. 4.13b exhibited the perception of the respondents with regard to women's cultural role. The male managers perceived the role of women to educate and nourish the children whereas women managers perceived their role to be dual - career as well as family.

The social role of men and women in the society is exhibited in their selection of jobs. The general perception is that it is women who choose the profession which best matches with their role and responsibility in the family. Thus, the respondents were asked,

To what extent the family obligations and duties affect the selection of jobs?

The responses were obtained in the case of husband and in the case of wife which is graphically displayed in Fig. 4.14

Family Obligations and Duties Affect the Selection of Jobs

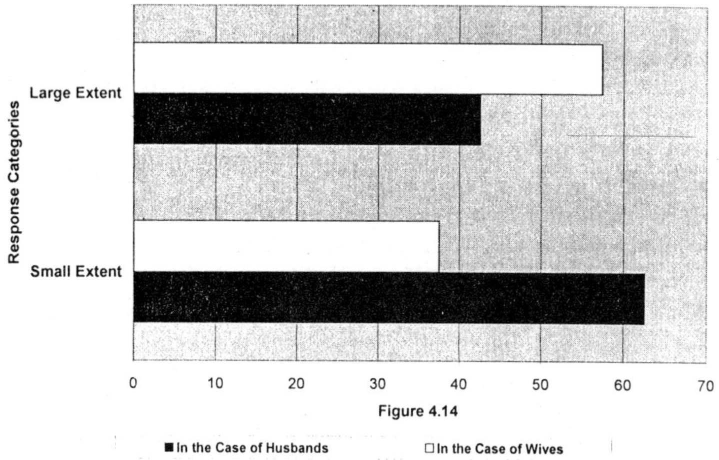

Figure 4.14

Fig. 4.14 suggested that family obligations and duties affected the selection of jobs to a large extent in the case of wife and to a small extent in the case of husband.

(2) The Perception of Women

The respondents were asked to express their views on, "what is your first reaction when a female joins the company in a managerial position?" The obtained views were content analyzed. The findings indicated that 45.84 per cent of the respondents felt that when a female joins the company in a managerial position, the first reaction is to know about her personal life. Only 25 per cent of the respondents were of the opinion that she is perceived as an administrator. A good number 29.16 per cent of the respondents expressed the feelings of appreciation for a female manager as she joins the company in a managerial position. The overall findings indicated a mixture of responses as a reaction to when a female joins the company in a managerial position. However, the most dominant reaction seemed to know about her past and family life.

(3) Women and Work

The next question that comes to mind is whether the allocation of work at the workplace is influenced by the sex differences. Therefore, the investigator tried to gather information pertaining to,

Do you take into consideration sex while allocating the work responsibility?

The respondents were asked to narrate one or two instances. The content analyses of the incidences indicated that 49.10 per cent of the managers who participated in the study perceived the prevalence of discrimination in allocating the work responsibility with respect to outside jobs. 32.72 per cent of the managers were found to hold the opinion that while allocating the work responsibility the priority is given to ability and expertise. A small number of managers (18.18 per cent) reported both to be true - discrimination as well as expertise, while allocating work responsibility.

The investigator further asked,

How often women are considered for assignments which demand greater involvement and commitment?

The findings indicated that 46.66 per cent of the respondents said that sometimes women are considered for assignments, which demand greater involvement and commitment. 22.23 per cent of the respondents hold the view to be very rarely as against 31.11 per cent who reported it to be very often.

(4) Success and Men and Women Managers

Attempts were made to understand the dimension of success in male and female managers.

(a) **Personality and success.** It is generally assumed that success goes with men. People believe that it is necessary to be aggressive in order to be successful. These are some of the common assumptions that people have. Therefore, the investigator asked the respondents,

Do you think it is necessary to be aggressive in order to be successful?

The obtained results are graphically displayed in Fig. 4.15

Is It Necessary to Be Aggressive in Order to Be Successful?

Figure 4.15

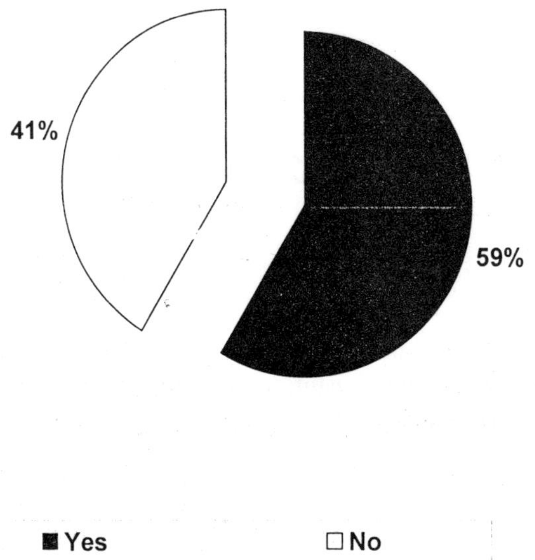

Fig. 4.15 disclosed that the majority believed that it is necessary to be aggressive in order to be successful (58.63 per cent). 41.37 per cent of the respondents negated the statement.

(b) **Criterion for being effective.** The respondents were further asked about the criterion for being effective in one's role as a manager, separately, in the case of male and female managers. The obtained percentage of responses after doing content analyses are graphically displayed in Figs. 4.16 and 4.17

(i) In the Case of Male Managers

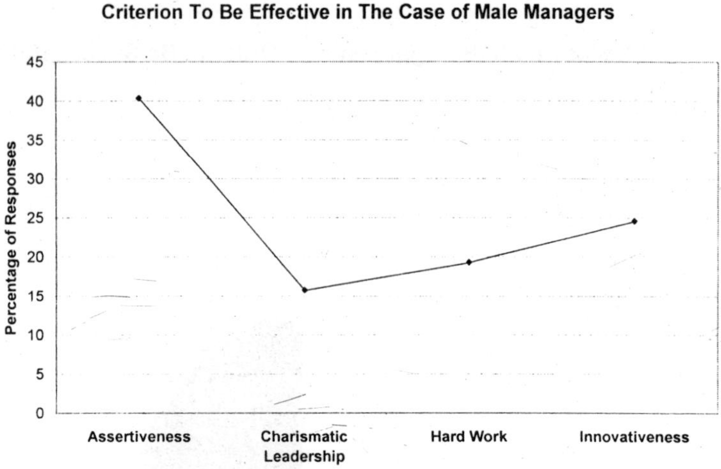

Figure 4.16

Fig. 4.16 suggested that the respondents perceived assertiveness to be the most preferred criterion for being effective in one's role as a manager. Innovativeness was reported to be the next important criterion.

(ii) In the Case of Female Managers.

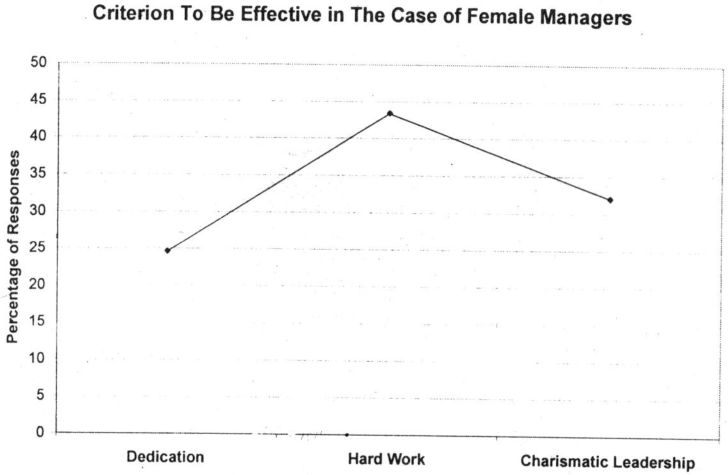

Figure 4.17

Fig. 4.16 indicated hard work to be most important criterion in the case of female manager in order to be effective in her role. Next criterion seemed to be charismatic leadership.

This clearly indicated the skewed perception of the respondents with respect to male and female managers in order to be effective in one's role.

The respondents were further asked regarding when is a female manager most effective—while working in a team, working individually or both. The findings clearly indicated that 56.9 per cent of the respondents believed that women managers are more effective while working in a team against 27.6 per cent of them who perceived that women managers are more effective when they work individually. A small percentage of respondents (15.5 per cent) reported it to be both - working in a team as well as individually.

(5) Competence and Male and Female Managers

The author was interested in examining whether female managers are perceived to be less competent as compared to male managers. The findings are displayed in Fig. 4.18

Are Women Managers Less Competent Than Their Male Counterparts

Figure 4.18

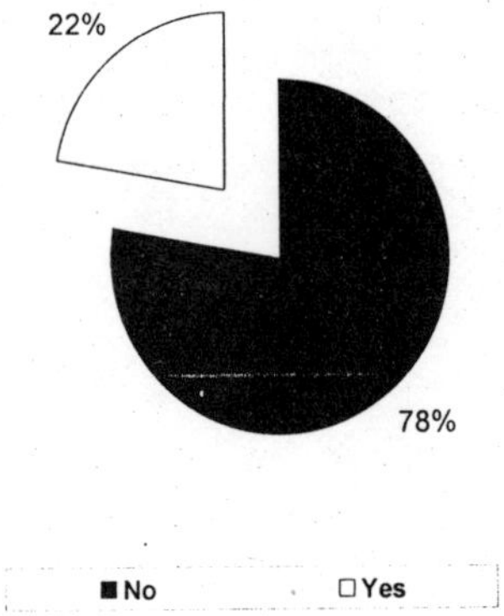

Fig. 4.18 highlighted that the majority (77.78 per cent) of the respondents reported that women managers are not perceived as less competent.

(6) Women and Assertiveness

This was examined with the help of a couple of items. First of all, attempts were made to examine whether there are female member in the Board of Directors. The obtained responses suggested that 67.3 per cent of the respondents reported that there are no women in the Board of Directors against 29.3 per cent of them who agreed to the presence of female member in the Board. A smaller percentage (3.4 per cent) did not respond to the item.

The respondents were further asked,

How do you perceive her behaviour to be:

(a) Assertive

(b) Neutral or

(c) Non-assertive

The findings showed that a good number of respondents (48.3

per cent) did not respond to this. 34.5 per cent of the respondents perceived the behaviour of women managers in the Board of Directors to be assertive against 1.7 per cent of them who reported it to be non-assertive. 15.5 per cent of the respondents reported it to be neutral.

Fig. 4.19 vividly presents the findings.

Women Managers and Perceived Assertiveness

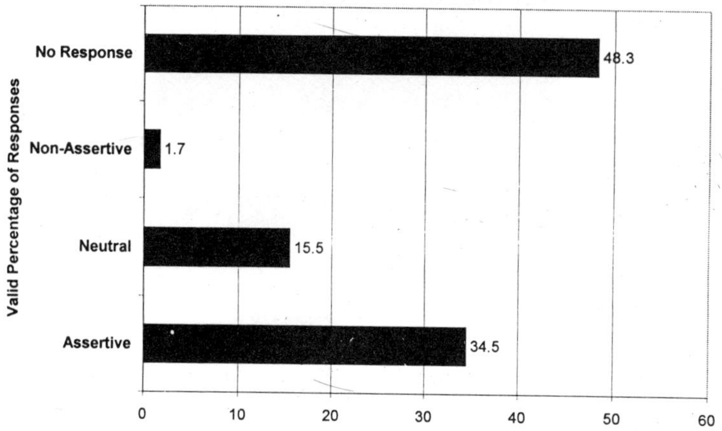

Figure 4.19

The author became further interested in understanding whether the women managers influenced the decision taken by the Board. 58.63 per cent of the respondents perceived it in an affirmative way. However, 41.37 per cent of the respondents felt it in a negative way.

Economic Development and Women Representation

The secondary source data have shown that the economic development of the country positively affects the women representation at the top. Therefore, the efforts were made get a general opinion on it. The respondents were asked,

Do you think that the level of economic development in the country influences the proportion of women in top managerial positions, if yes, how?

The findings indicated that all the respondents agreed to it. The expressed reasons were factor analysed and graphically displayed in Fig. 4.20

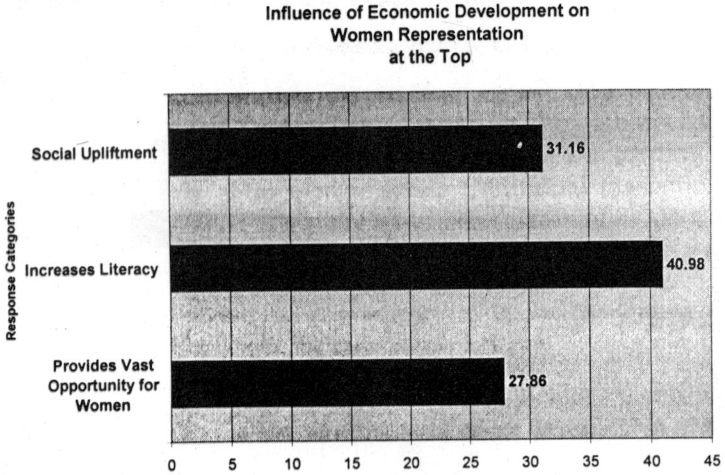

Figure 4.20

Fig. 4.20 indicated that the majority of them (40.98 per cent) believed that economic development increases literacy. 31.16 per cent of the respondents said that economic development leads towards social upliftment of the weaker sections of the society and granting them some amount of independence. 27.86 per cent of the respondents felt that economic development provides vast opportunity for women. All these affects women representation at the top in a positive manner.

Women in Management

Women Representation At the Top. The statistics show that women are poorly represented at the top. The volume highlights the reasons for it from a socio-cultural perspective and tries to link national culture with organizational policies in order to promote women at the top.

The book addresses some of the basic questions. The respondents were asked,

What in your opinion decides women's share in top managerial position?

The obtained views were content analysed and the findings are displayed in Fig. 4.21

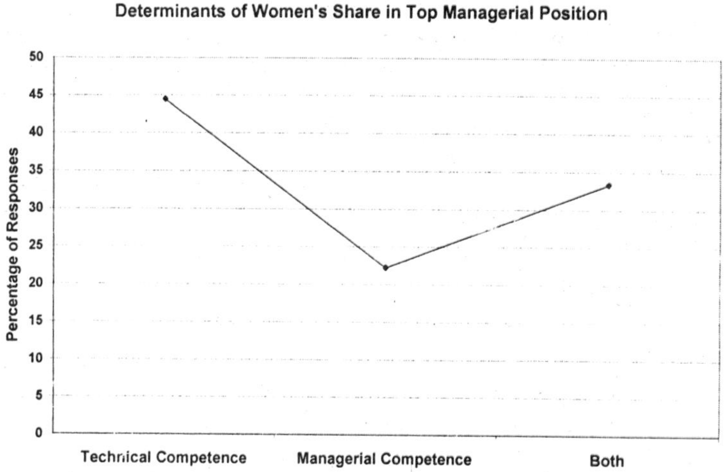

Figure 4.21

Fig. 4.21 showed that 44.44 per cent of the respondents reported technical competence to be the deciding factor of women's share in top managerial position whereas 22.23 per cent of the respondents felt it to be managerial competence. A good chunk of the respondents (33.33 per cent) believed that both the factors, technical as well as managerial competence, are responsible for women's share of representation in top managerial positions.

Women entry into management. The author further probed about when were women taken first into managerial positions in their respective organizations. The results indicated it to be a recent phenomenon. 54.85 per cent of the respondents reported it to be ten years against 29.03 per cent who said it to be twenty years. Women's entry into management was reported to be some thirty years back by 16.12 per cent of the respondents.

Meeting Work-Family Challenges

Women entry into organizations thus has a long history. Of course, the number has increased in the recent past. However, women representation at the top is still very low. Our social role seems to have a bearing on our structural role. Family still is the responsibility of women and they have to forgo many opportunities in their career to fulfill family duties and obligations.

Are the organizations aware of such constraints of the women? If yes, what do they do in terms of providing facilities and framing organizational policies in order to help women managers to overcome those constraints and obstacles? Let us see.

The author, therefore, tried to understand first, what support the organization provides to meet work-family challenges in order to have more and more women at the top in terms of childcare, flexi-time, special leaves, etc.

The results indicated that the organizations have still not moved towards adopting family friendly organizational policies, i.e., leave arrangements, childcare, etc. 82.15 per cent of the respondents reported that the support provided by the organization are the special leaves only. Flexi-time seems to be absent in the Asian organizations and very few organizations provided childcare facilities.

Promoting flexibility and autonomy. The findings hinted that the organizations in South-East Asian countries seemed not to adopt family-friendly programmes in order to support the women to overcome the major constraints of meeting work-family challenges. Therefore, the author became interested in understanding whether at all the organization promotes flexibility and autonomy and if they do then how? The obtained responses were content analyzed. The procured percentage of responses indicated that 49.03 per cent of the respondents perceived the autonomy promoted by the organization to be with respect to work, against 27.45 per cent of them who thought it to be with respect to time. 17.64 per cent of the respondents reported the organizational effort to promote flexibility with respect to time against 5.88 per cent who reported it to be with regard to work.

Empowering women managers. The respondents were further asked,

What does your company do for empowering women managers?

The findings obtained (on the basis of content analyses of the responses) indicated two broad stream of responses which can be graphically viewed in Fig. 4.22.

Company's Contribution for Empowering Women Managers

Figure 4.22

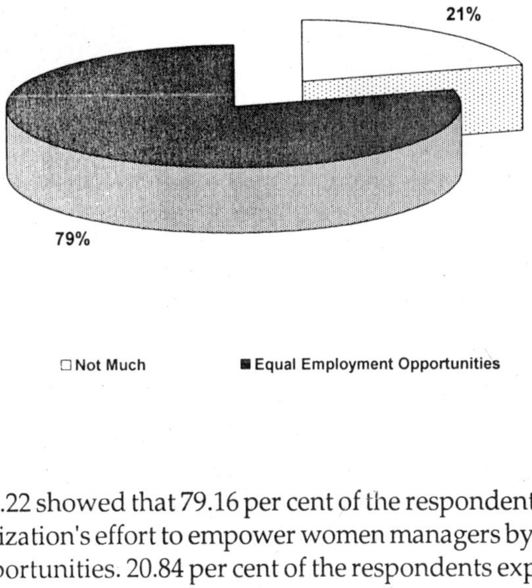

Fig. 4.22 showed that 79.16 per cent of the respondents reported the organization's effort to empower women managers by providing equal opportunities. 20.84 per cent of the respondents expressed the view that not much has been done by the organization to empower women managers.

Is the adoption of Equal Employment Opportunity sufficient enough to increase the women's share of representation at the top? Or does it require preparing and training them in order to achieve managerial positions. Hence, efforts were made to understand,

How often women managers are sent for different training programmes in order to achieve top managerial positions?

The findings are displayed in Fig. 4.23.

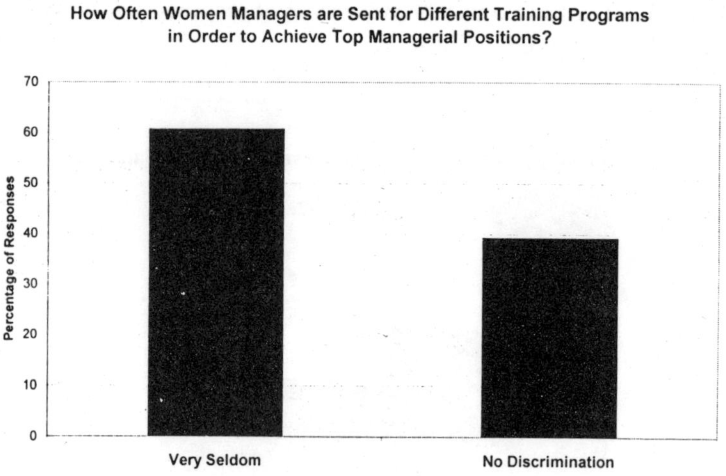

Figure 4.23

The majority (60.72 per cent) of the respondents perceived it to be very seldom. Only 39.28 per cent of the respondents told that there is no discrimination.

Sum Up

The under-representation of women in managerial and administrative positions is a global phenomenon. Such an uneven sex distribution in management is often attributed to the barrier women encounter in the organization.

Our assumption was that the socio-cultural factors influence women representation in managerial positions (Singh-Sengupta, 2000b). The overall results showed the basic difference in the motivation to work between male and female. The male reported to work to meet economic needs and the females for self-realization. This seems to have its roots in the socio-cultural realities, which focuses male as breadwinner. The perception towards work and career seem to be guided always by this sex role stereotypes.

No significant differences were reported in the qualifications or the personality of the male-female managers. The patriarchal nature of the society, which gives priority to male, seemed to have its spillover into the organizational culture too, as both the levels of respondents reported the organizational culture to be favoured towards men. Career is more important for men and family for women this is the general perception in the collectivist societies. This creates lots of conflict in women managers.

The adoption of work-life integration model suggested by Rosalind (1999) is likely to help women to take out some time for her career. A lot needs to be done at organizational levels. The findings of the study indicated that to address these concerns, changes in deeply rooted cultural beliefs and management practices need to be rethink.

Management would have to reject the traditional notions of masculinity and femininity and move beyond its fixation on face time rather than on productivity and output. This will help to marry the formal policies and informal corporate culture.

5

Discussion

An Overview

Social and employment trends indicate that increasing number of women today are entering occupation and profession traditionally labeled as masculine even in developing countries. Though it is found that women's participation has increased to a great extent in occupations, such as, nursing, teaching, medicine, community services and secretarial and white-collar jobs on one hand. On the other hand it is found that its representation in managerial jobs is growing but not to the extent as the earlier mentioned occupations and this is the scenario for Asian countries, which differs in this respect to the rest of the world. There are women who are satisfied with conventional occupations like teaching, nursing, secretarial and clerical jobs, etc. and are prone to choose such occupation generation after generation without any hesitation (Grey, 1999).

The intensification of global competition has a major influence compelling firms to view women managers as a competitive advantage rather than as a legislated necessity. Global competition challenges corporations to maximise the effectiveness of their human resources. The opportunity cost of prejudice of rejecting women and limiting selection to men is much higher than in previous economic environments. The recent decades have witnessed a huge increase in female labour market participation. Yet numerous studies report the persistence of inequalities and segregation between men and women in organizations (Poggio, 2000). The patriarchal ideology, based on the superior position of men, is evident in both government and the corporate world. The division of labour is often based on stereotypical gender roles. Sex role stereotypes are culturally based beliefs prescribing appropriate and inappropriate behaviours for the two genders. This significantly affects their career choice.

The present volume was an attempt to examine the socio-cultural determinants of women leadership in Asian organizations and establish linkages between national culture and organizational processes and practices that arguably act upon the constraints and opportunities women encounter in the workplace.

General Findings

Socio-Cultural Determinants of Women Representation at the Top

The overall results clearly reflected the perception of patriarchal society in the responses of the respondents. The collective orientation of the society was highlighted. The results provided support to the fact that Asian Organizations are hierarchically structured (Singh-Sengupta, 2001). The society provides a superior position to male members and the secondary position to female members. The role of men was perceived as breadwinner and that of women as to look after the family. The respondents significantly differed on the personality dimension of implacable on the basis of sex. In the Asian society men are perceived to be assertive and commanding whereas women are expected to comply, obey and be submissive and docile.

To add, in one of her recent studies (Singh-Sengupta, 2002) the author found that in Indian context the male and female perceive themselves to have different roles in the social space. Men are supposed to maintain external contacts, whereas women are primarily expected to fulfill their family responsibilities. These research findings were further validated in the present work when the male managers reported the economic basis to be the motivation to work (For illustration - Most individuals primarily work to be financially independent and meet family needs). Interestingly, female managers attributed it to be self-satisfaction (i.e., Work helps one to achieve self-satisfaction and make use of educational abilities). Going ahead on the same line of interpretation women attached greater importance to self-actualization and men to happiness as values that they wanted to realise in their workplace.

But the question arises are the female managerial folk able to realize self-actualization through their work activities? The strongest barrier for dual-career couples to reach the top ladders of organizational hierarchy is work-family management. The results showed that the female respondents reported family to be central in their lives as comparison to the male respondents who told it to be work. Therefore, family and related activities consumed most of her time. Male managers seemed to spend their time on work related activities, personal care, sleeping, etc. Quite natural, the women managers emphasized the importance of family support in order to achieve the career goals. Often (as the findings indicated) it is women who have to sacrifice promotions for family commitments.

Hence, the social role seemed to dominate the structural role, particularly in the case of women managers. The gyroscopic 'I' was perceived more as a part of the self by male managers than that of female managers. Women's role was perceived differently by men and women respondents. Male managers perceived the role of women to educate and nourish children. However, the female managers perceived their role to be of dual career. Both, men and women (who participated in the study) believed that career is more important for men and family for women. Therefore, the former attached greater importance to career aspirations as compared to the latter.

To add, the reluctance of the international companies to recruit women managers for overseas assignments is another example of the bearing of social role over structural role in the organizations. For both sexes, family issues are the number one reason for turning down an assignment abroad. Of course, this issue is compounded for women because of her family responsibilities. This does not however mean a women will automatically turn down the opportunity to have a career-enhancing experience overseas. While male partners in dual-career couples will be approached without reservation, managers often assume the women will turn it down. The result is women are not often given the opportunity to even consider such a move (Segal, 2001).

The results in the present study revealed some very interesting findings. The male managers who belonged to nuclear family, participated in the household chores and seemed to believe in hierarchical relationships perceived international companies to recruit women managers for overseas assignments. Whereas, the women managers who experienced significant improvement in their occupational status over the last five years felt that international companies are likely to recruit women managers. Thus, two things become clear: (a) Family support and (b) Importance to career.

This clearly emphasizes the importance of integrating work and life goals together, which need to be shared by both parties of the dual-career couples. The family demands have to be harmonized with the demands of two workplaces, each with its own requirements. The assumptions underlying work - life integration model is that "...a good job benefits both the employee and the spouse, and a bad job impairs the functioning of not only one but two workers. Thus every employer benefits if all employers institute effective work-life policies that support dual-earner couples" (Rosalind, 1999, p.151).

Economic Development and Women Representation at the Top

Although the percentage of employed women is increasing in most countries the number in management remains disproportionally low and the number holding executive positions remains negligible, almost everywhere. This pattern holds across oriental and occidental cultures across communist, socialist and capitalist systems and also among the developing countries. Evidence suggest that the under-representation under the utilization and skewed distribution of women managers is neither coincidental nor random but rather a function of systemic cultural sanctions, educational barriers, legal restrictions and corporate practices. The single most outstanding statement to make in this regard is that women in management are very few.

The findings indicated that individualistic societies, which are high on human development index, provide greater opportunities for women to enter the managerial positions. This suggests societies, which practices and believes in high power distance between males and females will provide unequal opportunities for the females. Masculinity was found to be negatively related to all the factors, except individualism (though insignificantly). Expectedly, individualistic countries contributed positively to GNP per capita income and negatively to the PDI scores.

The empirical evidences (the findings of the present study) showed that the majority believed that economic development increases literacy. Some said that economic development leads towards social upliftment of the weaker sections of the society and grant them some amount of independence. A few even told that economic development provides vast opportunity for women.

Thus, there seems to be a direct relation between economic development and gender empowerment. But the experience of many women striving to hit the top levels in business across the globe is that they must work harder, often struggling with extraordinary demands on their personal lives, to earn the same recognition or success as men. A tightening labour market is opening up now chances of top women to go ahead. The reported technical competence to be the major deciding factor of women's share in top managerial position. Whereas some felt managerial competence to be the factor. A good chunk of the respondents believed that both the factors, technical as well as managerial competence, are responsible for women's share of representation in top managerial positions. This clearly indicated a mixed response on why women are so poorly represented at the top and what decides her share in top managerial positions.

There are similar findings that report mixed views regarding the issue of why so few or lesser number of women reaches the top. The optimist believes that in the past women were excluded from full participation in the labour force and education. Once they are given the opportunity to acquire the necessary credentials and experience backed by supportive legislature, they will inevitably move into positions of authority and power and this is a time. The pessimist argues that the situation is complex and resistant to change. They believe that the optimist give little attention to prejudice, male and female resistance to changing roles, the effects of competition for desirable positions, as to who will perform the many unpaid tasks that women have traditionally done. They felt simply allowing women into college and the workforce will not necessarily and result women moving into positions of authority.

Specific Findings

The low representation of women at the top was substantiated by the fact that majority of the respondents reported absence of women in the Board of Directors. Though the history of womens' entry into management seems to be pretty old. Of course, it is only recent event that more and more women are coming forward to work in the profession that was traditionally perceived to be male-dominated.

The organizational culture was reported to be perceived as men-favoured. Interestingly, the male respondents perceived it to be greater as compared to their female counterparts. Therefore, quite obvious the first reaction when a female enters the organization is that of female first and then as a manager. The findings showed that people become more interested in knowing her personal life. This clearly indicated that the social reality exists as it is.

Hence, the question arises, are the organizations aware of the constraints and obstacles of the women managers which restrict their movement up the ladder. If yes, what do they do in terms of providing facilities and framing organizational policies in order to help women managers to overcome those constraints. On the whole, the findings showed that the organizations in Asian countries have still not moved towards adopting family friendly organizational policies. The most widely applicable work-life policies available in Asian context are still only maternity leave. Recently, the system of childcare at workplace premises has been introduced in some organizations. Other than these, there seem to be no other corporate policies, which can help the dual-career couples to overcome the barriers of advancement.

The results further showed that the organizations provided autonomy and flexibility only with respect to work and not with regard to time. To add, the organizations have followed Equal Employment Opportunities with respect to female managers, but still no concrete measures were reported to be adopted by the organizations in Asian countries in order to promote women managers at the top managerial positions.

If this is the scene a lot needs to be done. The author based on the findings of her research puts forth a twofold suggestion: One at the individual level and other at the organizational level. To put them,

(a) At individual level by adopting Life-Role Model, and

(b) At organizational level by promoting family-friendly organizational policies.

(a) Towards Work - Life Integration Model

Interest in research on process linking work and family is of relatively recent origin. Traditionally organization and family were treated as two discrete domains of an individual's life and the interdependence between the two was largely ignored. This "myth of separate worlds" (Kanter, 1977) perpetuated an image of compartmentalization between work and family life which overlooked the complex reality of inter-linkages between the two domains, even employees refused to acknowledge the possibility of conflict or competition between their work and family (Piotrkowski, 1979). Such segmentation, according to Voyadanoff (1980, p. 2) enabled the corporate world to "disclaim responsibilities of workers and to expect the family to fit the needs and demands of corporate organizations". Although scholars like Pleck (1977) introduced the concept 'work-life role system' to understand the inter-linkages between work and family roles, in many of the studies, the family was treated as the dependent variable and the effect of work environment was studied on family variables such as for instance, household task performance.

The phrase "work-family" emerged in the 1980s, a time when married women's labour force participation experienced a steep increase and when the spheres of work and family were more clearly separated than they are today (Barnett, 1999). More recent studies have however explored the potential reciprocity of work and family roles in a more comprehensive manner maintaining that neither the family nor work are closed systems, and changes in one should influence the other. The above researchers have probed such independence from a variety of perspectives. There are studies that have explored the family contributions to work commitment and reported a significant relationship of job commitment with organizational support for families, and the support provided by immediate families.

The separate sphere model. Corporate responses to work - family issues reflected the demographic and attitudinal realities of the time. The study by Rosabeth Kanter (1977) had concluded that the spheres of work and family were not separate but there was spill over between them. These understandings are not incorporated in our organizational policies. In practice the two worlds of work and family were conceptualised as totally separate and in competition. The separate sphere model was reinforced by the then-dominant corporate culture that explicitly required family matters to be left at the workplace door.

Prevailing values and attitudes. There has been a major shift in sex role attitudes—a shift away from traditional roles of male and females. This shift which has enormous implications for work-life policies, is just now making its way into popular awareness. With the full participation of women in the labour force, and with the reality that women's economic contribution is critical to the support of the family, new pressures and new rewards have surfaced for today's young adults. Increasingly, men and women are entering marriage with a new contract, one that honours the importance to both of them of their careers. This new contract dramatically affects work-related decisions and the traditional gendered division of labour in the house (Barnett, 1999).

Work-life integration model. Today in every dual-earner couple, family demands have to be harmonized with the demands of atleast two workplaces each with its own requirements. Rosalind C. Barnett (1999) advocates this model as depicted in Fig. 5.1.

This Work - Life Integration Model

Fig. 5.1

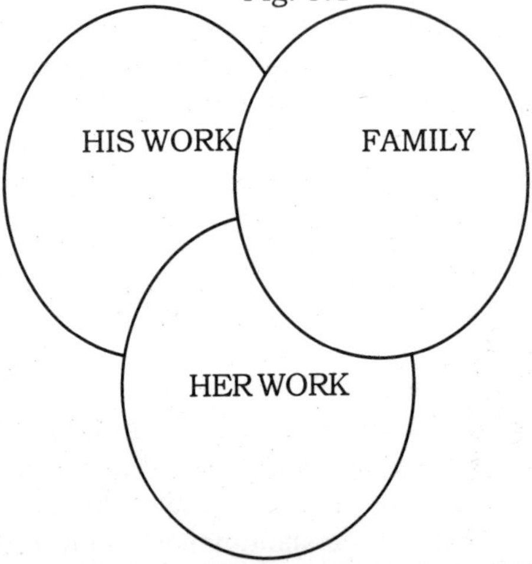

Source: Rosalind C. Barnett, 1999.

Assumptions

The clear assumption of this model is that a good job benefits both the employee and the spouse, and a bad job impairs the functioning of not only one but also two workers. Thus, every employer benefits if all employers institute effective work-life policies that support dual-earner couples.

The realization that men and women can successfully occupy numerous work and non-work roles has been accompanied by a revised model of human energy. According to this new view, the more roles one occupies, the better are one's chances of gaining important psychological inputs. Rather than focusing on role demands, this model focuses role rewards, or income. Thus, although one expends energy when one assumes additional roles, one experience a net gain in energy because of the benefits associated with multiple roles. The degree to which there is a positive gain depends, in part, on which roles on occupies and on the quality of those roles - some combinations may be more beneficial than others. The benefits of multiple role involvement include monetary income, heightened self-esteem, the power to delegate onerous role obligations, opportunities for social relationships, and challenge (Barnett, 1999, p. 152).

The singular focus both at the workplace and in the work-life policies on the worker and his or her needs has over time given way to the realization that most workers are partnered and that the needs and wishes of the partner also have to be considered. It appears that corporate values are catching up with the values expressed by increasing number of employees. Now the expressed aim is to help men as well as women better integrate their work and non-work lives in order to attract and retain outstanding workers and optimize their productivity.

The adoption of work-life integration model is likely to help women to take out some time for her career.

(b) Rethinking Employment: Family Friendly Organizational Policies

With dual-earner families partners are negotiating traditionally gendered roles to adapt to new realities and expectations (Lewis, 1994). Although women continue to retain the majority of family caring work (Hooyman and Gonyea, 1995), there are nevertheless shifts in men's family involvement and their willingness to modify work and family, particularly among younger generation (Wilkinson, 1994; New Ways to Work, 1995). Increasingly, then, the workforce is composed of women and men with responsibilities for both the care and the economic support of families, who seek a balance between their work and private lives.

Technological developments and the globalization of markets have brought great changes in the nature of work and employing organizations. Technology has eliminated the need for many routine jobs and blurred the boundaries between work and non-work time (Lewis, 1996). Employing organizations are also facing new challenges within the global market place. There is a drive for greater productivity and quality and a need for a flexible workplace, which can respond rapidly to new technology and changing markets. Restructuring may provide opportunities for greater flexibility for employees to manage their work and non-work lives, or may be used to achieve flexibility in numbers from the employers' perspective, creating insecurity and disempowering employees in managing their personal lives (Lewis, 1996).

It has been suggested that there is now a new psychological contract between employers and employees (Herriot, 1992). Workers, it is argued, no longer expect jobs for life, but do expect opportunities for self-development. This is usually interpreted in terms of employability but given the interdependence between work and family, also encapsulates opportunities to balance work and family in an optimal way.

The findings of the study indicated work-family management to be the major constraint for women managers to climb up the organizational ladder. Management practices need to be rethought in the context of deeply rooted socio-cultural beliefs. This is the right time that the management should reject the notion of masculinity and femininity and move beyond its fixation on face time rather than on productivity and output. This will help to marry the formal policies and informal corporate culture.

Linking family policies into organizational policies. Over the last 20 years or so, the issue has been addressed by the United Nations (1979 UN Convention on the Elimination of All Forms of Discrimination against Women; the Forward-Looking Strategies for the Advancement of Women; the Action Programme for the 1994 UN Conference in Cairo on Population and Development); the International Labour Organization (Convention 156 concerning equal opportunities and treatment between workers with family responsibilities, 1981), the council of Europe (resolution on policies to accelerate the achievement of equality between men and women,

1989); and the OECD (in a report entitled, "Conducting Structural Change: The Role Women" 1991). These reports share a broad approach to family responsibilities, covering not only children but other family members who need care and support; propose a wide range of measures and conditions to enable and support reconciliation, including terms of conditions of employment, working hours, tax and social security, leave arrangements and childcare services, and in most cases recognize the need for family responsibilities to be shared more equally between men and women (for example, the preamble to the 1979 UN Convention refers to 'a change in the traditional role of men as well as the role of women in society and in the family (being) needed to achieve full equality between men and women', paragraph 14). The interest of all these international bodies like EU is to provide equal opportunities to men and women and improve the position of women in the economy and society (Moss, 1996).

Work-Family at the Crossroads

In the light of changing socio-political landscape, the primary challenge today is how to reposition work-family within the corporation so that it is not just perceived as a benefit for the employee, but is also seen as a benefit for the corporation - that is, adding to the 'bottom line' of business. By most accounts, work-family has settled into a relatively comfortable niche within corporate life, perhaps best exemplified by the term 'family-friendly corporations'. Work-family has gained an enormous presence in American corporations.

Despite these success work-family does not rank as a primary business issue or concern. In the minds of most CEOs or corporate officers, the centrality of work-family to the organization remains very much in question. Instances where corporate leadership has driven the work-family issue into the organizations core identity and/or business strategies are rare (Lehman, 1995). It is our argument that within the Asian countries the evolution of organizations to family-friendly environments remains incomplete. Hall (1990) suggests that at the heart of the work-family issue is the question of corporate values. He argues that framing work-family balance as a 'parent problem' as opposed to a 'corporate problem' allows companies to look progressive by working on family issues without confronting important issues of discrimination—based not just on gender, but also race, ethnicity, and other kinds of differences (1990,

p. 13). A Company that defines work-family balance as a corporate balance, Hall asserts, fosters the adoption of an organizational or structural change approach rather than an individual accommodation strategy.

In attempting to have work-family balance redefined as a central business concern, professionals in the work-family field might heed the words of re-engineering advocates, Hammer and Champy (1993), that getting people to accept that the workplace will undergo radical change 'is not a war won in a single battle'.

Defining Work-Family Initiatives as Strategic Tools for Competitive Advantage. In a climate of global competition and cost cutting, human resource personnel must demonstrate to corporate leadership that investing in human capital is, in fact, linked to corporate success. Therefore, the next critical stage is the recasting of work-family initiatives within the corporate culture from being viewed as primarily 'corporate welfarism' or strategies of individual accommodation into being perceived as 'strategic tools for competitive advantage'. To do so stronger links will need to be created between work-family and business concerns of productivity and competitiveness. Such efforts will include defining the contribution of work-family to core business issues in the following ways:

(a) **Linking Work-Family to Employee Recruitment, Retention and Work Performance.** Even in a downsizing environment, recruiting and retaining a high-caliber workforce is a major concern of management. There is growing evidence that issues of work-family balance strongly influence individuals' choices about particular employment opportunities (Galinsky, et al., 1993; Ransom et al., 1989; Marquart, 1988; Lambert et al., 1992). Reframing work-family from an employee benefit to a strategic business concern affecting such issues as recruitment and retention creates a new perspective for both work-family professionals and firms. Moreover, the timing for such a transformation could not be more propitious. The re-engineering and work redesign movements leave in their wake enormous opportunities to create new policies and structures by which organizations can address the new realities of worklife. Whereas, 'traditional' work-family benefits have been targeted toward childcare resources, the new strategic approach could use the unfreezing of the organization through re-engineering to change a more basic set of structural and cultural barriers, which continue to impede healthy and productive individuals and families.

(b) **Linking Work-Family to Valuing Employee Diversity as a Competitive Advantage.** If workforce diversity is to be seen as a competitive advantage the challenge to corporations is to support strategies that enable employees to bring their whole selves to the job, their skills, experiences, values and attitudes. Broadening the concept of "flexibility" beyond the typical dimensions of time, space or style, Parker and Hall suggest that flexibility can also be a means of promoting 'psychological availability': 'A flexible workplace enables employees to bring their "full" selves to work and to be psychologically engaged in the tasks, activities, and relationships that make-up their jobs' (1993, p. 124). Based on this philosophy, flexibility becomes an approach of valuing differences and is linked in the organizational culture to core business outcomes. Employees who can bring their whole person into the workplace will be more productive workers (Gonyea and Googins, 1996).

(c) **Work- Family as a Component of a New Employer-Employee Social Contract**

> Few companies can today ask for employee loyalty and many no longer seem to want it. In turn, employees have entered an era of 'free agency', in which they are being advised to keep their skills and resumes current and be prepared to move on when and where they can. We can only wonder whether the cynicism washing over the workforce might reach the point where corporate proclamations about the 'value of people' are going to be perceived as 'corpocrisy' - hypocrisy in corporate life (Mirvis, 1993, p. 239).

A new social contract between employer and employee might be constructed around the concept of 'mutual flexibility' - recognizing that both employers and employees have need for flexible arrangements (Hooyman and Gonyea, 1995). For the corporation, changing technology and intense global competition require a flexibility to respond quickly to shifting market conditions. For employees, faced with unpredictable events such as sick children, ill parents, school plays and sports events, flexibility becomes an essential ingredient for achieving balance between work and home demands. For the firm, flexible staffing enables adaptability to insure a competitive advantage. For the worker, flexible scheduling enables the delicate juggling act to maintain a sense of equilibrium between work and home life.

Limitations of the Present Study and Suggestions for Future Research

A critical appraisal of the sample design, procedure, analyses and interpretations disclosed some of the constraints of this study. The limitations and possible future advice may be as follows:

The variables. The study was an attempt to examine the socio-cultural determinants of women leadership in Asian organizations. In this process the author made an effort to identify the factors at micro and macro levels. However, if the existing organizational policies were evaluated and taken into account it might have yielded a sharper picture of low representation of women at the top.

The future researches may be planned to analyse the organizational policies and its contribution towards the women representation at the top.

Further, efforts were not made specially to analyse and understand the leadership styles of men and women managers. Future researches can be directed in this direction.

There is a need to examine the personality profile of men and women managers at the top. Do they have different personalities? Is success related with sex? etc. etc.

The setting. The major parts of the data were collected from India. Out of 200 respondents 113 belonged to India and 67 belonged to Nepal, Bangladesh, Sri Lanka and Korea. It was not possible in this study to have a wider representation of Asian countries. It is advisable that a detailed study covering Japan and China should be taken up.

The sample. The selected sample consisted of different levels of managerial people working in different organizations. The convenience sampling (Sekaran, 1984) was adopted as the study had to be adopted in a limited time period. If the study had a wider dispersion of sample with respect to different types of organizations, i.e., male-dominated organizations (manufacturing, work organizations, etc.), organizations having a mixed representation of both sexes (for example, financial institutions, IT consultancy firms, etc.) and organizations preferred most by women (i.e., teaching, nursing, etc.) then it might have produced more specific findings. The nature of the organization is likely to influence the women participation at the top. Future researches may be carried out in this direction.

Procedure. The questionnaire method often yields socially loaded responses, in spite of best efforts. This seems to be a general flaw. To moderate this effect the author used open-ended items. Further, the findings were substantiated with the secondary source data.

The use of participatory method might have helped in overcoming the limitations of the questionnaire method. The participatory pattern of collecting data requires that the investigator should stay in the organization long enough to become more or less a part of it. This requires much time to be spent in the organization that was not possible in the present study.

Analyses. Some sophisticated statistical techniques can be applied to get more vivid picture of the findings.

Summary

The cultural values attached with the social role of a woman significantly affect her career choice. Conventionally, managerial jobs have been defined as largely a matter of instrumentality, autonomy and result-orientation, which fit the stereotypes of men rather than those of women. For that reason, male stereotypes have predominated in the world of management. Given, these women are perceived as lacking management skills and leadership abilities, and thus they are denied access to managerial positions. Nevertheless, sex stereotypes are culturally based beliefs prescribing appropriate and inappropriate behaviours for two genders.

Against this backdrop the author in this volume made a humble effort to examine the socio-cultural determinants of women leadership in Asian organizations.

The research was based on several assumptions. First, the low representation of women at the top in Asian organizations was analysed from a socio-cultural perspective. Secondly, the author took the stance that since managers control the bulk of power in organizations and largely determines a firm's human resources practices like recruitment, selection, placement, promotion and compensation, therefore, the extent to which managerial positions are filled by women has important long term implications for women employees. Finally, based on the findings of the study some intervention strategies are suggested at individual and organizational level in order to establish linkages between national culture and organizational practices that arguably act upon the constraints and opportunity women encounter in the workplace.

Certain hypotheses were advanced based on literature review. To put them,

Hypothesis 1. Socio-cultural factors will have direct effect on women's share in managerial positions.

Hypothesis 2. Higher the level of economic development in a country greater will be the proportion of women in managerial positions.

Hypothesis 3. Larger the power distance in a society lower will be the proportion of women in managerial positions.

Hypothesis 4. There will be an interaction effect of economic development and national culture upon women's representation in management.

The data were collected with the help of a structured schedule. Two separate questionnaires were framed which were a combination of, Likert type scales and open-ended items. The first questionnaire was designed to examine micro-level issues pertaining to the research theme. Hundred twenty-nine male and seventy-one female managers working in South-East Asian Countries (India, Bangladesh, Nepal, Sri Lanka and Korea) participated in the study. Out of which 32 respondents were from Sri Lanka, 20 from Nepal, 20 from Bangladesh, 15 from Korea and the majority 113 were from India. Convenient sampling was used to collect the data. The purpose of the study was to understand the socio-cultural determinants of the low representation of women in Asian organizations therefore an effort was made to get the responses from a wide variety of organizations ranging from IT Consultancy Firms, Financial Consultancy Firms, Banking to hard core manufacturing organizations. Our interest was not to examine the organizational differences but to have a holistic understanding of the research issue.

The overall findings of the present study indicated that both the levels of respondents perceived the societal culture to be proactive in nature. This indicates the collective orientation of Asian countries. Further, the managers who participated in this study reported the organizational culture to be men favoured. The perception seemed to be stronger in male respondents as they were found to believe more in hierarchical relationships. This provided support to the notion that Asian societies are hierarchical in nature and it has a bearing on the interpersonal relationships of the people in the organizations (Singh-Sengupta, 2002). The society provides a superior position to men and the secondary position to women. In the Asian society men are perceived to be assertive and commanding whereas women are expected to comply, obey and be submissive and docile. To add, in one of her recent studies (Singh-Sengupta, 2002) the author found that in Indian context the male and female perceive themselves to have different roles in the social space. Men are supposed to maintain external contacts, whereas women are primarily expected to fulfill their family responsibilities. These research findings were further validated in the present study when the male managers reported the economic basis to be the motivation to work (For illustration - Most individuals primarily work to be financially independent and meet family need). Interestingly, female managers attributed it to self-satisfaction (i.e., Work helps one to achieve self-satisfaction and make use of educational abilities). Going ahead on the same line of interpretation women attached greater importance to self-actualization and men to happiness as values that they wanted to realise in their workplace.

But the question arises, Are the female managerial folk able to realize self-actualization through their work activities? The strongest barrier for dual-career couples to reach the top ladders of organizational hierarchy is work-family management. The findings of the present study highlighted that the women managers of the sample reported family to be central in their life as compared to male managers who reported it be work. Therefore, family and related activities consumed most of her time, whereas, in the case of male managers it was found to be work related activities or personal care, sleeping, etc. Expectedly, women managers emphasized the importance of family support in order to achieve the career goals. Often (as reported in this study) it is women who have to sacrifice promotions for family commitments.

The social role perceptions seem to have a bearing on the structural role in the organizations, which, can be very well-supported by the reluctance of international companies to recruit women managers for overseas assignments.

For both sexes, family issues are the number one reason for turning down an assignment abroad. Of course, this issue is compounded for women because of her family responsibilities. This does not however mean a women will automatically turn down the opportunity to have a career-enhancing experience overseas. While male partners in dual-career couples will be approached without reservation, managers often assume the woman will just turn it down. The result is women are not often given the opportunity to even consider such a move (Segal, 2001).

The results in the present study revealed some very interesting findings. The male managers, who belonged to nuclear family, participated in the household chores and seemed to believe in hierarchical relationships perceived international companies to recruit women managers for overseas assignments. Whereas, the women managers who experienced significant improvement in their occupational status over the last five years felt that international companies are likely to recruit women managers. Thus, two things become clear: (a) Family support and (b) Importance to career.

This clearly emphasizes the importance of integrating work and life goals together, which need to be shared by both parties of the dual-career couples. The family demands have to be harmonized with the demands of two workplaces, each with its own requirements. The assumptions underlying work-life integration model is that "... a good job benefits both the employee and the spouse, and a bad job impairs the functioning of not only one but two workers. Thus every employer benefits if all employers institute effective work-life policies that support dual-earner couples" (Rosalind, 1999, p. 151). Currently the most widely applicable work-life policies available in Asian context are still only maternity leave. Recently, the system of childcare at work place premises has been introduced in some organizations. Other than these, unfortunately there are no other corporate policies, which can help the dual-career couples to overcome the barriers of advancement.

Implications of the Study

The study has far reaching implications. Men and women have different worldviews, which has its root in their socio-cultural milieu. If a company can link its prosperity or profitability back to wise management decisions from the standpoint of personnel, not necessarily guys then it can have the brightest people (Solomon, 2000).

The findings of the study indicated that family is still perceived to be the core responsibility of women. Therefore, women want more flexible work schedules. It has been discussed earlier in this paper that men and women are indistinguishable as far as qualifications are concerned, therefore, women want guidance from senior managers on how to succeed.

In South-East Asia, "women in general are disadvantaged, simply because they are women," said Khadija Haq, president of the Islamabad-based centre. Although women in the region work longer hours than men, they are practically invisible in the economy, earning just 30 per cent of what men bring home for the same work. South

Asia is one of the few areas in the world where men outnumber women, the report said. China and parts of Arab world show similar trends, it added (Women Mantra, 2000).

If the economic boom of the late 1990s rides out the fiscal crisis in Asia, corporations will have no choice but to initiate new strategies to hire, develop, and retain managers. Economic expansion that generates a tight labour market can only benefit women managers. Even in the face of structural discrimination, business necessity will force organizations to reach out to their women managers (Brett and Stroh, 1999). It will be up to the women managers to take advantage of these opportunities as they materialize and to push for the restructuring of jobs to make balancing work and family possible.

Suggestions for Policy Makers

Today's changed workforce includes women and men interested —in varying degrees and ways - in combining family involvement with work and career commitments. A variety of societal and workplace policies can support the integration of these family and work activities and in combination can constitute varying levels of family-friendly employment. However, the structure of what has been constructed as standard work involves practices such as long hours and rigid, uniform work schedules that can obstruct time for family caring, disempower family members and create the potential for stress.

Further when the organizations are willing to moderate hours and rigid schedules these facilities often can only be used at the risk of accepting career constraints. In this context, the organizational development challenge is to become family- and career-friendly by constructing equitable pluralistic work and career arrangements that provide time for family caring and which are institutionalized equivalents to standard work and career forms. However, change in the nature of work need not be seen as benefiting the employee only at the expense of the employing organization. Long work hours and rigid work and career requirements can undermine motivation, creativity and work quality, and therefore can be dysfunctional and counterproductive. Conversely, equitable pluralistic work and career arrangements can be seen as more congruent with achieving quality work outcomes. A point worth mentioning here is that although mechanistic, standard modes 'can work', pluralistic forms are likely to be more appropriate and yield better outcomes, particularly with the juncture of changes in work (the increased importance of motivation, innovation and quality productivity) and the changed workforce (with broadened active family involvement) in advance industrial societies.

Making Change Happen

Both the top women and top men in major corporations believe that companies, as well as women, have a responsibility to address women's needs in an evolving managerial workforce. Corporate India has begun to undertake effective initiatives to foster gender diversity in leadership. The three strategies listed below are key to successfully developing and retaining talented women:

Groom High-Potential Women for Advancement

In theory, this is simple. Employers need only examine how high-potential men are typically groomed-whether through formal mechanisms like executive education stints at top business schools, or informal means such as key assignments or mentors—and ensure similar opportunities for talented women.

In practice, of course, this approach often involves profound cultural change within organizations. Providing a female manager with a "stretch" assignment essential for her development may mean putting her in charge of a function or a factory or an international operation that has never before reported to a woman. To address this challenge, some companies have launched formal programmes to identify and develop high-potential managerial talent-usually not exclusively for women, but with women well-represented among programme participants. In 1990, ICICI began its Advanced Development Programme (ADP), which identifies each year, through an elaborate nomination and screening process, ten high-potential managers for participation. The programme may last from three to seven years and involves a series of rotational assignments, the opportunity for exposure to senior management through presentations and attendance at key company events, and coaching by a senior executive who serves as a mentor. Typically, at least half of ADP participants are women.

Build Diversity Objectives into Succession Planning. Many large companies have developed well-structured succession planning processes to ensure development and continuity of leadership. One effective way to foster diversity in senior management is to incorporate diversity into the succession planning process, by ensuring that the executive feeder pool includes women and people of colour. This may require linking succession planning to career development practices (such as the grooming of high-potential talent) at lower levels in the organization than are customarily considered.

Motorola built diversity into a well-established succession planning process known as Organizational Management and Development Review. In considering potential successors for top jobs, the company's leadership now reviews a list of three possible candidates for each position, at least one of whom is a woman or minority manager. Executive advisors coach the candidates on managing their careers and gaining critical experience. As a result of this disciplined focus, the number of female vice presidents at Motorola has risen from 2 to 32 since 1989.

Plug Leaks in the Pipeline. Many companies are losing female talent at a disproportionate rate, often after investing significant resources in women's training and development. Prudent financial management alone calls for addressing the attrition of high-potential women. One strategy for reducing turnover is to improve the performance and management review process so it provides employees with more feedback and managers with periodic pulse-checks to identify early-warning signs of disaffection. It also helps simply to let high-performing women know they are valued. Catalyst studies find that feeling under-appreciated is a major cause of voluntary resignations.

It's important to know why valuable employees leave. Because workers are often less than candid about their true reasons for quitting before they're gone, some companies conduct post-exit interviews that yield forthright information about why employees leave, which in turn suggests ways to reduce turnover. This information can be particularly useful for retaining women, who are often assumed to quit for personal reasons such as staying home with children. Women themselves may foster this largely incorrect assumption by citing such "acceptable" reasons rather than facing the unpleasantness of explaining work-related reasons for quitting. When Catalyst conducted a study for the Big Six accounting firm

Deloitte & Touche in 1992, it revealed that 90 per cent of former female professionals, even those with young children, had continued their careers elsewhere. More than 70 per cent were working full-time; 20 per cent had part-time arrangements. This information surprised firm leaders, who had assumed most were at home caring for their children and they adopted more flexible work policies.

Given people and organizations' innate resistance to change, corporate leaders must present a persuasive case for meaningful change to take place. Before they do this, they must be genuinely convinced themselves that it is the right thing to do. Catalyst asked senior women about what factors should motivate companies to increase the representation of women in senior management. The biggest reason why companies should support advancement initiatives for women in management, according to female executives, is because they're already there, in the management pool. Seven in ten executive women strongly agree with this proposition. Another reason, strongly endorsed by 61 per cent, is that women have a unique perspective to contribute to business decision-making and problem solving. A third reason why companies should boost the representation of women in senior management, according to female executives, is because they reflect the demographics of the consumer marketplace: that is, women represent more than half of the adult population and an increasing share of buying power. However, fewer than half of women in senior management think that bowing to pressure from customers, or from shareholders or the law, for that matter, should be a driving force behind women's initiatives. And they are split down the middle on the issue of whether companies should support the advancement of women out of a corporate sense of social responsibility. Half say yes; half say no.

Ultimately, the single best reason to have women running companies is because they can do it. "The winners are going to be the organizations that view diversity as truly a mechanism to gain competitive advantage," says a Fortune 500 CEO. "If you have a richer senior management decision-making process, where more views are easily expressed and incorporated, you're going to wind up with better decisions."

Guidelines in Hiring Women Managers

In considering hiring local women managers, leading transnational firms also follow a few consistent guidelines to increase their chances of success:

1. Companies use the flexibility afforded foreign firms, which need not limit their hiring and promotion practices to those of the local culture. Foreign firms have considerably more flexibility to tailor human resource decisions to those that best fit the firm's needs, including hiring both women and men for managerial and executive positions, even in countries whose local companies hire primarily men.

2. Companies take advantage of the low demand for women managers. They do not limit their selection pool to those people targeted by most other local and foreign firms—that is, they do not limit their recruitment to men; they draw from the best people available, including both women and men. Because of the lower demand, it is often easier to attract a top quality woman manager than a top quality man.

3. They do not confuse women managers and executives with women workers. The family and educational background of most potential managerial and executive candidates is completely different from that of most women in a country. They do not use general population characteristics, such as literacy rates, to predict the potential availability of women managers and executives.

4. They offer a working environment that is attractive to women managers and executives. Professional women working outside India often find different organizational and career characteristics attractive from those valued by Indian women. For example, in many parts of the world, highly educated women—those targeted for potential managerial and executive positions—come from upper class families in which they have relatively easy access to household help. Therefore, work-family dilemmas are neither the same as they are for most Indian women nor the same as they are for less advantaged local women workers. Offering day-care centres in such environments, for example, might not be as highly valued as it would be in similar settings.

Strategies to Promote Women into Management

Regulatory mechanisms and legal frameworks are necessary to eliminate discrimination on the grounds of sex. Affirmative actions and guidelines should be implemented to genuinely change attitudes while taking existing diversities into account. Enterprises, institutions and governments should take appropriate steps to ensure that employees are aware of obligations and rights stemming from fundamental rights, equal employment laws, where applicable, and related legal requirements.

Recruitment and promotion procedures and criteria should be transparent and based objectively, on competence and merit, and not result in discrimination in practice. For this, it is essential that clearly defined job descriptions are established free of gender bias and that there is an objective system of job evaluation and a well-structured management performance appraisal system. It is good for enterprises, institutions, organizations and governments to set targets and goals and to monitor progress.

Women should be given opportunities for strategic assignments and job rotation to improve their promotion prospects to high echelons of management and breaking the glass ceiling. Upward mobility and career progression should be more flexible to allow women more opportunities based on their ability and competence. Career and succession planning and the tracking of women in enterprises and organizations help them gain visibility and experience, as well as provide a mechanism for monitoring their progress. Adopting objective policies of internal recruitment combined with the necessary job and coping skills training can give more opportunities to women to advance in their career.

Positive action and equal opportunities policies play an important role in leveling the playing field and ensuring equal opportunities and treatment for women in recruitment and promotion. These policies and actions help women bridge the gender gap through the provision of special training or assistance with family care needs. For those aspiring to management jobs, equal access to assertiveness and leadership training, as well as the development of decision-making skills are especially relevant. Life-long learning and on-the-job training should be accessible to women and men on the same terms. The qualifications, diplomas and level of education of women should be valued in the same way as men's. Given the tension between the demands of family/private life and work at certain periods over the life cycle, ways need to be devised to enable not only women, but men too, to build a career and raise a family. This can include more flexible working hours, reduced hours of work and adequate child- and elder-care facilities and arrangements. A good balance between managerial and family/ private life responsibilities not only benefits the health of the individual, the family and therefore society, but may well contribute to more creative and efficient management styles and better business decisions and results.

Ensuring women's equal access to networks both formal and informal, not only in the enterprise but beyond, can provide support and visibility, and as well be a source of invaluable information. Mentoring women, not only by other women, but also by men, could provide advice and assistance in coping skills, as well as in business strategies, leadership, public speaking, assertiveness and team building skills. The benefits to the enterprise of a mentoring programme include increased job satisfaction, efficiency, creativity and reduced staff turnover. The employee gains confidence and self-knowledge, understands better her role and the corporate culture and has the opportunity to express how she and others think and feel about company practices. Mentoring also helps a future manager define career goals and increase professional skills.

Diversity management conceived as a response to specific needs, career aspirations, contributions and lifestyles of the workforce, can be an important strategy to promote women to the top and may be good for business. As this is a new and evolving concept, however, further consideration should be given to this new managerial approach, taking into account the cultural and social context and implications. When analyzing the subject of diversity management and equal employment opportunities approaches, the focus should be on the actual results with regard to women breaking through the glass ceiling.

Commitment of top executives to gender equality, making middle managers aware and accountable, and adopting a range of measures are central in ensuring the success of equal opportunities policies at the enterprise level. Recognition of best practice through awards at the national level can be important incentives to enterprises in promoting women. The appointment of corporate officers in the personnel departments of enterprises, who are responsible for the monitoring and promotion of equal opportunities throughout the enterprise, is an important means of sending a message throughout a company or organization and of making managers at all levels accountable for promoting women.

A Road Map for Futuristic Thinking

There are certain apprehensions that need to be thought over by the readers. The apprehensions are based on the trends of the findings. Broadly, three major trends of the results emerged:

1 Societal Trends

2. Organizational and

3. Individual and Family Trends.

1. Societal Trends

(a) Will traditional norms about women and men's role disappear?

(b) Will EEO laws become modified in practice and if so, in what direction?

(c) Will the sex difference in socialization experiences disappear?

2. Trends in Organizations

(a) Will gender stereotyping of workers end?

(b) Will organizations make it easier for employees to satisfy family needs?

(c) Will more organizations try to achieve equal opportunity?

(d) Will more organizations succeed in achieving equal opportunity?

3. Individual and Family Trends

(a) Will the sex difference in occupational choices disappear?

(b) Will women and men's careers become equally affected by family concerns?

A number of trends have been raised as likely to have a significant effect on the future of women and men in management. Most of these trends have been stated in positive versus negative terms. That is, it has been suggested that (a) if the trend goes one way its effect will be to promote equal opportunity in organization, to reduce sex differences, and to improve female / male work relationships, and (b) if the trend goes the other way, its effect will be to discourage equal opportunity in organizations, to maintain or increase sex differences and to fail to improve or worsen female / male work relationships.

But the question arises, are these extreme scenarios? Very much so. The first scenario depicts a positive image and the second one a negative image.

Which one more reflects today's realities? I believe the second one. What do you believe?

Which one would be better to achieve? I vote for the positive scenario. By now, I am sure that you do too.

Towards which scenario have we been heading in recent years? I believe the positive scenario, primarily because women have made substantial progress in entering male-dominated professions such as management and the difference in women's and men's typical career patterns in management has been reduced. The sustained sex segregation of occupations and sex difference in earnings argue in favour of lack of progress, however, and suggest the negative scenario.

Toward which scenario are we more likely to proceed as a society? It is hard to tell. This depends on how we address this question. Further, research is needed that will give us more guidance on how to eliminate sex discrimination and minimise the relevance of sex as an individual characteristic in the workplace? This can only be possible by adopting work-life integration model at the individual level and promoting family-friendly policies at the organizational level. This will help each other in their pursuit of satisfying careers, sharing family responsibilities and enjoying life maximally.

References

Adler, N.J. (1996). *Women in management worldwide. International Studies of Management and Organization,* No. 3.

Adler, N.J. and Izraeli, D.N. (1994). *Competitive frontiers: Women managers in a global economy.* Cambridge, MA: Blackwell.

Adler, N.J. and Izraeli, D.N. (1988). Women in management. In N.J. Adler and D.N. Izraeli (eds.), *Women in Management Worldwide* (pp. 3-16). Armonk, NY:ME Sharpe.

Agarwal, K.G. (1976). Self, role and status: Towards stratification theory of work motivation. New Delhi: National Labour Institute.

Alvesson, M. and Billing, Y.D. (1997). *Understanding gender and organizations.* London: Sage Publications.

Antal, A.B. and Izraeli, D.N. (1993). A global comparison of women in management: Women Managers in their homelands and as expatriates. In E.A. Fagenson (ed.), *Women in Management* (pp. 52-96). Newbury Park, CA: Sage Publications.

Arputhamurthy, S. (1990). *Women, work and discrimination.* New Delhi: Ashish Publishing House.

Barnett, Rosalind (1999). A new work-life model for the twenty-first century. The Annals of *The Academy of Political and Social Science,* Vol. 562, pp. 143-158.

Bem, S.L. (1977). On the utility of alternative procedures for assessing psychological androgyny. *Journal of Consulting and Clinical Psychology,* 45, pp. 196-205.

Boyacigiller, M. and Adler, N.J. (1991). The parochial dinosaur: Organizational science in a global Context. *Academy of Management Review,* 16, pp. 262-290.

Boyd, J. (2000). Firms work to keep women - Flexitime, mentoring programs intensify retention Efforts in IT. *Internetweek,* Special Issue No. 839, pp. PG 88- PG 90.

Brett, J.M. and Stroh, L.K. (1999). Women in management : How far have we come and what needs To be done as we approach 2000? *Journal of Management Inquiry,* 8, pp. 392-398.

Broverman, I.K. et. Al (1972). Sex role stereotype: A current appraisal. Journal of Social Issues, 28, pp. 59-78.

Business World (1998). April Issue.

Cannings, K. and Lazonick, W. (1994). Equal employment opportunity and the "managerial women" In Japan. *Industrial Relations,* 33 (1), pp. 44-68.

Chattopadhyay, G.P. (1975). Dependence in Indian culture: From mud huts to company board Rooms. *Economic and Political Weekly*, 10, pp. M30-M38.

Chattopadhyay, S.N. & Rao, T.V. (1970). Aspirations and apprehensions of small industry personnel and their relationship with apparent productivity. *Indian Journal of Psychology*, 45, pp. 39-52.

Charles, M. (1992). Cross-national variation in occupational sex segregation. *American Sociological Review*, 57, pp. 483-502.

Clark, R. (1991). Contrasting perspectives on women's access to prestigious occupations: A cross-national investigation. *Social Science Quarterly*, 72, pp. 20-32.

Cooper, C.L. and Maarshall, J. (1978). *Understanding executives stress.* London: MacMillan Press.

Cooper, C.L. and Payne, R (1978). *Stress at work.* Chichester: John Wiley and Sons.

Cussler, Margret (1958). *The women executive.* Harcourt Brace.

Czarniawska Joerges, B. (1991). Culture is the medium of life. In P. Frost et al. (eds), Refraining Organizational Culture. Newbury Park, CA: Sage.

Davidoff, L. (1986). The role of gender in the "first industrial nation": agriculture and England 1780-1850. In R. Crompton and M. Mann (eds), Gender and Stratification. Cambridge:Polity Press.

Deetz, S. and Kersten, S. (1983). Critical models of interpretive research. In L. Putnam and M..Pacanowsky (eds), Communication and Organizations. Beverly Hills, CA: Sage.

Dayal, I. (1976). Cultural factors in designing performance appraisal system. New Delhi: SRC Industrial Relations & Human Resources.

Deal, J.J. and Stevenson, M.A. (1998). Perceptions of female and male managers in the 1990s: Plus Ca change. *Sex Roles*, 38 (3/4), pp. 287-300.

De, N. (1974). Conditions for work culture. *Indian Journal of Industrial Relations*, 9 (4), pp. 587-598.

Devanna, M.A. (1987). Women in management progress and promise. *Human Resources Management*, 26 (4), pp. 469-481.

Dipboye, R.C. (1975). Women as managers - Stereotypes and realities. *Survey of Business*, May-June Issue, pp. 22-26.

Donnell, S.M. and Hall, J. (1980). Men and women as managers: A significant case of no significant difference. *Organizational Dynamics*, 8, pp. 60-77.

Fagenson, E.A. (1990). Perceived masculine and feminine attributes as a function of individual's sex and level in the organizational power hierarchy: A test of four theoretical perspectives. *Journal of Applied Psychology*, 75, pp. 204-211.

Fernberger, S.W. (1948). Persistence of stereotypes concerning sex differences. *Journal of Abnormal and Social Psychology*, 43, pp. 97-101.

French, J.R.P. Jr. and Caplan, R.D. (1973). Organizational stress and individual strain. In A.J. Marrow (ed.), *The Failure of Success* (pp. 30-66). New York: AMACOM.

Galinsky, E.; Bond, J. and Friedman, D. (1993). The changing workforce: Highlights of the national Study. New York: Families and Work Institute.

Ganesh, S.R. and Malhotra, A.K. (1975). Work values of Indian managers. *ASCI Journal of Management*, 4 (2), pp. 147-162.

Gomez-Mejia, L.R. and Welbourne, T. (1991). Compensation Strategies in a global context. *Human Resource Planning*, 14, pp. 29-41.

Goneyea, J.G. and Googins, B.K. (1996). The restructuring of work and family in the United States: A new challenge for American Corporations. In Suzan Lewis and Jeremy Lewis (eds.), *The Work Family Challenge* (pp. 63-78). Thousand Oaks: Sage Publications.

Grant, J. (1988). Women as managers what they can offer to organizations. *Organizational Dynamics*, 16 (1), pp. 56-63.

Greenhaus, J.H. and Beutell, N.J. (1985). Sources of conflict between work and family roles. *Academy of Management Review*, 10, pp. 76-88.

Greenwood, J.W. and Greenwood, G.W. (1979). *Managing executive stress*: A system approach. New York: John Wiley.

Grey, C. (1999). We are all managers now: We always were: On the development and demise of management. *Journal of Management Studies*, 36 (5), pp. 561- 585.

Hall, D.T. (1990). Promoting work - family balance: An organizational change approach. *Organizational Dynamics*, 18, pp. 5-8.

Hammer, M. and Champy, J. (1993). Re-engineering the corporation: A manifesto for business Revolution. New York: Harper Business.

Heilman, M.E. (1983). Sex bias in work settings: The lack of fit model. In B.M. Staw & L.L. Cummings (eds.) *Research in Organizational Behaviour* (Vol. 5, pp. 269-298). Greenwich CT: Jai Press.

Heilman, M.E.; Simon, M.C. and Repper, D.P. (1987). Intentionally favoured, unintentionally harmed? The impact of gender-based preferential selection on self-perceptions and self-evaluations. *Journal of Applied Psychology*, 72, pp. 62-68.

Heilman, M.E.; Block, C.J.; Martell, R.F. and Simon, M.C. (1989). Has anything changed? Current characteristics of men, women and managers. *Journal of Applied Psychology*, 74, pp. 935-942.

Heilman, M.E.; Lucas, J.A. and Kaplow, S. R. (1990). Self-derogating consequences of preferential selection: The moderating role of initial self-confidence. *Organizational Behaviour and Human Decision Process*, 46, pp. 202-216.

Heilman, M.E.; Rivero, J.C. and Brett, J.F. (1991). Skirting the competence issue: Effects of sex-based preferential selection on task choices of women and men. *Journal of Applied Psychology*, 76, pp. 99-105.

Helgesen, S. (1990). The female advantage. New York: Doubleday.

Henning, M. and Jardim, A. (1977). The managerial woman. Gaarden City, NY: Anchor Press /Doubleday.

Herriot, P. (1992). The career management challenge. London: Sage.

Hines, R. (1992). Accounting: Filling the negative space. Accounting, Organization and Society, 17(3-4), pp. 314-341.

Hofstede, G. (1991). *Cultures and organizations: Software of the mind.* London: McGraw Hill.

Hostede, G. (1980). *Culture's consequences: International differences in work related values.* Beverly Hills, CA: Sage.

Hooyman, N.R. and Goneyea, J.G. (1995). *Feminist perspectiveson family care*: Policies for gender Justice. Newbury Park, CA: Sage.

http: / /www.catalystwomen.org

Joshi, Rama, J. (1988). Women at work: Implications for organizations. *Indian Journal of Industrial Relations*, 23, (4).

Kakar, S. (1979). *Indian childhood: Cultural ideals and social reality.* New Delhi : Oxford University Press.

Kakar, S. (1978). *The inner world: A psycho-analytic study of childhood and society in India.* New Delhi: Oxford University Press.

Kahn, R.L. and Quinn, R.P. (1970). Role stress: A framework for analysis. In A. McLean (ed.), *Mental Health and Work Organization.* Chicago: Rand McNally.

Kahn, R.L.; Wolfe, D.M.; Quinn, R.P.; Snoek, J.D. and Rosenthal, R.A. (1964). *Organizational stress:Studies in role conflict and amiguity.* New York: Wiley.

Kalleberg, A.L. and Rosenfeld, R.A. (1990). Work in the family and in the labour market: A cross-national reciprocal analysis. *Journal of Marriage and the Family*, 52, pp. 331-346.

Kanter, R.M. (1977). *Work and family in the United States: A critical review and agenda for research policy*. New York: Russell Sage Foundation.

Katz, D. and Kahn, R.L. (1966). *The social psychology of organizations*. New York: Wiley.

Khandwalla, P.N. (1984). *Fourth eye: Excellence through creativity*. New Delhi:A.H. Wheeler & Co.

Kim, Son-Ung (1999). Determinants and characteristics of the corporate culture of Korean enterprises. In Henry S.R. Kao, Durganand Sinha and Bernhard Wilpert (eds.), *Management and Cultural Values* (pp. 86-101). New Delhi: Sage Publications.

Kluckholm, F. (1954). *Culture and behaviour*. New York: Free Press.

Komarovskay, M. (1950). Functional analysis of sex roles. *American Sociological Review*, 15, pp. 508 - 516.

Kopelman, R.; Greenhaus, J. and Connolly, T. (1983). A model of work-family and inter-role conflict: A construct validity study. *Organizational Behaviour and Human Performance*, 32, pp. 198-215.

Kossek, E.E.; Noe, R. & DeMarr, B.J. (1999). Work - family role synthesis: Individual and organizational determinants. *Inter-national Journal of Conflict Management*, 10 (2), pp. 102 - 129.

Kothari, R. (1970). *Politics in India*. New Delhi: Orient Longman.

Lachman, R.; Nedd, A. and Hinings, B. (1994). Analyzing cross-national management and organizations: A theoretical framework. *Management Science*, 40 (1), pp. 40 - 55.

Lambert, S.; Hopkins, K.; Easton, G. and Walker, J. (1992). Added benefits: The link between family responsive policies and work performance at Fel - Pro, Inc. Chicago: University of Chicago.

Lau, C.M. and Ngo, N.Y. (1996). One country many cultures: Organizational cultures of firms of different origins. *International Business Review*, 5 (5), pp. 469 - 486.

Laurent, A. (1986). The cross-cultural puzzle of international human resource management. *Human Resource Management*, 25, pp. 91-102.

Lehman, E. (1995). Business must do for working parents. *Parade Magazine*, 26th February, pp. 12-13.

Lenney, E. (1981). What's fine for the gender isn't always good for the goose: Sex differences in self-confidence as a function of ability area and comparison with others. *Sex Roles*, 7, pp. 905 - 923.

Lewis, S. (1996). Rethinking employment: An organizational culture change framework. In S. Lewis and J. Lewis (eds.), *The Work - Family Challenge* (pp. 1- 19). Thousand Oaks: Sage Publications.

Lewis, S. (1994). Role tensions in dual career couples. In M. Davidson and R. Burke (eds.), *Women in Management: current research issues*. London: Paul Chapman.

Lunnenborg, P.W. (1970). Stereotypic aspects in masculinity feminity measurement. *Journal of Consulting and Clinical Psychology*, 34, pp. 113 - 118.

Marriot, K. (1977). Changing identities in South - Asia. In K. A. David (ed.), *The New Wind: Changing Identities in South Asia*. The Hague : Aldine.

Marshall, J. (1993a). Organizational cultures and women managers: Exploring the dynamics of Resilience. *Applied Psychology: An International Review*, 42 (4), pp. 313 - 322.

Marshall, J. and Cooper, C. L. (1979). Executive under pressure: A psychological study. London: MacMillan Press.

Marquart, J.M. (1988). A pattern matching approach to link program theory and employer-sponsored childcare. Ann Arbor, MI: University of Michigan.

McClelland, D. (1975). *Power: The inner experience*. New York: Irvington.

McKee, J.P. and Sherriffs, A.C. (1959). Male versus female discussion leaders. *Personnel Psychology*, 23, pp. 455 - 461.

McMohan, I.D. (1982). Expectancy of success on sex-linked tasks. *Sex Roles*, 8, pp. 949 - 958.

Mirvis, P.H. (1993). A competitive workforce: The issues and the study. In P.H. Mirvis (ed.), *Building the Competitive Workforce* (pp. 220 - 247). New York: Wiley.

Moore, G. and Shackman, G. (1996). Gender and authority: A cross-national study. *Social Science Quarterly*, 77 (2), pp. 273 - 288.

Moss, P. (1996). Reconciling employment and family responsibilities: A European perspective. In S. Lewis and J. Lewis (eds.), *The Work-Family Challenge* (pp. 20 - 33). Thousand Oaks: Sage Publications.

New Ways to Work (1995). Balanced lives: Changing work pattern for men. London : New Ways to Work.

Nivea, V. F. and Gutek B.A. (1981). *Women and work: A psychological perspective*. New York: Praeger.

Norris, J.M. and Wylie, A. M. (1995). Gender stereotyping of the managerial role among student in Canada and the United States. *Group and Organization Management*, 20, pp. 167 - 182.

Offerman, L. R. and Hellmann, P.S. (1997). Culture's consequences for leadership behaviour. *Journal of Cross - Cultural Psychology*, 28 (3), pp. 342 - 351.

Orser, B. (1994). Sex role stereotypes and requisite management characteristics: An international perspective. *Women in Mana-gement Review*, 9, pp. 11 -19.

Pampel, F.C. and Kazuko, T. (1986). Economic development and female labour force participation: A reconsideration. *Social Forces*, 64, pp. 599 -619.

Pareek, U. (1983). *Role stress scale manual*. Ahmedabad: Navin Publications.

Pareek, U. (1976). Inter-role exploration. In J.W. Pfeffer and J.E. Jones (eds.). *The 1976 Annual Handbook for Group Facilitators* (pp. 211-224). Lajolla, California: University Associates.

Parker, V.A. and Hall, D.T. (1993). Workplace flexibility: Faddish or fundamental. In P.H.Mirvis (ed.), *Building the Competitive Workforce* (pp. 122 - 155). New York: Wiley.

Perera, B. (2000). Policy alternatives for balancing employed women's roles. In Kalpana Sinha's (ed.), *Empowerment of Women in South Asia* (pp. 76-84). Hyderabad: AMDISA.

Piotrkowski, C.S. (1979). *Work and the family system*. New York: Free Press.

Poggio, B. (2000). Between bytes and bricks: Gender cultures in work contexts. *Economic and Industrial Democracy*, 21 (3), pp. 381 - 402.

Powell, G.N. (1993). *Women and men in management*. Newbury Park, CA: Sage.

Powell, W.W. (1990). Expanding the scope of institutional analysis. In W.W. Powell and P.J. DiMaggio (ed.), *The New Institutionalism in Organizational Analysis* (pp. 183 - 204). Chicago: The University of Chicago Press.

Powell, W. (1990). Neither market nor hierarchy: Network forms of organization. *Research in Organizational Behaviour*, 12, pp. 295-336.

Powell, G.N. and Butterfield, D.A. (1994). Investigating the 'glass ceiling' phenomenon: An empirical study of actual promotions to top management. *Academy of Management Journal*, 37, pp. 68 - 86.

Powell, G.N. and Butterfield, D.A. (1989). The "good manager": Does androgyny fare better in the 1980s? *Group and Organizational Studies*, 14, pp. 216 - 233.

Powell, G.N. and Butterfield, D.A. (1979). The good manager: Masculine or androgynous. *Academy of Management Journal*, 22, pp. 395 - 403.

Pleck , J. (1977). The work family role system. *Social Problems*, 24, pp. 417 - 427.

Ransom, C.; Ashbacher, P. and Burud, S. (1989), The return of the childcare investment. *Personnel Administrator*, 34, pp. 54 -80.

Ritzer, George (1972). *Working - conflict and change.* Englewood Cliffs, NJ: Prentice - Hall Inc.

Roland, A. (1980). Toward a psycho-analytic psychology of hierarchical relationship in Hindu India. Bombay: Indian Psychoanalytic Societies.

Rosalind, B.C. (1999). A new work - life model for the twenty - first century. *The Annals*, 562, pp. 143 - 158.

Schein, V.E. (1975). Relationship between sex role stereotypes and requisite management characteristics among female managers. *Journal of Applied Psychology*, 60, pp. 340 - 344.

Schein, V.E. (1973). The relationship between sex role stereotypes and requisite management characteristics. *Journal of Applied Psychology*, 57, pp. 95 -100.

Schor, S.M. (1997). Separate and unequal: The nature of women's and men's career building relations. *Business Horizons*, September - October Issue, pp. 51 -57.

Schor, J. (1995). Brave new world: Patterns of work, family, time and consumption for the 21st century. *Paper Presented at the Work / Life Issues Conference.* Northeastern University, World Trade Center, Boston, MA, March.

Schneider, S.C. and DeMeyer, A. (1991). Interpreting and responding to strategic issues: The impact of national culture. *Strategic Management Journal*, 12, pp. 307 - 320.

Schneier, C. and Bartol, K.M. (1980). Sex effects in emergent leadership. *Journal of Applied Psychology*, 65, pp. 341 - 345.

Scott, S. G. and Lane, V.R. (2000). A stakeholder approach to organizational identity. *Academy of Management Review*, 25 (1), pp. 43 - 62.

Shweder, R.A. and Levine, R.A. (1984). Culture theory: Essays on mind, self and emotion. New York: Cambridge University Press.

Schwartz, F. (1989). Management women and the new facts of life. *Harvard Business Review*, 67, pp. 65 - 76.

Segal, N. (2000). We want you: Why women aren't going global and why they should. http://International.monster.com/workabroad/articles/women

Sekaran, Uma (1984). *Research methods for managers: A skill building approach.* New York: John Wiley and Sons.

Selye, H. (1956). *The stress of life.* New York: McGraw - Hill.

Seth, Mira (1998). A manager and a mother. *Business World*, 22nd April, pp. 72 - 75.

Silverstone, R. and Audrey, W. (1980). Careers of professional women. Edited Book. London: Croom Helm.

Singh-Sengupta, Sunita (2002). Cultural determinants, gender and self. In M. M. Mboya (ed.), *Self Concept Theory, Research and Practice : International Perspectives* (pp. 287 - 306). South Africa: Iiitha Publishers, Pretoria.

Singh-Sengupta, Sunita (2001). Women managers in global economy: An Asian perspective. *Paper Presented in The Tenth European Congress of the Work and Organizational Psychology*, Praha, May 16-19, 2001.

Singh-Sengupta, Sunita (2000). Management Development Programme on "Women in Management and Leadership", February 7-9, 2000 at Indian Institute of Management Calcutta, India.

Singh-Sengupta, Sunita (2000a). The positive face of power. A Research Report.

Singhsengupta, Sunita (2000b). Socio-cultural determinants of women leadership. In Kalpana Sinha's (ed.), *Empowerment of Women in South Asia* (pp. 124-139). Hyderabad: AMDISA.

Singh-Sengupta, Sunita (1990). *The emerging patterns of power distribution*. New Delhi: Commonwealth Publishers.

Sinha, J.B.P. (1990). *Work culture in Indian context*. New Delhi : Sage Publications.

Sinha, J.B.P. (1980a). The nurturant - task leader. New Delhi: Concept Publishing House.

Sinha, J.B.P. (1980b). Power structure, perceptual frame and behavioural strategies in dyadic relationship. Paper Presented to the International Association for Cross-Cultural Psychology. Bhubaneswar, India.

Sinha, J.B.P. (1970). Development through behaviour modification. Bombay: Allied Publishers.

Solomon, C.M. (2000). Cracks in the glass ceiling. *Workforce*, 79 (9), pp. 86 - 94.

Spencer, A. and Podmore, D. (1983). Life on the periphery of a profession: The experience of women lawyers. *Paper Presented to British Sociological Association Conference*. University College, Cardiff.

Steinhoff, P.G. and Tanaka, K. (1994). Women managers in Japan. In N.J. Adler and D.N. Izraeli (eds.) *Women Managers in a Global Economy* (pp. 79 -100). MA: Blackwell.

Stephens, G.K. and Greer, C.R. (1995). Doing business in Mexico: Understanding cultural differences. *Organizational Dynamics*, 24 (1), pp. 39 - 55.

Stover, D.L (1994). The horizontal distribution of female managers within organizations. *Works and Occupations*, 21, pp. 385 - 402.

Stroh, L.K.; Brett, J.M. & Reilly, A.H. (1992). All the right stuff: A comparison of female and male managers' career progression. *Journal of Applied Psychology*, 77, pp. 251-260.

Strykowska, M. (1995). Women in management in Poland. *Women Studies International Forum*, 18 (1), pp. 9-12.

Tabak, F. (1997). Women's upward mobility in manufacturing organizations in Istanbul: A glass ceiling initiative. *Sex Roles*, 36 (1/2), pp. 93-102.

Tharenou, P.; Latimer, S. & Conroy, D. (1994). How do you make it to the top? An examination of influences in women's and men's managerial advancement. Academy of Management Journal, 37, pp. 899 - 931.

Voyadanoff, P. (1987). *Work and family life*. Newbury Park: Sage.

Ward, K.B. and Pampel, F.C. (1985). Structural determinants of female labour force participation indeveloped nations, 1955-75. *Social Science Quarterly*, 66, pp. 654-667.

Wilkinson, H. (1994). *No turning back: Generations and the genderquake*. London: Demos.

Women Mantra (2000). For South Asian Women Bias Begin Before Birth.

http://www.siliconindia.com/women/

Wright, H.B. (1979). Executive ease and disease. Essex: Gower Press.

Yates, J.E. (1979). Managing stress: A business person's guide. New York: AMACOM.

ANNEXURE - 1

The Factor Analysis of the Items Pertaining to Social Values

Factors / Item Description	*Loading*
Collective Orientation	
1. Children are taught to conform and be team players.	.432
2. People are comfortable taking orders from those with higher positions.	.503
3. People in society are comfortable taking tasks.	.663
4. The society values working together as a group.	.815
5. Work is considered an important part of people's life.	.735
Being independent is valued.	.509
6. People like to socialize and get to know each other before doing business.	.491
Eigen Value	3.22
Pct. of Variances	16.95
Reactive Culture	
1. People do not schedule more than one activity at a time.	.787
2. People feel comfortable questioning their supervisor's decision.	.547
3. Personal characteristics, such as age, gender and family background determine who will go ahead.	.461
4. People welcome specific directives from someone with higher authority in carrying out their work	.580
5. People rely mainly on use of words to convey meaning.	.683
Eigen Value	2.73
Pct. of Variances	14. 37
Emphasis on Normative Behaviour	
1. Women are expected to be subservient to men.	.542
2. In this society there are clear rules as to how one should behave.	.558

(Contd...)

(Contd...)

3.	People sit or stand close to one another in carrying out their daily activity.	.656
4.	Not being on time for meeting or for conducting daily business activities is acceptable.	.643
	Eigen Value	2.22
	Pct. of Variances	1.51

Believe in Proactive Culture

1.	People believe that hard work leads to high achievement.	.391
2.	Men and women are given equal employment opportunities.	.662
3.	People value being direct and speaking their mind freely.	.532
	Eigen Value	1.51
	Pct. of Variances	7.94

ANNEXURE - 2

The Factor Analysis of the Items Related to Perception of Organizational Culture

Factors / Item Description	*Loading*
Men Favoured Organizational Culture	
1. Meetings are run more effectively when chaired by men managers.	.484
2. It is more important for men to have professional career than it is for women to have professional career.	.671
3. Women don't value recognition and promotion in their work as much as men do.	.732
4. Men usually solve problems with logical analysis whereas women solve problems with intuition.	.594
5. Solving organizational problems usually require the active forcible approach which is typical of men.	.622
6. It is preferable to have man in high position rather than women.	.779
7. There are some jobs which a man can always do better than a woman.	.617
8. Women are more concerned with social aspects of their jobs than they are with getting ahead in their career.	.578
Eigen Value	3.51
Pct. of Variances	26.93
Work Motivation	
1. Most individuals primarily work to be financially independent and meet family needs.	.611
2. Work helps one to achieve self-satisfaction and make use of educational abilities.	.769
3. In modern times many individual work for societal and development of country's economy.	.617
4. People choose profession according to their educational background.	.712
5. Women value working in a friendly atmosphere than men do.	.439
Eigen Value	2.45
Pct. of Variances	18.88

ANNEXURE - 3

The Factor Analysis of the Items on Values Grid

Factors / Item Description	Loading
Inner Happiness	
1. Act on my own.	.447
2. Discover develop or design new things.	.685
3. Have a high standard of living by my earning.	.587
4. Do work that gives me inner happiness.	.708
Eigen Value	3.52
Pct. of Variances	16.75
Work Values	
1. Use all my skills and knowledge in work.	.813
2. Reach a high standard in my work.	.767
3. Be able to get promotion.	.656
4. Find pleasure in the beauty of my work.	.662
Eigen Value	3.23
Pct. of Variances	15.36
Work Centric Caring Relationship	
1. Help others with personal problems at the work place.	.460
2. Work in my own style.	.475
3. Develop as a person through my work.	.650
4. Get a lot of exercise in my work itself.	.509
5. Have power and prestige in society because of the kind of work I do.	.506
6. Have a comfortable life in work place.	.787
7. Oblige those who work around me.	.603
Eigen Value	2.89
Pct. of Variances	13.78

Factors / Item Description	Loading
Variety At Work	
1. Tell others what to do.	.463
2. Take risky decisions in my job.	.615
3. Entertain friends and relations during working hours.	.715
4. Have a network of friends and relations in my work place.	.687
5. Do a number of difficult things in a typical workday.	.558
Eigen Value	2.51
Pct. of Variances	11.92

ANNEXURE - 4

The Factor Analysis of the Items on Perception of Security / Insecurity Scale

Factors / Item Description	*Loading*
Self Orientation	
1. I do not mind using sarcasm if it helps me making a point.	.50
2. I find it easier to ask for help.	.60
3. I can express pride in my accomplishments without being boastful.	.70
4. I can express my true feeling to someone I really care for.	.68
5. I feel confident in my ability to stand up for my rights.	.73
Eigen Value	2.64
Pct. of Variances	14.71
Other Orientation	
1. If others interrupt me when I am talking, I suffer in silence.	.71
2. People take advantage of me.	.63
3. I tell people what they want to hear if it helps me get what I want.	.56
4. When I feel angry with other people, I bottle it up rather than express it.	.65
Eigen Value	2.56
Pct. of Variances	14.43
Implacable Behaviour	
1. If people are rude, I will be rude right back.	.65
2. I ask for a raise when I feel I really deserve it.	.54
3. I lend things to others even when I do not really want to.	.46
4. I win arguments by dominating the discussion.	.76
5. If people criticize work, I find a way to make them back down.	.64
6. When I criticize someone else's work, they get mad.	.45
Eigen Value	2.55
Pct of Variances	14.17

(Contd...)

(Contd...)

Factors / Item Description	*Loading*
Low Confidence	
1. I respond with more modesty that I really feel when my work is complimented.	.76
2. Other people find me interesting.	.46
3. I find it difficult to speak up to a group of strangers.	.58
Eigen Value	15. 21
Percentage of Variances	8.45

APPENDIX - 1
NAME OF THE COMPANIES THAT PARTICIPATED IN THE STUDY

QUESTIONNAIRE -1

1. CANARA BANK
2. GRIDCO
3. VXL LANDIS & GYR.
4. NATIONAL BANK FOR AGRICULTURE AND RURAL DEVELOPMENT
5. KPMG
6. SCHNEIDER ELECTRIC INDIA LIMITED
7. SONI ENTERTAINMENT
8. TATA STEEL
9. VESUVIUS INDIA LIMITED
10. SOCIAL MARKETING COMPANY(BANGLADESH)
11. SINGER BANGLADESH LIMITED (BANGLADESH)
12. ISPHANI MARSHALL LIMITED (BANGLA DESH)
13. EVEREADY
14. LARSEN & TOURBO INDIA LIMITED
15. DORNIER INDIA MEDICAL SYSTEMS
16. FOSROC CHEMICALS INDIA LTD.
17. GAS AUTHORITY OF INDIA LTD.
18. HDFC
19. BANK OF BARODA
20. GONTERMAN PIEPERS (INDIA) LTD.
21. INDIAN ALUMINIUM LIMITED
22. BALAJI DISTILLERIES LTD.
23. INDIAN OIL CORPORATION LIMITED
24. ITC HOTELS LIMITED
25. NESTLE INDIA LIMITED
26. KOREA ELECTRIC POWER CORPORATION

NAME OF THE COMPANIES THAT PARTICIPATED IN THE STUDY
QUESTIONNAIRE -2

1. GONTERMAN PIEPERS (INDIA) LTD.
2. TATA STEEL
3. BRITANNIA INDUSTRY LTD.
4. ALLAHABAD BANK
5. BANK OF BARODA
6. SHALIMAR PAINTS
7. MARICO INDUSTRIES LIMITED
8. VXL LANDIS AND GYR.
9. EVEREADY
10. INDIAN ALUMIMIUM LIMITED
11. BANK OF TOKYO AND MITSUBISHI
12. HDFC
13. INDIAN AIRLINES
14. HINDUSTAN PETROLEUM
15. RESERVE BANK OF INDIA
16. BALMER LAWRIE AND COMPANY LIMITED
17. MONSANTO TECHNOLOGIES INDIA LIMITED
18. FRITO LAY (INDIA) LTD.
19. JOHNSON & JOHNSON LTD.
20. INDIAN OIL CORPORATION
21. PRICE WATER COOPERS
22. BONAGION REFINERY AND PETROCHEMICAL LTD.
23. GAS AUTHORITY OF INDIA LTD.
24. DORNIER INDIA MEDICAL SYSTEM PVT. LTD.
25. FOSROC CHEMICAL INDIA LTD.
26. BALAJI DISTILLERIES INDIA LIMITED
27. ITC HOTELS LIMITED
28. POWER FINANCE COPRPORATION LIMITED
29. KOREA ELECTRIC POWER CORPORATION

30. OCIAL MARKETING COMPANY(BANGLA DESH)
30. SINGER BANGLADESH LIMITED (BANGLADESH)
31. ISPHANI MARSHALL LIMITED(BANGLA DESH)
32. NESTLE INDIA LIMITED

The data from the companies functioning in Nepal were collected through National Productivity and Economic Centre, Nepal and from the companies functioning in Sri Lanka through P.G. Institute of Management Columbo, Sri Lanka.

Index